MAT 111

MAT 111

DONG XOAI, VIETNAM 1971

STORIES FROM 33 QUEBEC'S TOUR OF DUTY

JIM ROBERTS

CONTRIBUTIONS BY
GEORGE MILMAN, JIM RICE, AND
GARY WEINREICH

Vietnam is not a great war.
It isn't even a good war.
But it's the only war we have.

C-130 heading down the strip.
Airborne daddy gonna' take a little trip.
Stand up, hook up, shuffle to the door.
Jump right out and count some more.

If I die in a combat zone,
Box me up, and ship me home.
Am I right or wrong?
             You're Right.
Are we going Strong?
             You're Right.
Sound off.
     1   2
Sound off.
     3   4
Bring it on down.
     1   2   3   4
     1   2   3 4

To Linda who is my wife, my partner, my friend.

Where would I be without you?

DEDICATION

A deep and sincere thanks to the men who served on Special Forces A Team 342 at Dong Xoai during the late 1960s. Their training of the Regional Force (RF) companies at Dong Xoai is the main reason I am here to write this set of stories.

A very similar set of thanks to the following:
The men on MAT 111 and the District Team at Dong Xoai. Their professionalism and dedication to duty continued to maintain the military capabilities of the RF companies with whom we lived and worked.

Sergeant First Class L J Turner with whom I operated in the field during the first part of my tour at Dong Xoai. Working with me, a green Lieutenant, he taught me much of what I would need to survive in the jungles of Phuoc Long Province after he returned to the States and retired from the Army.

Sergeant Gary Weinreich (YB) — our friendship began one night in May, 1971 during the attack that was the first combat experience for both of us.

Captain Jim Rice, the team leader of MAT 111 who set the tone for the team and allowed me to be what I hope was an asset to the team.

Todd DePastino, the founder of the Veterans Breakfast Club in Pittsburgh, Pennsylvania, whose thoughtful and probing questions at one of their meetings started me thinking about events that had long been buried and forgotten. While I am totally responsible for any errors in these writings, Todd is responsible for them being written.

Table of Contents

PROLOG

"Read the appendices first if you want to understand this book," was the first comment from most of the readers of the early drafts of this memoir. If you do not believe them, read the first sentence of the Forward.

These memories are from a time fifty years ago when I was in a foreign land working as a member of a small military unit in a jungle village. Telling these stories from that time requires the use of the terminology of the work and the political structure of Vietnam. Unless you are a Vietnam veteran or a serious reader of that history, the terminology could be a problem.

The first draft of this work contained phrases such as, "Even with our PRC77s connected to a two-niner-two, we could not establish commo with Province." At the suggestion of early readers, this phrase now reads as, "Even with our portable field radios connected to our long-range antenna, we were too far from Province Headquarters to make radio contact."

Even with similar changes, a great deal of military and political terminology remains in the stories. One reader marked both appendices with paper clips so he could quickly refer to those pages when he forgot something.

The language we used in Vietnam to express ourselves was often far from what is considered politically correct today. Some of that language is in these stories because that was the reality of those times. These instances are not meant to insult or demean anyone, and I hope you understand why they are in this work.

As I wrote the first story (not Story 1), another memory returned; then another. It continued throughout my writing leading to this collection of stories. These stores are the ones in which I thought you might be interested and some are stories that have rarely if ever been described by the few books about teams like mine that have preceded this work.

FORWARD

I am 33 Quebec.

I am not a writer, and what follows is not a work of literature as you will soon come to realize.

In 1971, I was an Infantry Lieutenant in Vietnam, but I was not part of a "regular" or typical Army unit that you see in the movies and documentaries. I was on a Mobile Advisory Team — MAT 111; five men living with the Vietnamese in the village of Dong Xoai advising the local military units: the Regional Force (RF) companies and the Popular Force (PF) platoons — the Ruff Puffs.

Very little has been written, and knowledge about MAT teams and the advising they did during the last five years of the war is rare. The web site, MACVTeams.org has one set of web pages for each Advisory Team in the Provinces of Vietnam. The introductory page of their site introduces the teams with these words,

"MACV Teams were out there alone — not on base camps, air bases or at sea. Small groups of Americans often in remote areas supported only by Vietnamese forces whose capabilities and loyalty were sometimes suspect."

These are stories from actual events during my tour with MAT 111. This is a work of non-fiction with dialog, character, and setting details filled in to the best of my memory; a memory, that I have to admit, is clouded by the passage of 50 years. I have tried to tell these stories in a manner that allows you to stand next to me, see what I saw, hear what I heard, and feel the mosquitos biting the back of your neck while you experience the events. It is not my intention to aggrandize these stories or the people in them. The only heroics here were every day soldiers doing their every day jobs trying to accomplish the mission and protect the soldiers around them. The wins, losses, good decisions, bad mistakes, good luck, and misfortunes are found in these stories. I have tried to keep this as historically and militarily accurate as possible, but errors still exist in the writing, and they are solely my responsibility.

33 Quebec

Story 1 - Arrival at Dong Xoai

The journey from West Virginia where I enlisted to the village of Dong Xoai had lasted almost two years and involved varied and intensive training at seven different locations in the States and Vietnam. My actual travel to Vietnam was no different from that of many of the soldiers who made the same trip: a twenty three hour flight with two stops for fuel and leg stretching; a very steep aircraft dive towards the ground before landing[1]; hot, humid, fetid air rolling into the cabin when the door opened; the bus ride with protective wire mesh over the windows; the issuing of our clothing, web gear, weapons — it was the same set of carbon copy experiences for most of 2.7 million men who served in Vietnam. My "copy" happened at MACV Annex (Military Assistance Command Vietnam) in Saigon, the first stop for newbies processing into the giant war machine as advisors.

The next stop was two weeks at Di An (pronounced Zee Ahn) for a school that attempted to compress my previous six months of training (three months at Ft. Bragg with the Special Forces and three months at the Defense Language Institute studying Vietnamese) into two weeks. For many of the advisors in this two-week school, it would be their only introduction to and training for what they were about to undertake in the next eleven months. Those of us who had the extended advisor training sequence before arriving in country were very fortunate. I cannot imagine how my tour would have turned out with only two weeks of training.

From Di An, Air America flew me north to Phuoc Long Province

---

[1] The dive was necessary to avoid Viet Cong ground fire and possible anti-aircraft missile attack from the jungle around Tan Son Nhut airport outside Saigon.

PHUOC LONG
PROVINCE ADVISORY ORGANIZATION
MACV ADV TM 67

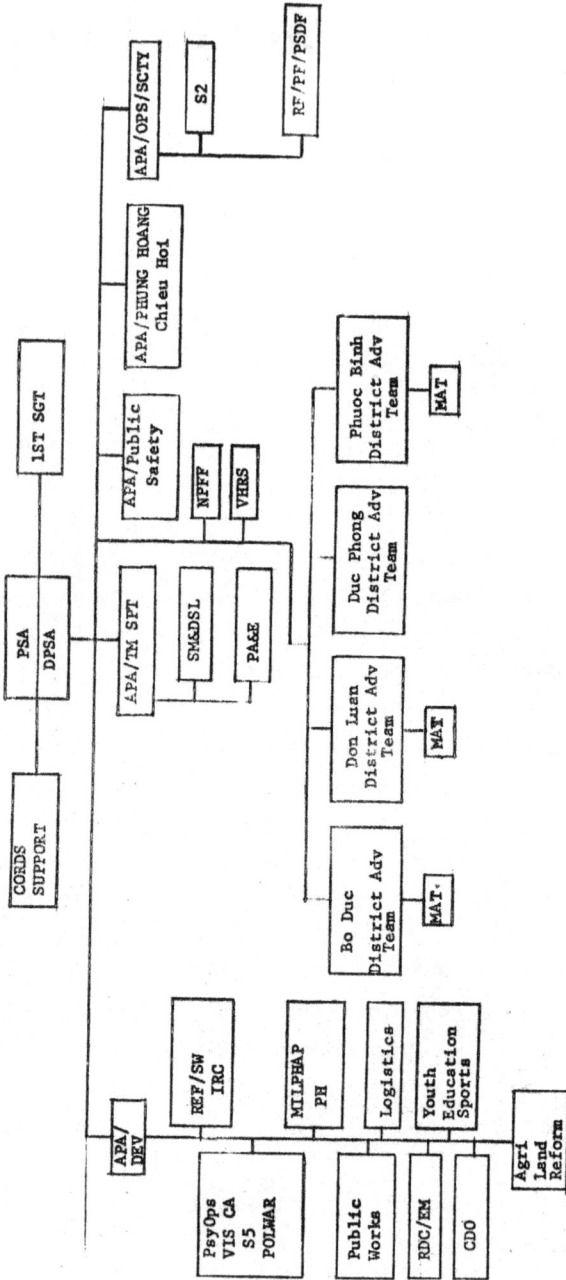

CORDS SUPPORT

PSA
DPSA

1ST SGT

APA/DEV

PsyOps
VIS CA
S5
POLWAR

REF/SW
IRC

Public
Works

MILPHAP
PH

RDC/EM

Logistics

CDO

Youth
Education
Sports

Agri
Land
Reform

APA/TM SPT

SM&DSL

PAGE

APA/Public
Safety

NPFF

VHRS

APA/PHUNG HOANG
Chieu Hoi

APA/OPS/SCTY

S2

RF/PF/PSDF

Bo Duc
District Adv
Team

MAT.

Don Luan
District Adv
Team

MAT

Duc Phong
District Adv
Team

Phuoc Binh
District Adv
Team

MAT

Figure 1.1 Team 67 organization chart for 1971.

which was situated along the Cambodian border. The plane landed at Song Be[2], province capital and the location of the headquarters for Advisory Team 67 which was responsible for all advising activities in the province. Province level advising was multifaceted in all areas of government. Military advising was just one part of this effort. Almost all of the tactical operations involved the MAT teams at the district level.

I was met at the air strip and driven to Team 67's compound where I would be for the next two days as part of my ongoing in-processing. I reported to the Province Senior Advisor's (PSA) office. He was a Colonel, and he gave me the standard brief welcome a new Lieutenant usually receives. Then he turned me over to the care of his First Sergeant who gave me a brief tour of the camp and introduced me to some of the officers with whom I would be working; the Province S-2 (the Intelligence Officer — a Major) and the Province S-3 (the Operations Officer — also a Major).

The S-2 and S-3 worked together with their Vietnamese counterparts to plan operations against the Viet Cong who operated in the province. Much of my communications with Province HQ during my tour would be with the S-2 and S-3. The next stop was the S-4 shop (Supply — run by a senior NCO) where I was issued more equipment and ammunition for my rifle.

Then the First Sergeant took me to the small mess hall and made a group introduction to the few men who were there. He left me there to have some lunch. While I was sitting there eating, I noticed that unlike what I saw in Saigon, everyone's jungle fatigues here were unpressed and faded to a much lighter green than my newly issued fatigues. Nothing here was wrinkle free or even close to being starched. The color difference stood me apart from the others in the mess hall in a way that I found unsettling. A messenger found me (easy to do given my fatigues) and bringing me back to reality, told me to report to the S-3 shop.

---

[2] Song Be as a village does not exist today. If you search for Song Be with Google Earth, it will take you to the middle of the Song Be River delta. To explore this area today with Google Earth, search for Nui Ba Ra, the mountain close to the former site of Song Be.

The S-3 told me to get my field gear[3] together and report to the aid station. I was going out on a Med-Cap this afternoon. A Med-Cap was a Medical Civic Action Patrol. I was both excited and nervous. I was going on my first operation — granted only as an observer on my first day in province. I assembled my web gear, filled my canteen, and loaded 28 cartridges into each of the four magazines for my M-16.

The mental image that I formed of the Med-Cap while organizing my gear turned out to be very different from the actual Med-Cap. Expecting to find at least a squad, if not full platoon of Vietnamese soldiers riding in trucks for protection and a doctor, what I saw when I got to the aid station was a medic sitting alone in an idling jeep outside the aid station building. He greeted me as I walked up and said, "Good, you brought your M-16." I was to be the protection for this operation.

Driving much faster than I would have (then), the medic headed out of the compound and down a rutted, muddy road to a Montagnard village a few miles away. During the drive to the village, the medic asked

Figure 1.2   A typical Montagnard long house.

---

[3] Field Gear: Everything I needed to go on an operation.

what I had done in civilian life, and I told him that I had been a biology teacher. He asked if I could take blood pressures, pulses, and give injections. I replied that I could, and he smiled.

Based on my training, the village was what I expected. The Montagnards lived in long elevated communal houses with their various animals living beneath the houses. Before the war the Montagnards were nomadic, moving from place to place, and their houses were temporary. The political situation today made their villages more permanent.

Arriving at the village, we were surrounded by children waiting for the medic to hand out candy bars that he carried in one of his many bags. With that done, the Village Chief met us, and the medic communicated with him using a few words and a lot of hand gestures and pointing. These Montagnards spoke Stieng, but did not speak Vietnamese, much less English, so our Vietnamese language skills were useless.

Figure 1.3.   A Montagnard child.

The medic spread a green army poncho on the hood of the jeep. Then he laid out his supplies, a stethoscope, and blood pressure cuff, and the villagers lined up for our clinic. He greeted each person, gestured "What is wrong?", and made a visual evaluation. Then he listened to their hearts with the stethoscope, and if he thought it was necessary, passed the stethoscope to me to take a blood pressure. If he thought a shot was needed, he would tell me what medicine and what dosage to use. The shots were limited to antibiotics and vitamins. Unless the medicine was a single dose, pills were out of the question. The Montagnards did not understand, "Twice a day" or similar. If they were given an envelope with 14 pills to be taken twice a day for a week, they would simply take all of them at once. Rashes received a smear of ointment; minor cuts and abrasions some antibiotic cream and a bandage. For serious cuts and sprains I assisted him as he treated and dressed them. Fortunately, there were no broken bones this time. That would have meant driving the villager back to a civilian hospital at Song Be for treatment, and then returning him or her to the village. One trip

5

down a jungle road was usually safe because any nearby Viet Cong would not be expecting you. The second trip was risky — they might be waiting for your return. A third and fourth trip could be very bad.

After this was over, we were invited to a celebration that I had heard about during my training. A villager brought out a large clay jar with a long neck and a long hollow reed which would serve as a straw. The pot contained some type of fermented Montagnard brew that did not have an inviting smell. The Village Chief put the reed down into the neck of the jar and pulled it out measuring the level of the liquid. Then he put the reed back in the pot and took a long swig with the reed. Pulling it out, he measured the new level of the liquid with his fingers. Holding two fingers apart to show the amount he had drunk, he handed the jar to the medic who was obligated to repeat the action. This time when the medic drank, the villagers urged him on to drink more and more, and they cheered when he finished. All of this was fascinating to me. Culturally it was quite educational, and I was pleased to be a firsthand witness to the ceremony — until the medic, holding two of his fingers apart to show how much he had managed to drink, passed the jar and the reed to me. There was no way out. This is what advisors in Vietnam did; win the hearts and minds of the people. I copied the Village Chief and the medic putting the reed into the jar and withdrawing it to mark the level. Then I put the reed back into the jar, exhaled as deeply as possible, and did my best to drink as much as I could. My total body reaction to this vile brew as I struggled to drink my share generated a loud and hearty reaction by villagers.[4] The only good side effect of this stuff was that it made the drive back to Song Be much less worrisome, and the road seemed smoother.

The next morning, I was tasked to take a resupply of ammunition by helicopter to a fortified camp near the Cambodian border in an area called Bu Gia Mop. The soldiers had been in heavy contact the previous night and needed a resupply of everything. Sitting on the edge of the open doorway with my legs hanging down near the skids of a helicopter

---

[4] This ceremony was often a source of hepatitis among advisors. I was fortunate to avoid it.

Figure 1.4   Two camps: a remote outpost and Dong Xoai.

that was flying over rolling terrain at treetop level to avoid enemy rifle fire was a thrill even though the terrain and vegetation of the area looked very inhospitable.

The heavily fortified camp was too small to land the helicopter so the pilot dropped the cargo net that carried most of the supplies outside the barbed wire. Then the ship's crew chief and I had to lay on the floor to hand the additional supplies carried in the cabin down to the soldiers standing on the ground, while the chopper pilot hovered trying to keep the machine stable and in one place. I wondered if my eventual posting was going to be like this one.

After lunch the S-3 again summoned me and told me that I was going to join MAT 111 at Dong Xoai that afternoon as their assistant team leader. The chopper would drop me there on the return trip to its base.

"Welcome to Dong Xoai, L T."[5] were the first words I heard when I got off the helicopter after it had settled down on the small asphalt blotch serving as a landing pad at the camp. The young Sergeant who shouted those words over the THUMP, THUMP, THUMP of the Huey's rotor blades extended his hand to shake mine. There would be no saluting between officers and NCOs here. Salutes identified leaders to others, including enemy snipers. This was the first time I had been ever addressed as, "L T," and it is among one of the proudest moments of my service.

After shaking my hand, the Sergeant took my duffle bag, threw it on the hood of the jeep, and drove us the short distance to the team house where the introductions began. Compared to the camp in Bu Gia Mop, Dong Xoai was a luxury resort — or so it seemed.

---

[5] L T instead of "Sir" was the informal way many Lieutenants were often addressed in an Infantry unit.

Story 2 - I don't Talk to Lizards

WARNING
This story repeatedly uses a word that many consider to be an extreme obscenity, but it must be used to tell the story.

I had just arrived at Dong Xoai (DX) by the work helicopter. I was joining MAT 111 as the Assistant Team Leader. The camp at DX was home to the Vietnamese District Chief, his staff, and their families and two Regional Force (RF) companies. Two 105 mm Howitzers crewed by the RF soldiers were also inside the perimeter. The families of the RF

Figure 2.1 The outer defensive perimeter showing the living accommodations for some of the soldiers and their families.

troops were housed within the camp's defenses; some in dismal conditions right next to the outer perimeter.

When the jeep pulled up to the team house, I was greeted by the MAT Team members: The Captain who was the team leader, the Lieutenant I was replacing, two senior NCOs, and the Medic.

The Lieutenant took charge of showing me around. He introduced me to the District Advisory Team that was composed of four men: The District Senior Advisor who was the boss — a Major, his NCO, the Intelligence Team Captain, and the Intelligence team NCO who had met me at the helipad. Members of both teams were cordial but not particularly warm, after all I was a green Lieutenant replacing a seasoned one. I knew that I was in for some kidding and had much work to do to earn their respect.

Both the MAT and District Advisory Teams were based within the inner defensive perimeter occupying two team houses capable of sleeping and feeding about 15 men. The larger house had a well-equipped kitchen and central area for eating, meeting, and planning. Connected to this large team house was an extensive bunker system with a medical room for treating wounded, a storage room, and a command center. The smaller team house, about twenty feet from the door to the kitchen was strictly bunk space. Everyone had a "room" which was partitioned off by a wooden frame and covered with woven palm fronds which provided visual privacy but nothing for sound. A snorer could serenade everyone. The Green Berets for whom this camp was built managed to scrounge and otherwise equip the two team houses very nicely. As I would learn, I was fortunate to be based here.

After eating dinner, I decided to take a shower. There was some water pressure in the shower provided by two raised water buffalos (trailers) but the only water heating was from the sun. I excused myself, got my things, and walked to the shower. The water was not too cold but not really warm. I got used to it and was washing off the day's dust and sweat when I heard a somewhat high-pitched sound,

aaarrrhhHH...aaarrrhhHH...aaarrrhhHH

Fuck You... Fuck You... Fuck You

aaarrrhhhh

There it was, the first ribbing or kidding by one of the teams' NCOs. I decided to ignore it.

Then again,

aaarrrhhHH…aaarrrhhHH…aaarrrhhHH

Fuck You… Fuck You… Fuck You

aaarrrhhhh

If I just stay quiet, he will get bored and go away. He has to have better things than to continue to try and get a response from me…

aaarrrhhHH…aaarrrhhHH…aaarrrhhHH

Fuck You… Fuck You… Fuck You

aaarrrhhhh

OK, that's it! I replied with three extremely loud, "Fuck You"s and kept on showering. I heard nothing further.

I walked back into the main room of the team house to find most of the team members there, and some were playing cards. Someone asked me to join them, so I took my stuff to my room and returned. As I sat down, one of the Sergeants looked up and asked, "L T, do you talk to lizards very much back home?" I asked him what he meant. Another Sergeant replied, "You were just talking to a lizard a bit earlier and we were just wondering." The others chuckled. I didn't get it at first and then it dawned on me. I replied, "That was no lizard; it was one of you. Don't worry, I'll figure out which one of you it was. You're not going to get me!" With this, they all laughed. The NCO next to me patted me on the shoulder as the cards were being dealt.

This lizard kidding continued the next few days, and I heard the call from time to time. I just figured that one of the Sergeants was making the call as a joke, and the others were playing along.

It was my eighth day at Dong Xoai, and I was pulling my first radio watch which is detailed in the next story. Sometime after the "rat on the shelf incident,"[6] I took my M-16, went outside, and climbed up on the top of the bunker. The concrete was still warm from the sun. It was very quiet; not a sound, no engines, no movement, nothing. And with no electricity in the camp or in the nearby village, it was DARK. There were no clouds, and the moon was not out. Laying back on the warm bunker roof, I could see the vast covering of stars extending to infinity. It seemed odd to me that this beauty could be the nighttime cover of a war zone.

Then I heard a slight noise; not enough to be made by a human, so I wasn't startled. Sort of a scurry of little feet; probably another rat. It seemed to be on the tin roof of the team house behind me. I sat up and turned around and looked towards the noise. More scurrying. Then I heard it;

aaarrrhhHH…aaarrrhhHH…aaarrrhhHH

Fuck You… Fuck You… Fuck You

aaarrrhhhh

Very slowly I removed the red lens cover on my flashlight, pointed the light at the sound, turned the white light on, and could see it but for only a moment before it scurried away. So, I had been talking to a lizard.

The next morning, after I gave my first Radio Watch report, one of the NCOs asked, "What did the lizard have to say last night, L T?" I replied, "We had a face-to-face meeting, saw eye-to-eye on the situation, and settled things." This produced a good round of laughs and a good way to begin the day.

---

[6] The "rat on the shelf incident" is also detailed in the next story.

Story 3 - Radio Watch

Our camp at Dong Xoai was the base for nine Americans. In addition to the five on the MAT Team there were four soldiers on the District Team led by the District Senior Advisor (DSA), a Major who was the "boss."

Part of the routine for daily camp life was radio watch. Everyone but the Major pulled radio watch, ideally in rotation once every eight days

Figure 3.1 Radio Watch monitored activity from this location in the team house. The door to the team house (not in the picture) is about five feet to the left. Part of the bunker entrance can be seen on the left side the picture. The door to the small briefing room where I sat at night (also not in the picture) is to the right.

which was often disturbed when one or two of us were out of camp on an operation, at Song Be for a meeting, or in Saigon dealing with something that required our presence.

Before going off watch in the morning, the last set of duties for Radio Watch was to go out to the generator area behind the team house at 0600 hours and start generator #1. Then he had to go into the bunker and turn on the radio that had the range to reach Song Be that was about 25 miles to our north. This radio did not run on batteries; it required 110 volts. He made a communication check with Province and tested the "Green Machine"; a scrambler that was used for secure voice communications. The rest of us, if we were not already up, got up when the generator started. While the radio checks were being made, we shaved, dressed and made our way to the dining area. Tei Lai, our cook had arrived earlier to start breakfast for the day. Outgoing Radio Watch gave a report to everyone at breakfast and turned the duty over to oncoming Radio Watch.

For the next twenty-four hours, Radio Watch stayed close to the radio terminal in the team house that was connected to the radio in the bunker. All calls were taken, logged and dealt with accordingly. If Radio Watch had to leave the area, he asked another team member to cover the radio. The radio must never be left unattended.

At some point in the day the Huey work helicopter would call to say it was inbound for some reason: delivering a visitor, bringing supplies and our mail. Radio Watch would pick up the mail sack and drive the jeep the short distance to the helipad to swap the outgoing mail sack for the incoming mail sack. He also picked up any other items being delivered. Once a month the Huey would deliver our supply of gasoline for the jeeps and the generators in 55-gallon drums, a butane cylinder for cooking if needed, and any other POL[7] supplies we had requisitioned. Radio Watch was responsible for gathering other team members to help move these supplies to their proper storage locations around the camp.

At noon, Radio Watch went to the bunker and called Province to inform them that we were going off the air. He would turn the radio and

---

[7] POL: Petroleum, Oil, Lubricants.

the green machine off. Then he would go to the generator area and shut down generator #1 and start #2. Back to the bunker to turn the radio and green machine on and call Province to say we were back on the air.

The same routine was repeated at 6:00 PM. We had three 10KW generators and ran each one six hours each day supplying electricity to our team houses, to the Regional Force[8] headquarters, and to the District Chief's offices. From time to time, we had to inspect the wires running to those two areas to clear parasitic taps made by the RF troops for some electricity. They did not need much — just a little for a light bulb. We did not like cutting those wires but the taps did degrade the overall system. Besides, they quickly replaced them.

The electrical system had a fuse block to protect both the generators and the radio equipment. The fuse block used cartridge fuses which were no longer available in Vietnam. Someone in the past discovered that plumbing solder, which was available, could be used as fuse wire because it melted at a fairly low temperature. Using the solder was simple. Pull a length off of a spool of solder measured by holding the end of the solder in one hand and the solder spool in the other. Then you unroll the solder by stretching your arms apart as wide as possible and cut the unspooled length from the roll. You wrap the solder around the fuse cartridge contacts in the fuse block closing the circuit. Hopefully, you had shut down the generator first. If too much power was moving through the circuit, the solder melted protecting the generator and the electrical equipment it powered.

At midnight Radio Watch went to the bunker and reset the keys on the green machine with the new security pattern and called Province to check the key pattern. If it did not work, the procedure was repeated. Once it worked, Radio Watch told Province that Dong Xoai was going off the air until 0600 hours tomorrow. Then he shut down the radio and green machine. Next, he set up a fresh pot of coffee that would start brewing tomorrow morning when he started generator #1. With this done he went to the generators and turned off #3.

---

[8] The RF company was analogous to our National Guard responsible for security in the district.

At that point everything in the camp went quiet — dead silence with only the sounds of the insects that had managed to survive the chemical dosing for mosquitoes and other pests. With camp activities settled down for the first time in eighteen hours, he went back to the team house, turned on a battery powered field radio[9], lit a kerosene fueled Coleman lantern, and spent the next six hours alone with only the dim light of the lantern waiting for dawn.

The six hours between midnight and 6 AM were extremely quiet except for the hourly pipe clanging at defensive positions on the perimeter by the soldiers on watch to indicate they were awake. Usually, outgoing harassment and interdiction artillery firings by the 105 mm howitzers were finished. After this, any explosive sounds meant incoming shells from a Viet Cong mortar attack, a harassing ground probe, or a full-scale ground assault. If that happened, Radio Watch went out to the top of the bunker and started the emergency generator so the radios could be brought back on line and Province could be contacted. Because the field radio was too weak to send a transmission that far, communication with Province during an attack required 110 volts of electricity.

At 0600 hours the next morning Radio Watch wrapped up his duties as explained earlier. Then, maybe a shower (cold — of course), breakfast, and hit the bunk for some sleep. The rest of the day was duty free if the situation permitted (which was often not the case…).

My first radio watch was probably 8 days after I arrived in Dong Xoai since I would have been added to the bottom of the rotation. I remember having thoughts of a Viet Cong bursting through the team house door with a pack of high explosives and a short fuse on his back. The location of our team house was not a secret, so the local force Viet Cong knew where we were. American advisors were high priority targets

---

[9] The field radio was too weak to reach Province. We could receive Province, but they could not receive our calls. It was also used for emergency calls from other units that might be in the area and from passing air traffic. Because Dong Xoai was black at night; there were no lights to identify the camp's location from the air.

for the Viet Cong. It was not uncommon for the Viet Cong to offer a reward for the death of an advisor. That I am writing this shows no one collected a reward for me. Nor was it collected for any of the other eight advisors at Dong Xoai, though it came close to happening on several occasions. This did happen at province headquarters before I arrived. During an attack, a Viet Cong soldier carrying an explosive backpack managed to enter the province command center and detonate his backpack killing a number of senior advisors including the well-respected Province Senior Advisor.

Throughout my tour I used radio watch nights in various ways. I wrote letters home to my wife, my parents, and others. If it wasn't raining, I sat outside on top of the bunker in total darkness to get some air (and mosquito bites) and to make cassette tapes to send home. Inside I would sit in the darkened entrance to the small dark briefing room adjacent to the radio area with my M-16 in my hands waiting for that Viet Cong to charge through the door.

But my first radio watch was much different; I almost shot up the kitchen. A bit nervous and more than a bit scared, I was sitting in the briefing room entrance waiting for that Viet Cong when I heard a crash in the kitchen. I got up from the chair flipping my M-16's safety to AUTO, and peered out of the briefing room looking towards the door between the team room and the kitchen. The Coleman lantern provided very little light in that area, so it revealed nothing. I waited a while, nervously listening for any sounds and heard nothing. Moving out of the doorway to the briefing room over to the radio watch desk, I picked up the flashlight with a red lens cover[10] and crept towards the kitchen — still listening carefully for any sounds of movement. When I got to the kitchen, I slowly opened the screen door as quietly as possible. Hearing nothing, I stepped into the room. There was nothing. Still shaken, I returned to the darkened doorway and kept an even more vigilant eye out for that Viet Cong with the exploding backpack.

---

[10] The red lens cover allowed us to maintain some of our night vision though it was already somewhat compromised by the light from the Coleman Lantern.

The next morning, after starting the generator, I related this along with the talking lizard experiences to the team during my report at breakfast. It provided some amusement among the veterans. One member then explained that the kitchen noise was probably a rat moving on one of the shelves in the kitchen where canned food was stored pushing a can off the shelf onto the floor — apparently a common nighttime occurrence. After breakfast I checked with the cook, and there was a can on the floor when she came in that morning.

I still wonder to this day what would have been the consequences if I had sprayed the kitchen wall with 28 rounds of M16 ammunition. It is quite likely that this set of stories about being a member of MAT 111 would be significantly shorter.

For my entire tour, I spent radio watch with the same attitude always waiting for the Viet Cong with the explosive backpack to come through the team house door.

Story 4 - The First Haircut

The Army does not like long hair. The first haircut of basic training was a rite of passage for every enlisted soldier. During the six months in Infantry OCS (Officer Candidate School), I had my hair cut twice a week whether it was needed or not. Vietnam was not a good place for long hair either. It was hot, sweaty, and on a five-day operation became a filthy mess.

I had been at Dong Xoai about two weeks. The Lieutenant I replaced was gone. I had stood my first radio watch and I felt I was beginning to settle into the administrative aspects of being the assistant MAT Team leader. New experiences continued to present themselves, and my first hair cut at Dong Xoai was one of those occasions.

Roughly twice a month the local village barber came to the team house, often with a friend to help him carry things. We did not allow very many Vietnamese into the team house or in our area of the inner perimeter. When they were in the house, a number of documents, pieces of equipment, and maps were covered with cloth. Allowing civilians into the area allowed a possible Viet Cong spy to mentally map the layout of our area and to measure distances by counting the steps it took to walk into and out of the area. At least that was my thinking, but hey, I was just a new Lieutenant. I tried to keep my thoughts about this and other similar issues to myself, offering advice only when asked.

The barber set up shop in the main team room. His helper brought over a stool that usually sat in one corner of the room. The barber spread his tools out on a table and was open for business. Electricity was not readily available in the village so he had to use hand powered clippers in his shop. Here, though, it was different. Generating our own electricity for eighteen hours each day allowed him to use a set of electric clippers that we owned. Apparently mailed to the team by the family of a past team member, they were a luxury item to him. He would walk over to the clippers that were laying on the table and pick them up. Turning them on and listening to the hum of the blades, he would look at us and say in the tonal way Vietnamese is spoken, "Numbah one". These clippers were probably the real reason he came to cut our hair.

Every Vietnamese I encountered had "numbah one" along with, "numbah ten" in their vocabulary. Number one was VERY GOOD while number ten was VERY BAD.

Most of the advisors were there, and as the newbie at Dong Xoai, I had the honor of going first. I climbed up on the stool, and the barber covered me with a cloth apron. Turning on the clippers, he began to cut my hair; the sides, the back, the top. There were no mirrors, so I had no idea how much he was removing or what I looked like, but since none of the others were laughing, I figured that I was ok.

The clippers switched off and I felt something cold and wet on my neck — shaving cream — for the final trim.

Then I heard it — the sound of metal sliding on leather, a straight razor on a razor strop, a CUT THROAT RAZOR!

What felt like a strong jolt of electricity sat me upright — it was total abject fear — and I was off the stool, on my feet, and starting to move away. One of the Sergeants, apparently anticipating my reaction stepped in front of me blocking my exit and said, "It's ok, L T."

Two thoughts immediately came into mind: another set of laughter and ribbing was coming, but I heard nothing. Looking around at the team and into their faces, I did not see humor; I saw concern, possibly from a flash back to the memory of their first time sitting on that stool. There would be no laughter about this now or ever. The other thought was about how the barber and his helper were reacting to my behavior. Was my reaction typical? Part of my job was to convey trust and respect of the Vietnamese people and culture; to win their hearts and minds. My behavior conveyed a lot of things but definitely not that. Were these two men thinking that I just saw them as just a couple of dinks who are friends during the day and Vietcong at night?

Embarrassed and not wanting to face the two Vietnamese, I backed up and sat down on the stool, closed my eyes tightly and endured the longest shave of my life.

Finally, the barber wiped off my neck, removed the apron, and shook the hair from it. I stood up, pulled some Vietnamese currency from of my pocket and handed him his fee for the haircut without looking him in the eye. Then, possibly to assuage my embarrassment of my reaction to the razor, I gave him another bill. I do not remember how much it was but it must have been big. The barber took it, looked at it, and then looked at me and smiling, said in his tonal, sing-song tone, "L T numbah one."

Story 5 - First Contact

It was late May, and I had been at Dong Xoai a little less than a month. I had just been promoted to First Lieutenant in a brief ceremony with the other MAT Team members and the District Team attending. The Major read the orders for my promotion and handed me a pair of silver bars, while the Team Captain pinned one black bar[11] on my collar. The party was simple — beer for everyone and I was buying; at 10¢ a can for Budweiser, 5¢ for everything else, it was a cheap party.

Things were settling into a routine, and I thought I was close to adjusting to the reality of this world. That night the generators had been off for a while, but I was not fully asleep when I heard the pops; 3, maybe 4? I knew that I had about ten-seconds before the mortar shells those pops had launched hit their targets — **US.** Then I heard the weapons: **AK47 rifle fire and Viet Cong machine gun fire.**

How could I, a green First Lieutenant, a newbie, recognize those sounds so quickly and accurately? During my Advanced Individual Training (AIT) for the Infantry, "Tiger Land" at Ft. Polk, Louisiana made things as realistic as possible for us. One of the training phases, "Crack and Thump" put my squad[12] in a shallow hole in the middle of an open field — no cadre[13] — just trainees. The hole was surrounded by a row of sandbags. If you got up on your knees, you could see over the top of the

---

[11] Black bar: We wore "subdued" insignia on our jungle fatigues to better blend in with the jungle foliage and present less of a target to the Viet Cong. Black was the subdued version of silver colored rank 1LTs wore. A dirty bronze was the subdued version of gold colored rank insignia 2LTs wore. The other collar end had black Infantry Crossed Rifles insignia.

[12] I was a trainee squad leader. A squad was composed of 11 men and the leader.

[13] Cadre: Drill Sergeants, Training NCOs and Training Officers.

sandbags. We had a radio with a loud speaker so all of us could hear it. As squad leader, I made the required replies when needed. The voice on the other end of the radio explained what we had to do and what was about to happen.

We were told to lay down on our back looking up and stay there. That was the easy part. Then they told us that the next thing we would hear was a mortar firing two 81 mm rounds at the maximum range for the weapon — about 3000 meters (3 KM). They were not firing at us or over us so the rounds would explode at a safe distance. We were told to count the seconds, "One thousand and one, one thousand and two, ..." until we heard the explosions, so we would know how much time we had to react before the shells exploded. That is how I recognized the pops that night and knew about how much time I had to react.

Then the voice told us what each subsequent sound would be. The crack would be the sound of the bullet passing closely over our heads as we lay on our backs in the hole. The thump which we would hear a bit later would be the sound from the weapon that fired the bullet. The time delay between the crack and the thump would indicate how close or distant the shooter was. Then they shot at us. First, the US weapon, then the corresponding Viet Cong version: M-16 and AK-47, M-60 machine gun and VC machine gun, .50-caliber machine gun and .51 caliber machine gun. That is how I knew what was shooting at us that night.

<u>Back to Dong Xoai</u>. I had practiced my reaction for this numerous times in daylight. I rolled out of my bunk onto the concrete floor. Laying there waiting for me were my carefully placed and arranged steel helmet, trousers, boots, web gear, flak jacket, and weapon all within easy reach and easily donned. Or so I thought. The helmet was easy. However, in the darkness my pants were a problem, but I finally got them on. The boots were next but the lacing would have to wait. Then the web gear, flak jacket and finally my rifle. All of this was done while trying to stay on my back as close to the concrete floor as possible.

During this time the enemy weapon firing continued; now joined by M-16 and M-60 machine gun return defensive fire. The first mortar rounds had hit exploding somewhere nearby and there were more pops; more incoming mortar rounds. Grabbing my rifle, I was ready to move. Stooping up rather than standing up, I opened the door, stepped into the hallway, turned left, and headed towards the main team house checking each room as I passed by to insure it was empty. Everyone had moved much faster than me.

The gap between the two team houses was only about twenty feet but it seemed much larger that night. I waited alone at the door before crossing because I could hear machine gun fire.

Again, Ft. Polk had done a good job. A well-trained gunner operates his weapon in a manner that is much different from the way John Wayne, Rambo, or Schwarzenegger do in the movies. The attacker cannot fire long, extended bursts. He cannot carry that many bullets. If he did, the recoil of the extended burst would cause very inaccurate results in his targeting after the first few rounds, and he would risk melting the barrel of the weapon. An attacking force uses the machine gun to suppress the defense's machine gun fire. The gunner fires 5-7 round bursts using the tracer rounds (rounds that are filled with phosphorous and glow brightly

Figure 5.1 This is the gap between the two team houses that we had to cross during attacks on the camp. The main team house is on the left. YB and I along with two other team members bunked in the smaller team house on the right. After the second attack we added the two rows of oil drums filled with gravel for protection against small arms fire and shrapnel.

as they travel — our tracers were red and theirs were green) to direct the fire. The gunner would fire one or two bursts and then switch targets if no return fire was received.

One of the enemy gunners was targeting the .50-caliber machine gun position behind the main team house near the space between the two team houses. The first crack of bullets with green tracers passing through the space between the two team house came a few seconds after I got to the door followed by their corresponding thumps. The gunner was not too close. After a pause, a second set of tracers passed between the two team houses. There were no tracers or cracks before the next set of thumps so I made a quick crossing to the main team house.

We were to rally at the radio position, and I was the last to arrive. Then someone asked, "Where is YB?" I muttered, "Shit" and said, "I'll get him." I had just made a major mistake as an Infantry Lieutenant. As the ranking officer — in fact the only officer — in the other team house it was my duty to clear the house before leaving it. I was supposed to be the last man out of the house. Instead of turning left upon leaving my room, I should have turned right and moved to YB's room first and checked his status. That mistake came close to killing me and so very much closer to killing YB.

YB was the Intelligence Team NCO — the young Sergeant who met me with the jeep when I arrived at Dong Xoai. His nickname, "Y B" had an interesting origin but this is not the time to go into that...

I repeated the process for crossing back over to the other team house: waiting, counting, listening, and observing machine gun bullet tracers to time the crossing as safely as possible. As I ran down the hallway, I remember yelling, "**YB**" and hearing his reply — he was ok. I moved further down the hall towards him and ... I remember trying to get up off of the concrete floor. All of this was happening in total darkness, and now the air had a heavy smell of dust and explosives. I groped my way towards YB's room and heard him trying to speak, but it was garbled and pained. He sounded like he was rolling around on the floor. My first thought was that there was a VC in his room, and YB was fighting with him. I vividly remember my next thought, "Damn, I'm gonna' die tonight!" I dared not use my M-16 because I could not see; any gunfire would probably hit YB. So, I pulled my bayonet and entered his room.

YB was alone. He began to speak just a bit more clearly and mumbled that he thought he could walk. Helping him up, we headed back towards the team house door. When we got there, YB mumbled, "Rifle" and disappeared in the darkness heading back towards his room. Army training — never get separated from your weapon.

I waited at the door for YB to return counting machine gun bursts and watching more green tracers. A flash of light from something somewhere within the inner perimeter shined briefly on a sweaty bare back of a human form carrying a rifle and crouching at the corner of the other team house. I had moved the selection lever on my M-16 from SAFE to AUTO when I heard two whispered words, "L" "T". The figure was one of the team's NCOs, wearing only his shorts, trying to find out what was happening. I called back that YB was hit and to get the medic ready. I would bring him over in a few seconds.

By this time YB had rejoined me at the door. We counted machine gun cracks, watched the green tracers, and crossed the 20-foot space safely to the main team house where the medic was waiting. He asked if I was ok and I replied, "Take care of YB."

I rejoined the rest of the MAT Team and the District Team at the radio. Things were chaotic. The emergency generator did not start up as it should have. The District NCO was outside exposed to weapons fire and mortar shells trying to start it. Without that generator, we had no way of contacting Song Be to call for help.

The VC attack failed to penetrate the outer perimeter, and the fighting ebbed. Then it was quiet. We relit the Coleman lantern in the team house and checked each other out, I found out why I had trouble putting my pants on. They were on in-side-out which provided a good laugh to the team veterans and another mark against green Lieutenants.

I still think about my failure to clear YB's room first. Had I done that, both of us would have been in the main team house when the mortar hit his room and YB would not have been wounded. And I would not have come within a half second of killing one of the Sergeants on my team. I honestly believe that the list of mistakes I made in Vietnam is extremely short, but I am troubled that this is number one on that list.

Jim Roberts

YB was the youngest American at Dong Xoai. He was a Sergeant E-5; the first of the five Sergeant or NCO ranks in 1971. This rank is commonly called "Buck Sergeant". This gave him the nickname, "Young Buck" which soon became "YB."

Story 6 - First Contact
The Next Day

A medical evacuation helicopter flew in at first light to pick up YB. He had a hole through his cheek, and the medic had removed a three-inch-long shrapnel splinter from his tongue. The medic was worried that a small fragment might have penetrated his skull and was evacing him for X-rays and further treatment. The medic asked me if I needed to get checked but I declined. I had pulled a shrapnel splinter out of the base of my right hand, but I was fine and there was work to be done. I found some metal splinters in my flak jacket and in the cloth covering of my steel helmet. Years later I developed what looked like the beginning of an abscess beside the third knuckle of my left hand. One day I squeezed it and a small rough piece of metal a bit larger than a BB worked its way out. It had been there all that time. I was very lucky.

The morning light also revealed the details hidden by the darkness. The attack was typical. The mortar fire and small arms fire was supposed to distract and drive the defenders into their bunkers. While this was happening, a group of Viet Cong (VC) soldiers, almost naked so their clothing would not catch on the barbed wire defenses was supposed to crawl through the wire and the mine field in another part of the perimeter. Once inside the wire, some of these soldiers who were carrying bags of grenades would throw them in random directions at intervals. From inside a bunker, the pop of the mortar tubes would not be heard, but the explosions of the grenades would have sounded like exploding mortar shells. This was supposed to keep the defenders in their bunkers and allow the remaining VC, each carrying an explosive backpack with a very short fuse to enter the command bunkers and other important positions within the inner perimeter, and detonate the explosives in suicide attacks.

Apparently two things happened that thwarted their attacks:

- Our defenders did not retreat into bunkers but stayed at their positions and engaged the enemy delaying the VC soldiers' attempt to crawl through the wire and mine field that was protecting the outer perimeter.

- The VC planned on using a rocket propelled grenade (RPG) launcher to destroy the defending machine gun positions. The first rocket propelled grenade fired by the Viet Cong was apparently bad and detonated immediately when it was fired, destroying the launcher and killing the VC. With these two occurrences, the attack failed and the VC withdrew.

The District Team NCO went to work immediately on the emergency generator to see why it did not start. When he was finished, it would start easily the next time we were attacked, and Radio Watch would not needlessly be exposed.

Inspecting YB's room, we saw that the shell had hit a wooden support

Figure 6.1 YB's quarters.

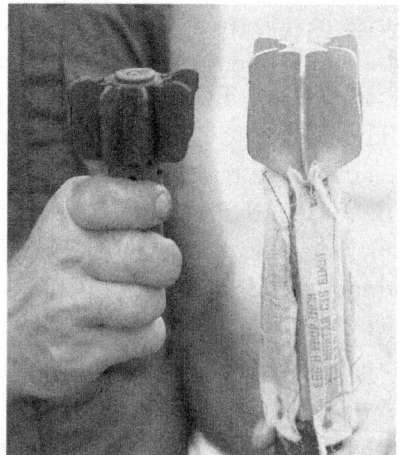

Figure 6.2 The fin sections of the VC mortar round that hit YB's quarters on the left and an unexploded US mortar round of similar size on the right.

member of the roof over his head and exploded about 5 feet away from him (Figure 6.1). When he heard the mortar pops, he had rolled out of his bunk onto the floor. He was on his knees putting on his flak jacket in such a way that it blocked the shrapnel that could have killed him. The blast knocked him down, wounding and stunning him. He was on the floor trying to gather his senses when I entered his room. The metal splinter in his tongue had made it difficult for him to speak. We also found the fin section of the exploded shell.

YB returned by chopper in the afternoon with a very sore tongue, a hole in his cheek, ringing in his ears, and a bottle of antibiotics, but otherwise, with a clean bill of health. The first thing he did, after checking in and assuring everyone that he was ok, was to gather his things and move into the larger team house. Looking at the topo map, it was clear that YB's end of the smaller team house was the closest point to the probable location of the Viet Cong mortar position, and that the shell that hit his room had probably traveled the maximum possible distance. Moving to the other team house seemed like a safe thing to do.

Last night's attack was the first attack on Dong Xoai in a long time. Our response to the attack began with a review of SOPs[14] with an eye to revising them and setting up new ones. During the discussions, I decided that the last place I wanted to be during an attack was inside a bunker or in the team house near the radios with a group of advisors. That sounded like too much of a target. With the image of a VC with an explosive backpack bursting into the room in my mind, I decided I'd rather take my chances outside with the incoming mortar rounds and small arms fire.

YB agreed with this thinking, so we suggested and the team agreed that he and I would move to an unused fighting position near the far end of the smaller team house where YB had slept.

When an attack began, we would check in at the radio watch position. Then YB and I would move back through the small team house to the fighting position with an M-60 machine gun and a portable field radio.

It wasn't much of a position. It was not constructed of concrete with

---

[14] SOP: Standard Operating Procedures.

Figure 6.3   A fighting position on the outer perimeter.

overhead cover like the outer perimeter position in Figure 6.3; rather it was a very small building built from stacked logs with sandbags on the top. The area inside the structure was originally used for storing ammunition to keep it out of the weather. We never entered this area. Using a flashlight, we leaned in and inspected what we could see but we did not step in. Why not? Chuck-No-Neck, Charlie-No Shoulders, Jake the Snake, Charlie-2 Step. All nick names for a pit viper named fer-de-lance that was endemic to this area of Vietnam. It was called Charlie-2 Step because some GIs thought that if you were bitten, you were dead by the time you took two steps. While its poison was not that quick, without an anti-venom injection, death was certain. We did not have anti-venom and getting it in time would be impossible. So, we just looked in and could not see ammunition or any type of explosive inside the structure. The top of the fighting position was in sad shape. The three rows of sandbags ringing the top were badly frayed from the harsh sunlight.

Firing the M-60 during an attack would be unlikely. The camp was defended by two perimeters. The outer perimeter was an extensive maze of barbed wire and land mine patterns. The Regional Force (RF) troops were positioned and lived in bunkers with their families just inside this outer perimeter. Raised, fortified fighting positions with overhead cover were located at intervals on this outer perimeter.

The barbed wire and mine field of the outer perimeter were initially kept clear of vegetation with the use of Agent Orange. Use of Agent Orange stopped in late 1970, and the jungle was rapidly reclaiming the area. The mine field prevented us from having the vegetation cut, and burning the areas would set off the mines. Even with the mine field, this growth provided sufficient cover for the VC to get close enough to the perimeter to bring effective fire on our positions.

The advisors' two team houses, the original .50-caliber machine gun position, and our new position were within an inner perimeter of barbed wire. We could only engage the enemy directly if and when they breached the outer permitter and began moving towards the inner perimeter. Otherwise, we would be shooting into the backs of the RF defenders on the outer perimeter. Our new position could also cover the road that passed through both perimeters to the center of the camp — a road that, in my humble Lieutenant's opinion was too lightly defended. Our primary mission would be to provide situation reports by radio for our sector of the perimeter to those back in the team house bunker. YB and I hoped that the failure of this attack and strong response by the RF troops would discourage future attacks for some time to come. It was a hope that would not last very long.

Story 7 - More Attacks ...

The time intervals between these first attacks are lost. Some dates are certain: when we arrived in country and at Dong Xoai, when we left. YB's Purple Heart citation gives us the exact date of the first attack. Few other dates of events are this exact. The Team Captain, YB, and I are certain that the second attack occurred soon after the first one, but the exact amount of time between them is not clear.

In the days after the first attack, things were a bit more settled, and the "normal" routine was slowly returning. Since YB and I were going to take a position away from the rest of the team and send back situation reports to the Major in the bunker, we needed a radio. The MAT Team had two field radios — an older model and its successor. They looked identical, but the older radio had a glass tube and the newer one was all solid state — a new development in 1971. All of the accessories were interchangeable and the range was the same (11 KM) for both. The newer model was more durable and the battery lasted a bit longer, so we used it when we were in the field. YB and I pulled the team's older model out of the storage area of the bunker and tested it; it still worked. This was the radio we would take to the fighting position. Initially we put the radio in the bunker near the entrance next to the radio watch station.

We would use the M-60 machine gun which was part of the MAT Team's standard equipment. Even though the NCOs had checked YB out on the gun prior to my arrival, we returned to the practice range outside the perimeter and went over the use of the weapon. We put the gun in the bunker next to the radio watch position. We moved a number of cans of M-60 ammunition to the top of the bunker and placed some sandbags on top of them. Then we practiced our movements in daylight and then at night just to be sure we could do them under stress in the darkness.

In 1965,[15] Dong Xoai was almost overrun by a force of over 1000 Viet Cong. This was a time when there was more American support and backup available than we had now. While we had no intelligence indicating a similar attack was imminent, I could not help but wonder if the attack was a probe in preparation for more frequent attacks, if not a much heavier assault by a larger force. With this in mind, YB and I decided to make the radio part of an E&E (Escape and Evasion) backpack. Instead of using the radio's pack frame, we secured the radio to a regular rucksack frame and tied the canvas pack over the radio. We now had room for the gear we would need if we were overrun and had to escape the camp and evade the Viet Cong. Among other items, this included:

- A spare radio battery.
- The radio's collapsible ten-foot-long accessory antenna for greater range.
- A spare handset.
- Extra M-16 magazines (loaded — of course).
- An M-16 cleaning kit.
- A topographic map for Dong Xoai with marked pre-arranged rally points for pickup up if we had to escape and evade.
- Two star clusters (hand held/fired aerial flares) and two smoke grenades to mark our position for a circling helicopter.
- Extra first aid field dressings.
- A survival kit that included a small supply of amphetamine tablets to keep us going if sleep was not possible.
- A metal can of morphine syrettes.
- Two sticks of C4 plastic explosive, blasting caps, fuse, and igniters.
- Two ponchos and two poncho liners.
- Hershey's Tropical Chocolate Bars (see Story 14).
- Two canteens of water.
- Iodine tablets for purifying water.
- Extra mosquito repellant.

---

[15] Two Congressional Medals of Honor, one posthumously, were awarded after that battle. Search the web for, "The Battle of Dong Xoai".

Instead of keeping the radio in the bunker, I moved it to my room for immediate access and added it to my rehearsed pattern of getting geared up when we were attacked. Getting dressed in total darkness during an attack seemed like a waste of time, so I decided that I would sleep in a tee shirt, my fatigue trousers, and wear a pair of tennis shoes. Every night I would strap one pair of jungle boots and my jungle fatigue shirt to the outside of the radio pack. In the chest pocket of the fatigue shirt was a compass, the SOI (Signals Operating Instructions), and whiz wheel used to encrypt the coordinates of our location before radioing them over an unsecure channel. I practiced rolling out of my bunk and into this gear in the daylight and darkness so I would be ready for the next attack. Or at least I hoped I would. I wondered how long I would have to wait — hopefully a very long time... but that would not be the case.

Our rehearsals proved useful in a second attack. The pops of the mortar tube woke me up. I rolled out of my bunk and onto the floor. Quickly putting on my gear and the radio pack, I cleared the team house and checked in at the radio watch position. This attack was like the first one: small arms fire and mortars. YB retrieved the M-60 from the bunker and we crossed the space between the two team houses, back through the smaller team house to the fighting position where we called in situation reports by radio. The Team Captain and the District NCO moved to the .50-caliber machine gun position behind the main team house. The attack ebbed as quickly as it began with no casualties for the RF troops or the advisors.

While the District Team NCO had been firing the .50 cal machine gun on the probable VC mortar positions, the MAT Team Captain, acting as the assistant gunner was positioned near one of the wooden posts that supported the overhead concrete cover when he sensed something momentarily near his ear. The next morning, curiosity took him back to the machine gun position. He checked the post he had been near and found what appeared to be a fresh mark in the wood. Digging into the mark with his knife, he pried out an AK47 slug. Like YB in the first attack, the Team Captain was very lucky in this one.

A few days after the second attack, the two MAT Team Sergeants hooked the team's trailer to the team jeep and "disappeared" for part of the day. The Team Captain and I knew better than to ask where they were going or what they were up to.

Later that day they returned with the trailer that was now covered with a tarp. Saying nothing, they came into the team house and pulled cold sodas out of the refrigerator and went to get something to eat. YB and I went out to the trailer and removed the tarp. Laying there was a pile of scattered metal pieces and a cardboard box filled with parts. YB and I

Figure 7.1 Our "new" .50-Cal machine gun and spare parts.

removed the haul, cleaned the pieces and put them together. When those pieces were reassembled, we had our second .50-caliber machine gun, a tripod on which to mount the gun, plus some important spare parts.

The Viet Cong could not fire their mortar from just anywhere when they attacked. The mortar uses a tripod system for support. The main leg of this tripod is the mortar tube. The other two legs were used to aim the tube. The base of the tube sits on a heavy metal base plate that absorbs the recoil when the mortar is fired. Because of this, the base plate must be set on firm ground. Set it up on wet, swampy ground, fire the mortar, and the recoil drives the base plate deep into the mud. The mortar fires shells in a very high arc, so overhead clearance is needed. These two requirements meant that we knew the two probable locations of their firing position. One was about 1000 meters out and the other was about 3000 meters. Both were well within the range of the .50-caliber machine gun positioned at the main team house and the one at this new position. And because of the distance, the machine gun would have to be fired upward at an angle that would carry the rounds safely over the heads of the RF troops on the outer perimeter.

To effectively cover both high grounds from which the Viet Cong could mortar us, we sat the new gun up on top of the bunker and sandbagged the tripod to keep the recoil from shifting the gun. Firing the gun from the tripod at a known target in the dark is best done by adding a third element to the gun system called a "T and E". "T and E" stands for "Traverse and Elevation." It is a small device that connects the gun to the tripod securely holding it in a specific predetermined position. We did not have a T and E so we improvised. We went to the village sawmill and bought several pieces of rough-cut wood. We cut them to length and sandbagged them on the edge of the top of the bunker at the two heights needed to aim the weapon at both probable mortar locations. We drove spikes and nailed wooden stops into these boards to position the gun laterally in the direction of the target areas. This insured two things:

- We would not accidentally fire into the backs of the RF troops on the outer perimeter.

- We could fire on the VC mortar positions in total darkness

If the outer perimeter were breeched, we could kick these restraints

Figure 7.2   Our fighting position with the newly "acquired" .50 cal machine gun.

off the top of the bunker and engage the enemy soldiers directly. We could also swing the weapon laterally and cover the road that led into the perimeter.

When the third attack came, our practice and planning paid off. After checking in at the team house, YB and I moved to the position and fired the gun on the suspected VC mortar positions. The other machine gun at the main team house did the same thing.

The next morning the Regional Force (RF) Captain came over to the gun's position while we were cleaning it. He told us that his troops were very surprised to hear the gun firing behind them and pleased to see the tracers heading out towards the possible VC mortar positions. He suggested that his troops take charge of the position in the future and that we act as observers. As advisors we had no command authority within the RF command structure, and it was his camp, so we agreed. Besides, every VC carrying a machine gun and RPG would be aiming at the machine gun positions, so observing and sending situation reports back to the team house might be somewhat safer if we were not actually on the position. And we still had the M-60 if we really needed it.

Story 8 - Food, Soda, Beer, & Payday

Generally new Lieutenants have a lot of responsibilities but not very much authority. The gold or silver bars on our collars carried no weight with the officers above us and very little with the seasoned NCOs. After commissioning in OCS[16], my first assignment was as the Executive Officer (XO)[17] and Training Officer of a basic training company at Ft. Campbell, Kentucky. On my first day at the company, I learned that in addition to being the XO and the Training Officer, I was also the supply officer, mess officer, security officer, morale officer, morals officer, vector control officer[18], fire suppression officer plus a few I have forgotten. Fortunately, the company had competent NCOs who actually did the work and I just signed the paperwork — think of Colonel Henry Blake and Radar in the television series, "M*A*S*H".

When I arrived at Dong Xoai as the Assistant Team Leader of MAT 111, I learned a different story; Those various jobs were there, but there were no NCOs to do them. They were all mine. In addition to maintaining the readiness of the team in terms of weapons, ammunition and similar items, I was also responsible for acquiring everything else the District Team and the MAT Team might need to function at the camp. This included, gasoline for the jeeps and generators, butane for cooking, food, soda, and beer. The gasoline, butane, and bullets were easy — radio the S-4 (supply) NCO at Province and request a resupply.

---

[16] Officer Candidate School.

[17] Second in command of the company — a unit of about 200 soldiers.

[18] Vector Control: Think, "Disease Transmission" control or more simply, rat and bug killer.

Figure 8.1   Our medic shopping in the village market.

Figure 8.2   One source of protein in the village market.

But the food, soda, and beer were another thing. Our medic visited the village markets with our cook to buy fresh produce and rice. Our cook would not let him buy any of the meat, fish or other forms of protein in the market. To her, they were, "Numbah 10!" — very bad.

YB was buying the food before I arrived. The S-4 NCO outranked YB, and the process had some rough edges, especially when there were problems. In one incident YB had ordered 47 pounds of meat for a month's meals through the S-4 NCO (explained below) varying from hamburger to steaks and shrimp. When the S-4 NCO got to the general store, the only meat available was hot dogs. Since the teams had ordered 47 pounds of meat, he purchased 47 pounds of hot dogs. Both teams ate hot dogs, sauerkraut and weenies, pigs in a blanket, pizza with hot dogs on it, hot dog omelets and whatever else they could imagine for much of the month. By the last week of the month, the teams were so sick of hot dogs they couldn't face another one, so they started eating C Rations for lunch and supper. The District Senior Advisor (the Major) felt that putting an officer in charge would smooth situations like this out, and I was that officer.

The S-4 NCO at province headquarters explained the process to me when I went to Song Be for a briefing. Once a month before payday, he would send me a set of mimeographed pages with the food items supposedly available at the General Store. The General Store was just exactly that. A MACV (Military Assistance Command Vietnam) run supply point from which province teams could draw supplies. But the supplies were not free. Food items were cash and carry. Advisors who lived in the villages and did not have access to a military dining facility were paid a Rations Allowance, so they could purchase food "on the economy."[19] I would check off what and how much of the various items I wanted for the month and send it back in the mailbag the next day. The teams in the other three Districts did the same thing. The S-4 NCO would fly to the General store in Ben Hoa on the work helicopter and purchase the food items on the lists paying the bill in cash. Then using the work chopper, the NCO would deliver the food to the Districts and collect cash for the food — cash and carry. I would pay him for Dong Xoai's food when he delivered it. Pay him? PAY HIM? Where exactly was

---

[19] "On the economy": get what is needed from the village markets and shops.

I supposed to get the money to pay him? So, I asked him, "Is there a slush fund at DX?" The simple answer was, "No, L T. You pay for the food out of your pocket and then the team members pay you on payday. This is one reason I buy the food just before payday. You only have to float the loan for the food for a couple of days. That's how it's done." End of story. Well, not quite.

As the end of the month approached, I talked to the team members about what to order, and YB offered advice based on his experience. Then the list arrived in the mailbag; it was three pages long with lots of food choices, but there were no prices. Some of the choices were fantastic. It was almost too good to be true — which it would turn out to be. I checked off what we would eat for the coming month which included specific requests from the team members along with some things I thought would be great for the team. I was sure that everyone would be surprised and pleased with what I had ordered. Looking at the list, I smiled, congratulating myself for my planning of the next month's menu and put the list in the mailbag.

In the afternoon two days later, a call came over the radio. It was the S-4 NCO coming in by chopper with our food order. I drove the jeep to the landing pad and waited. I tossed a smoke grenade near the pad as the helicopter approached so the pilot could judge the wind direction and speed. Once the chopper settled down on the pad, I drove up and unloaded the supplies. There seemed to be less than I had ordered. The NCO handed me the original order list and the bill and I handed him cash; my first business transaction in Vietnam.

I drove the short distance back to the team house, where the cook helped me unload the boxes and we went over the bill. It was right. Then we compared the bill and the food to the original list, and much if it was not there. But there was other food I had not ordered. YB came into the kitchen and explained that the good stuff I ordered was not in stock, never is, and probably would never be. The Supply Sergeant substituted what he could buy for what I ordered, so we would be able to eat for the month. Fortunately, this time it was not hot dogs.

Soda and beer were purchased by the supply NCO on a different helicopter run. (The reason for a different run is explained below.) I paid 5¢ a can for soda and beer except for Budweiser which was 10¢ a can. In today's dollar that was about 32¢ or 64¢ a can. Thanks to some extra

Figure 8.3   The MAT Team Leader (left) and the District Chief (center) enjoy a Budweiser. The MAT Team interpreter is on the right.

special activities by the Special Forces who were at Dong Xoai before us, we had a second refrigerator for cold drinks. On the door was a list of names and you put a mark by your name when you took a can — two marks for a Budweiser. The system worked well and everyone was honest.

From time to time, we would take a case of Budweiser to a meeting in the village but I do not remember how we paid for that. Then again, I do not remember collecting money from the team members to pay for food purchased in the village or the cook and the house maids' wages but in recent correspondence, both the Team Captain and YB assure me that I did.

One month the entire shipment of soda was flat — absolutely no carbonization in any of the flavors. Apparently, the company (which I am not naming but is still a major player in the soft drink industry) had managed to bottle (actually can) an entire lot of flat soda. Instead of dumping it, they shipped it to Vietnam and sold it to the soldiers. We drank it anyway.

There were nine Americans in camp when everyone was present. If everyone drank two cans of beer or soda a day, that is 18 cans a day or 540 cans a month or 22.5 cases a month. And our three interpreters also drank the soda and beer, so that added 180 cans or 7.5 cases.

And this is not counting any beer and soda served to guests and the occasional case taken to the village. Our total beverage consumption was at least 720 cans or more than 30 cases a month. This is why the Supply NCO had a separate helicopter run for beer and soda to supply all of the outposts in the province.

Payday for the team was a typical Army payday, conducted in Vietnam just as it was done in the states. Every team member had most of their money sent home as an allotment to a bank account for their wives and family. For the remainder of the money, some of us had part deposited to a Bank America checking account and the rest paid to us in cash. No checks. On the last day of the month a helicopter would land on the pad and an officer from Finance wearing a 45 on his pistol belt would step out with a briefcase and a paper bag. The briefcase carried the necessary paper work and the paper bag had the money (cents were carried forward to next month) in the exact distribution of bills needed to pay each soldier exactly what he was owed.

We lined up in reverse rank order with the Major last — "Take care of your men before you take care of yourself." The Intel and MAT Captains were in front of the Major and I was in front of them. The Sergeants were ahead of us with YB at the front. One at a time everyone stood in front of the payroll officer and stated their name and serial number. He gave each team member a form to sign and counted out their money. Actually, I was not in line - I was supposed to be but I wasn't. I was sitting next to the payroll officer with a list of what each team member owed for food and drinks and their share of the cook and maid's wages. They paid me before they put their money away.

From time to time the paperwork for a team member indicated that he owed the Army money — usually some fantastic amount containing many zeros. Or the Payroll officer tried to pay him an amount that also had a lot of zeros. The Payroll Officer had no leeway — he had to deliver or collect the amount indicated on the form along with a signature. If the

Figure 8.4   The bunk room at MACV Annex for Captains and Lieutenants.

form showed that the team member was owed an extreme amount of pay and he signed the form and took the money, a payroll officer would be back next month demanding the return of the money. It was an insane game.

When this occurred, the team member would refuse to sign the form (signing it would mean that you agreed with the amount on the form) and no money exchanged hands. Such an event dictated the team member make an Air America trip to Saigon the next day and go to the Finance office to straighten things out. It happened once to me. The Army wanted a lot of money from me for something they said I had signed for but was not supposed to have — a 16-foot aluminum boat used by MAT Teams in the delta region 100 miles to our southwest. I made the trip to Saigon and the Finance office the next day and the problem was easily and quickly corrected. I stretched the trip out to cover two nights at the MACV Annex so I could eat well and sleep in an air-conditioned room with no mosquitoes buzzing and no mosquito net.

One thing we could not get was peanut butter. There were small, condiment size cans in some of the C-Ration meals that we ate in the field, but nothing big enough for the team. After a bit of badgering by the team, I agreed to try to solve the problem. In my next letter home, I asked my wife, Linda to find the corporate address for the Skippy Peanut Butter company. She did and put the address in her next letter. This was a two-week process — one week from me to her and one week for her return letter. Communication with the "World" was much slower in 1971 than it is today.

When I got the address, I drafted a letter to the company explaining our plight asking if I could purchase a supply of their "wonderful peanut butter that reminded us of home" directly from them and would they please provide the details for making the purchase by return mail. I put it

Figure 8.5 The peanut butter order.

in the outgoing mail and crossed my fingers. What I was actually hoping for was a shipment of free peanut butter for some beleaguered soldiers in Vietnam.

Probably a month or so later, a large and well cushioned carton arrived in the mail from the Skippy Peanut Butter company with 24 jars of peanut butter and a letter from someone in the upper levels of the corporation thanking me for the letter and the request, saying to enjoy the peanut butter at no charge. My letter actually worked!

I thought we could put a jar out in the team house next to the salt, pepper and catsup for use as desired, but the team members had other ideas. Right after this picture (Figure 8.5) was taken, everyone picked up their own jar and took it to their quarters. So, we decided to give a jar to each interpreter, our cook, our house maids and sent several over to the Regional Force headquarters. When we were done, there were no jars remaining.

YB took this picture which I returned to the person in the company who wrote the letter with a "Thank You" note signed by everyone on team including our interpreters, cook and house maids.[20]

---

[20] Understand that this was a very long process. We had to mail the film to Japan for developing and printing. Then the lab had to mail the prints back to us before we could send the picture to Skippy. From start (my original letter) to finish (Skippy's receiving of the Thank You note and picture) spanned months.

Story 9 - The Things We Carried

with apologies to Tim O'Brien

The idea of a typical MAT Team or typical operation was a fallacy. Nothing was typical about the teams or their missions. Each team adapted its tactics to its individual situation. And for every team, each operation was different. To deal effectively with all of this, a MAT Team tried to apply SOPs (Standard Operating Procedures) where possible to make things run as smoothly as possible. 33 Tango[21], the MAT Team Sergeant with whom I operated in the field and I followed several SOPs in preparation and planning for an operation. This is an example of our planning for one. It has more details than you really want to know.

This was my first combat operation in Vietnam and 33 Tango's first one since joining MAT 111. We were unknown to each other, to the others on the MAT Team and to our Vietnamese counterparts.

After we got our OP order (OPerations order — the mission details) and met with our Vietnamese counterparts, the two of us began to organize and plan what we would have to carry on the operation. We would be out five days, so everything that we needed on day five had to be in our packs on day one. What follows begins on the inside and works its way out.

Upon arrival in Viet Nam, every advisor was issued among other things five sets of underwear; olive green boxer shorts and tee shirts. Most GIs in the jungle never wore them under their jungle fatigues. The dampness from the humidity and the sweat created a perfect climate for rashes called, "Jungle Rot," and underwear contributed to this climate. Some soldiers did not wear socks in their jungle boots for the same

---

[21] 33 Tango was his radio call sign. 33 Quebec was my radio call sign. We never used rank or names in our radio transmissions.

reason, but I did wear socks putting a lot of fungicide laced Army issue foot powder in the socks.

My dog tags were on a chain around my neck. Early in the war GIs taped their tags together to keep them from rattling. The Army solved the noise problem by issuing clear tubing for the chain and two rubber rings into which each tag could fit. By the end of my tour, the inside of the tubing covering the chain holding my dog tags was green from some life form thriving in that environment. Also, on the chain was my P-38; the standard issue can opener for C-Rations.

Jungle fatigues were the standard uniform — loose fitting trousers with the usual pockets plus pockets on the side of each thigh and a loose blouse or jacket with four pockets. The breast pockets were slanted for easy and quick access by either hand. I carried my compass in the left breast pocket. The cord attached to it went around my neck. I carried my whiz wheel[22] with a cord that ran through the button hole of the pocket flap in my right breast pocket. In this same pocket I had a plastic bag that had the current SOI (Signals Operating Instructions), the unused whiz wheel sheets, a small tablet, a lead pencil[23] and a grease pencil[24], signal mirror, a picture of my wife, and my Geneva Convention Identification Card which the VC would want to see if they captured me[25].

Mosquito repellent and iodine tablets for treating drinking water were carried in my pants pockets.

The plastic laminated topographic map for the area in which we would operate was carried in the outer thigh pocket on my right side. I carried a sheath knife on the belt that held up my trousers.

---

[22] See Appendix 1.

[23] On an operation you can sharpen a broken pencil with your knife but when a ball point pen quits writing, you are out of luck, and pencils seemed to work better on damp paper.

[24] For marking on the laminated topo map.

[25] The Geneva Convention ID card probably would have been of no interest to the Viet Cong.

Next came a bandolier with four magazines for my M-16. Each magazine, designed to carry 20 rounds of ammunition, only had 18. Experience dictated that putting 20 rounds into the magazine could weaken the spring that fed the bullets into the chamber causing the last round to improperly feed jamming the weapon — something you did not want when you really needed that last bullet. A bandolier was made from olive green cotton and initially carried bullets in reloading clips that allowed them to be quickly shoved into a magazine. Once they were removed, the bandoliers were used for many things. Each bandolier had a circular strap and a large strong black safety pin. I used it to pin the middle of the strap to the middle of the bandolier making something resembling a bra. I put the straps over my shoulders with the magazines against my chest. If, for some reason I had to drop my pack and my web gear or I wasn't wearing them, I would always have these four magazines with me.

Next came what the Army called my, "TA-50." We called it our web gear. It consisted of a pistol belt with multiple brass ringed holes for attaching other elements of the TA-50. Attached to the belt was a pair of suspenders with various attachment points that shifted the weight of the equipment carried on the belt to my shoulders. A small pouch with a snap was attached at shoulder level. This carried a camouflage green field dressing — a large bandage with long strips for securing the bandage over a wound. The pouch was attached upside down so when the pouch was opened, the dressing would fall out for immediate use.

Attached to the pistol belt were two canteen covers. These were positioned on the belt near my kidneys. Inside each cover was an aluminum canteen cup and a plastic canteen. The cups were used for heating water to make coffee and for heating C-Rations or sharing food with the Vietnamese. Attached to the front of the belt were two magazine pouches. Both pouches carried three M-16 magazines. Each pouch had two attachment points for carrying fragmentation hand grenades. I carried four "frags." The last item on the side of the belt was the scabbard for my bayonet.

Everything else went into or on the rucksack. The rucksack consisted of a metal frame with a nylon bag attached to it. The bag had a large main compartment and two smaller outside compartments. Packing this was detailed and important. Both the weight and possible immediate need of each item had to be considered. Heavy items carried better if they were near the top of the pack but C-rations cans which were heavy did not have an "Immediate need."

The bottom layer had spare socks, extra mosquito and leech repellant, iodine tablets for water purification, and a survival kit that had, among other items amphetamine tablets to keep us going if sleep was not possible.

Following this was a hammock, poncho, and poncho liner. The poncho was used as a ground cloth or to cover the hammock during the night when it was raining, but we never wore the poncho. The poncho liner provided some warmth at night when I was wet. Next was the food. We did not take everything that came in a single C-Ration box. It was just too heavy and occupied too much space. Resupply during the five-day mission was not possible, so every meal we needed on day five had to be in the pack on day one; that was thirteen meals[26]. After winnowing the rations down to something that was almost reasonable to carry, I put the cans into a couple of socks and tied knots at the top. This kept them together and prevented them from shifting around in the pack and rattling. On top of this was a flashlight, a cleaning kit for my M-16, and a small metal container with a package of morphine syrettes.

The army issued each of us a small battery powered strobe light to be used to mark our position at night if we needed rescue by helicopter. The strobe flashed a bright white light at timed intervals. To use it, you turned it on and held it overhead pointing it at a passing or rescue helicopter. There were some problems with this. Early use resulted in some helicopter crews, seeing the flashes and thinking they were being fired on, returning fire with their door mounted machine guns — not good! Another problem was that bright flashes in the night tended to reveal your location to the nearby Viet Cong who were searching for you — also not good. The Army attempted to mitigate this by issuing a plastic tube to put over the strobe. The sides were black so it would not readily

---

[26] No breakfast on day 1 and no supper on day 5.

reveal your position to those nearby Viet Cong. There was a blue cover over one end of the tube which changed the color of the flash so it would not resemble the muzzle flash of a gun being fired at the helicopter. Nice try, but now to be seen, the strobe had to be pointed directly at the helicopter — which was flying at night with no lights visible so you really did not know where it was other than it was over head, and the strobing light was much dimmer. We chose to leave these in camp.

33 Tango and I made a list of other equipment we thought we would need on the mission. Once we finalized the list, we divided the items between us keeping the weight as close to even as possible. Some of the items included:

- Batteries for the radio. Batteries lasted one day and weighed three pounds each — we needed five. We would carry two each, and our interpreter would carry one.
- C-4 plastic explosive, blasting caps, fuses, and igniters. 33 Tango carried two blocks of C-4 and I carried the rest[27].
- Ten-foot-long extension antenna for the radio. 33 Tango carried this because our Vietnamese RTO would be with him.
- Smoke grenades; four colored and two white. The colored smoke grenades would be used for marking our location for a helicopter; the white grenades for hiding our movement.
- Two Star clusters. Hand held aerial flares for marking our location, especially at night.
- Machete. Carried but rarely used.
- Two entrenching tools (collapsible shovels).
- Two lengths of nylon cord.
- Several thin nylon boot laces.
- Small spool of trip wire — thin metal wire painted green that was useful for various tasks
(see Story 15).

---

[27] The C4 was very stable. The blasting caps were not, so carrying them was my responsibility. The weight of the caps, fuse, and igniters was less than the weight of the C-4.

These items along with others were packed on top of the main compartment and in the two outside pockets for quick access. On the outside of the pack, we each carried a 2 1/2-quart collapsible canteen. Even though it was rainy season, good water could be difficult to find and dehydration was a problem to be avoided at all costs — even at the cost of carrying an additional five pounds. Being collapsible eliminated the sloshing sound water would make in a partially filled canteen.

At the start of the mission with all of the food and full canteens, the pack was extremely heavy; probably close to seventy or eighty pounds. It was put on last over the web gear and the bandolier bra. The pack had two quick releases on the shoulder straps, so it could be quickly dropped in an emergency. If I did that, I would still have my web gear with the magazines and the fragmentation grenades. If, for some reason (sleeping at night) I had to move before being able to put on my web gear, I had the four magazines in the bandolier on my chest.

Next, my M-16. When I drew my weapon from the armory at MACV (Military Assistance Command, Vietnam) Annex in Saigon, I was issued four 30 round magazines for the weapon — no bullets, just empty magazines. The magazine pouches they issued were for 20 round magazines meaning that I could not carry all four magazines. So, when I arrived at Dong Xoai, I gave each of the other MAT Team members (not counting the medic) one of the 30 round magazines. I loaded 28 rounds in the magazine for the same reason I only put 18 rounds in the 20 round magazines and locked this magazine into my rifle. Any sudden, surprise use of my weapon would happen for only two reasons: we literally ran into Viet Cong coming the other way, or we walked into a VC ambush. In the initial seconds of either encounter, 28 bullets would be better than 18.

I started every mission with exactly 208 rounds of ammunition. There was no reason to carry more. Unless we were initiating an ambush where we had to bring maximum fire immediately on the enemy or I was the one being ambushed, I should not be firing my rifle. During contact, my job would be to observe and advise; the RF troops would be doing the shooting. If I had to fire my weapon at the enemy, we were in some very serious trouble. The other reason not to carry more ammunition was that the M-16 had a reputation for jamming after 200 or so rounds had been fired due to carbon buildup in the chamber. 208 bullets were probably more than I needed.

Some things are not mentioned here. Toilet paper is one of them. Each C-Ration meal came fully supplied with green toilet paper. Exactly THREE single sheets. That was it. Enough said…

33 Tango and I did not shave on operations. Our packs were heavy enough, and I did not want to risk the problem of an infected shaving cut or skin rash on my throat. The mosquito and leech bites were enough to deal with. Tango 33 was more than willing to follow "his Lieutenant's" lead on this. The Major, our boss was not pleased with this. Even though he expressed his displeasure, he never ordered us to shave while on an operation.

Having just returned from one mission, before either of us could clean up and shave, the Major brought it up again. As part of his comment, he said, "If you can carry what you need to brush your teeth, you should be able to carry a razor." Before I could think of something to say, 33 Tango remarked, "Sir, the L T carries the toothpaste, and I carry the toothbrush." With the other team members present doing their best to stifle their laughter, the Major turned and left the area. 33 Tango was retiring when his tour was finished, so he had nothing to lose.

The last things to go on were a floppy boonie hat and a green towel. The floppy hat was preferred because it did not have a regular shaped which is

Figure 9.1   One of the three figures at the Vietnam Memorial in Washington, DC with a towel.

unnatural in the jungle and is much easier to spot. The towel which can be seen in Figure 9.1 on the statue at the Vietnam Memorial in Washington, DC. was an incredibly useful and important part of the things we carried. Wiping the sweat from my face was only one use of the towel.

A full rucksack, M-16, magazines, grenades, and other items on our web gear had a combined weight approaching 80 to 100 pounds. This made movement through the jungle vegetation up and down the rough terrain extremely difficult.

Story 10 - The First Mission

Within the MAT Team, we formed two-man sub-teams; one officer and one NCO. MAT SOP dictated that the Team Medic not accompany us on operations. The Sergeant operating with the Team Captain was on his second tour. The Sergeant with whom I would operate — his radio call sign was, "33 Tango" — was on his third tour in Vietnam. With two and one-half years in the jungle, he had valuable experience and was the right Sergeant for me. He patiently taught me what I needed to know, and we developed a good working relationship. 33 Tango and I took the smaller operations — twenty to thirty men and the MAT Team Captain took the larger ops. This was not a formal arrangement between the Captain and me, but it was ok with me. An ego can get you killed.

Things had been quiet at Dong Xoai for quite a while before I arrived. Recent intelligence from Province HQ and the District Intel team had not generated enough information for a meaningful mission. Then the attack on the camp occurred; mortars, small arms, machine gun fire, an RPG, Viet Cong in the barbed wire.

Our first mission was probably a "training wheels" mission for the two of us — an entrance exam to the brotherhood. Although 33 Tango was a seasoned veteran, he was unknown to Captain Ky, the Regional Force (RF) company commander who was my counterpart for this mission. I was a green first Lieutenant with no experience and unknown to everyone. Captain Ky did not know how well his two new co vans (Vietnamese: advisors) would work together as a team with him. In addition, we would be within artillery and radio range of Dong Xoai the entire time. If we got into trouble and needed help, it would be available. We were accompanying the operation to act as liaison for any US support that might be needed: artillery fire, helicopter gun ship sweeps, and helicopter evacuation of the wounded.

The mission was to follow a specific line of march, looking for signs of infiltration moving south from the Cambodian border located about 25 miles north of Dong Xoai and for a possible overnight camp location and supply cache. It was possible that a Viet Cong squad (5-6 men) was moving through the area.

We left camp early morning on day one with a convoy of two deuce-and-a-halfs (two and one-half ton trucks) and two jeeps. I rode in the lead jeep with Captain Ky. As his counterpart, my place was to be near him as much as possible. 33 Tango rode in the second jeep with his counterpart at the end of the convoy. Captain Ky had volunteered one of his troops to be our RTO (radio telephone operator). This troop would carry the 16-pound field radio and battery0 and stay close to 33 Tango.

Our radio was in the last jeep as backup. Captain Ky assigned one of the two pre-sets on his radio to the MAT Team frequency, so I could use it quickly if necessary. Correspondingly, we assigned the RF's frequency to one of our radio's presets. If our jeep triggered a booby trap, a mine, or drove into an ambush, 33 Tango would still be operational with a working radio.

The troops in the two deuce-and-a-halfs traveled in the middle of the convoy. The road had not been checked and cleared for mines and booby traps, but the trip out was uneventful except that it began to rain — not a shower but a steady rain. After all, it was the rainy season. We arrived at our departure point, dismounted, and the four vehicles returned to Dong Xoai.

I had flown a reconnaissance mission over the area the day before and saw that it was covered with a thick low growth of vegetation despite heavy dosing by Agent Orange.[28] We moved as a single file column. Flank security to either side was not possible. Two RF troops moved ahead of the column as the point element looking for booby traps, ambush sites, and signs of enemy presence. Captain Ky was next followed by his RTO. I was behind the RTO and behind me was our interpreter. My responsibility was to be nearby if needed but not in his face. Just as we traveled in the convoy, 33 Tango was at the rear of the

---

[28] Phuoc Long Province had the second most heavy use of the defoliant (and cancer causing) Agent Orange in Vietnam.

column with our RTO. If the front of the column tripped a booby trap or triggered an ambush, he would be out of the kill zone and capable of making the call for help.

We moved steadily all morning, taking a short break every hour or so. When we stopped, 33 Tango moved to the front of the column with our RTO, so we could confer about our position on the map, and I could check in with the team at Dong Xoai.

We crossed numerous small streams, some large ones that were beginning to flood, and moved up and down the hills and valleys. The vines and growth made travel very difficult. Add to this a heavy pack and the wet jungle floor on the steep slopes, just remaining upright was a serious challenge.

The biggest problem for me, other than trying to remain upright was keeping track of where we were. Our topographic maps were very accurate in terms of the ups and downs and the location of the streams. But it is easier to track your course on a topo map if you move in a straight or nearly straight line. It also helps to be able to see more than 20 feet in front of you. Neither of those held true here and now. We had to know where we were in case we needed artillery or helicopter gunship support.

When we stopped to eat some lunch, the column formed a tight perimeter for defense. It was still raining. 33 Tango along with our RTO moved to the center of the perimeter and dropped his pack next to mine. We were kneeling near the command group looking at our maps when Captain Ky walked over to us and asked, "Chung toi a dau" (Vietnamese: Where are we?) Our interpreter was not close by — he was probably relieving himself on the perimeter's edge. I pointed to my map indicating where we were. Captain Ky smiled and said, "Rat tot" (Vietnamese: Very good). I replied, "Cam on" (Vietnamese: Thank you) as he went back to his command group. 33 Tango looked at me with surprise and asked, "You speak their language, L T?" I think my Sergeant and I had just passed the first part of our exam: we had moved silently through the thick vegetation and rough terrain with the column causing no delays, we had stayed out of their way, and we knew where we were.

It continued to rain — only harder now. We crossed more streams and worked our way through more jungle the remainder of the day finding nothing; the rain having washed any trace of enemy movement or activity.

We stopped about an hour before dark to eat. The tactic was to eat first and then move to the NDP — the Night Defensive Position. Moving into the NDP just before dark was done, so anyone tracking us would have difficulty locating us and leading others to our position in the dark. Captain Ky called our interpreter over and talked to him. The interpreter came back and said that if the three of us could contribute three cans of C-Rations to the pot, we could eat with them. And Captain Ky wanted to know if we had any C4 explosive. We each pulled a can of C-rations out of our packs and 33 Tango pulled out one of our two sticks of C4. We handed these to our interpreter who took them back to the command group.

Sometime later we were called over to the command group to eat. 33 Tango told our interpreter to ask Captain Ky if our RTO could eat with us. Captain KY nodded, "Yes," and like that, our lowly Vietnamese private, tasked to carry the co vans' radio was elevated in status to a place at dinner with the Captain. 33 Tango's request was very insightful. Because of it, we had just acquired a permanent and loyal RTO for future missions with Captain Ky.

33 Tango worked throughout the mission with our new RTO teaching him how to recognize our call signs, so he could listen to the radio and give the handset to one of us when we were called. The RTO was taught to say in a very interesting attempt at English, "Wait One, over," when he heard a call.

Somehow, some way, in all of this rain and dampness, the Vietnamese made a small fire under a low-strung poncho using a piece of the C4 as the starter. The fire was small, hot, almost smokeless. There was still enough light but the use of the poncho kept the fire from being a security risk. When we walked over, one of the Vietnamese returned most of the stick of C4 to 33 Tango. Two pots were there; one with rice and one with a soupy stew. We brought our canteen cups and the Vietnamese used large leaves as plates. Apparently, every time we paused during the day, several of the troops had foraged for roots, plants, and small scurrying things to be used in the stew. With our three cans of different C-Rations added to the mix, it looked good in a weird sort of way. We put some rice into our canteen cups and poured some of the stew over the rice. After a day in a constant rain, this hot food was very welcome. One thing I repeatedly heard in every different phase of training was to NEVER ASK what you are eating; just eat and try to enjoy it.

While we were eating, several troops were out scouting for a place to set up a defensive perimeter for the night — our NDP. Just as light was beginning to fade, we picked up our packs and began to move to the NDP. We walked for fifteen minutes or so before stopping. The column formed a perimeter just as they did at lunch and supper. Captain Ky and I walked the perimeter checking the troops positions and their firing lanes. I tried to provide a second set of eyes for Captain Ky, though he did not really need them.

Even though 33 Tango and I were carrying entrenching tools (shovels), we did not dig fox holes or fighting positions; it was too wet. Any hole we might dig would fill immediately with water. Sleeping on the ground was impossible for one reason — actually hundreds of reasons - LEECHES. They were everywhere and were desperately trying to find a dry spot; preferably a warm one with a blood supply. Because of the leeches and the soggy soil, we carried small nylon hammocks for sleeping. On a dry night, we would tie the hammock up, cover ourselves with mosquito repellant and try to sleep. On a rainy night, we strung our poncho over the hammock, did the repellant thing, and tried to sleep. To stop the rain water from running down the nylon cord that was holding up the hammock getting us even wetter, we tied a boot lace on each end of the hammock to divert the water — this worked poorly, but it was better than nothing.

The problem with all of this was the "tie up" part. I weighed about 180 pounds. 33 Tango, taller than me weighed in at a bit over 200. We were much heavier than the RF troops. Finding something strong enough to hold us off the ground was a challenge; especially in the fading light. On more than one occasion this arrangement began with me completely in the air, but by morning my butt was firmly grounded.

33 Tango and I placed our hammocks so our heads were near each

other. This allowed us to put the radio within reach of both of us. In this arrangement we took turns on radio watch through the night — alternating two hour shifts until first light. Considering the terrain, the rain, the food, the leeches and the sleep, it was a tough way to operate.

After the final radio check with Dong Xoai, we had one more task to perform. Both of us carried standard issue flashlights with red lenses that preserved our night vision and reduced the risk of being detected if they

Figure 10.1 A P38 can opener on the right and the paper packaging with the instruction illustrations telling the GI what a can is. The Vietnamese 5 Dong coin was worth about 1/5 of one cent in 1971.

were used in the dark. Without the red lens, the white light would have destroyed our night vision (our ability to see shapes in the darkness) for about twenty minutes. We removed the lights from our packs and hung them on our web gear. Then we took off our boots and wet socks, and using the red light, checked our feet and lower legs for leeches. I allowed myself the luxury of a second pair of socks stored away from the wet in two plastic bags. I had doused this pair of socks with Army issue foot powder that had a fungicide mixed in. I put these dry, almost warm socks on and then a plastic bag over each sock so they would not get wet and put my boots back on. I did not lace the boots hoping that this would help maintain some circulation in my feet. Tomorrow, I would remove these dry socks and put the cold wet ones back on. In that setting dry socks were a very real luxury to me. Next, we took off our shirts and checked our arms, and chest and each other's back looking for leeches. Finally, we dropped our pants (We did not wear underwear of any type because of the dampness.) and made the same leech check on our upper legs and groin area. I sprinkled the foot powder on my groin hoping to forestall any rash or irritation. Then in turn, we bent over and pulled our buttocks apart so we could check each other for leeches — a required intimacy in this situation. We redressed, covered our exposed skin with mosquito repellant and tried to get comfortable in the hammocks. Listening for anything out of place in the night, we took turns waiting for daylight.

At first light, we made a radio check with Dong Xoai and got out of the hammocks trying to loosen up and work out the cramps. I put my cold wet socks back on, put the dry ones in the plastic bag, packed everything away and had something to eat. Burning small heating tablets that could warm a canteen cup of water, we made coffee and using our P38s, opened a can of something to eat. The something varied, depending on what we carried: cake, crackers, peanut butter, jelly, cheese, fruit cocktail. It differed every morning. We met with Captain Ky and discussed today's march and where he wanted to spend the night. Finally, a police of the area to pick up anything that would reveal our presence last night. We carried machetes but rarely used them. The jungle would quickly recover from our trampling but cut vegetation would mark our passage for a significant time.

Day two was like day one complete with rain. Day three was like day two. On day four we found a small base camp with a cache of rice. The

RF troops loaded what they could carry on their rucksacks to take home. Since it was still raining, burning the remaining rice would not work, so the troops spread it across the ground to let it rot. We marked the location on our maps, so it could be targeted by the RF artillery battery as part of their nightly H & I (Harassment and Interdiction) firing.

Midmorning of day 5 Captain Ky sent encrypted coordinates for pickup by convoy, and we moved towards the road. It was still raining. The trucks arrived and picked us up. Our return to Dong Xoai was uneventful except the rain stopped while we were in route. The two jeeps delivered 33 Tango and me to the door of our team house where Radio Watch greeted us.

We stripped our wet clothes off outside the team house hanging them on the barbed wire near the team house door. We went to our rooms to get fresh clothes and a towel and then to take a cold shower. Wearing dry clothes, socks, and boots, we both drank cups of hot coffee while we cleaned our rifles and laid out our gear to dry. Then we had something warm to eat and gave a report to the team. I think we passed the exam.

Not all first missions go as smoothly. This one could receive a grade of 80% having failed only in one of the mission's five goals:

- We found evidence of Viet Cong presence when we located the small base camp.

- We logged the location of the base camp so the RF artillery could shell it as part of their H&I firing each day.

- We found a cache of rice that was either returned to Dong Xoai or scattered on the wet ground to rot so the Viet Cong could not use it.

- We did not encounter a stronger enemy force that could have destroyed us.

The shortcoming was that we did not find the Viet Cong squad and eliminate it.

The next story, written by the MAT team leader details his arrival at Dong Xoai, his first days, and his first mission after he took charge of MAT 111. His story compared to mine reinforces the idea that there was nothing "typical" about missions and experiences in Vietnam.

Story 11 - First Days at Dong Xoai for the MAT 111 Team Leader

Told by Jim Rice

I was an Air Defense Artillery (ADA) Officer put on orders for Vietnam shortly after I was promoted to Captain. Since there were few ADA units in Vietnam, I was placed on orders with training at Fort Benning, Georgia for 2 weeks. That is the home of the Infantry, and I attended a course called Infantry Officer Vietnam Orientation (IOVO). The idea was to give me some Infantry knowledge and training in preparation for joining an Infantry unit in VN as a staff officer of some sort. The course was not real informative but did give you some land navigation and weapons training and a lot of personal experience and knowledge from soldiers that had been in country and who knew about things such as booby traps and ambushes used by the enemy forces.

I won't go into my background other than to say I needed to log some command time to remain competitive for the next promotion, and they were not likely to give me command of an Infantry unit as an ADA Officer. I knew that people who were advisors to the Vietnamese units were credited with Command Equivalent time, and since they were in a combat zone, each month served was 2 months credit in the command. So a year of advisory duty could give me 2 years equivalent time for command!

There were 2 major commands in Vietnam for the US Army. USARV was US Army Vietnam which commanded all US units. The other was MACV or Military Assistance Command Vietnam, and it interfaced with all Vietnamese units and commanded all advisory efforts in Vietnam.

My orders were to USARV with no specific unit so when you arrived in country and in-processed, you were asked what specific unit you preferred to be assigned to. On that, "Dream Sheet" I indicated that I wanted to be an advisor. Everyone that came in country on my flight was housed in a barracks environment for a few hours to a day awaiting those final assignments, then they were picked up by the unit of assignment and taken out of the barracks. There was a bulletin board near the office, and everyone checked it several times a day to see where they were going. Everyone from my flight was gone the next day…except for me because I still had no assignment! A new flight unloaded and they occupied the same barracks space. They all got their assignments, left, and I was still sitting still. When I asked the folks in the office if they had forgotten me, they told me that since I had asked for a MACV assignment, they had to send the request up the chain of command to USARV HQ for approval to release me for assignment to MACV.

After 3 days I was approved, and a jeep showed up to take me to an in-country school at Di An for new advisors. I had been selected to lead Mobile Advisory Team 111 in the village of Dong Xoai which was an element of Advisory Team 67 in Phuoc Long Province. Most advisors were selected months if not a year before they arrived in country to give them time to get training in the United States on how to advise, Vietnamese culture, weapons used by the Vietnamese and even months of language training. I was going to get a total of 2 weeks of training and sent to work…talk about starting behind the power curve!

It was about a week before Christmas when I finished the school, and they put me on a chopper that dropped me in Song Be which was where TM 67 was located. I got a day of briefing and some equipment and put on a chopper for Dong Xoai. That was a 3-stop ride that dropped off supplies or personnel at other outlying advisor posts in route to mine.

When we landed at Dong Xoai, the chopper was met by a tall slim guy in jungle fatigue pants but only an OD T-shirt on the top and no hat. He asked if he could help me with my duffle bag or anything else, and I said, "Sure," and shoved a heavy bag to him as well as my weapon and another bag I had. He unloaded the supplies into the jeep he had brought and then told me to hop in. I thought he was being pretty informal considering my Captain's bars were easy to see. He asked what brings an ADA officer to this place, and I said I was the new MAT Team Leader for MAT 111. He stared at me and said, "I didn't know we had a new team leader coming in." I figured the District Senior Advisor (DSA) who was to be my boss knew I was coming but had not shared the information with the rest of the team.

When we stopped at the Team House to unload supplies and my stuff, he shook my hand, and said, "Welcome Aboard. I am the District Senior Advisor, Major R———." I was awful glad I hadn't chewed his butt for not showing me the respect I thought I deserved as a Captain, but I was also confused because he didn't even know I was coming. What a way to start my year of advising. Turns out that the Major was a tremendous Field Artillery Officer, who had been DSA for about 8 months. He was a valuable trainer for me, since I had missed so much training in my round-about assignment to this strange place and duty assignment.

My introduction to the day-to-day activities at Dong Xoai were just as interesting. Having arrived at Dong Xoai in late December, the first job the Major gave me was to go to Phuoc Vinh and get a Turkey for Christmas dinner. Phuoc Vinh was a village a few miles south of Dong Xoai and the home of a Cavalry Brigade. There was an American operations base with a number of American units.

As I look back on it, that was a tough mission for a newbie. The trip would be in a single jeep over a road that was unprotected and had spots in it where you just couldn't go very fast. I went with Sergeant Stewart, the District Team Medic and another NCO from the District Advisory Team. I rode shotgun with an M16 and Stewart driving with an M16 on his lap and the other NCO in the back with an M79 grenade launcher and lots of rounds.

When we got to the base, we went from mess hall to mess hall begging. We would put whatever we got in the trailer, cover it with a tarp and go to the next one. We ended up getting 2 or 3 rolled Turkey roasts but no whole Turkey.

We stopped in a First Cavalry communications shop, and the NCOs asked if they had a serviceable field radio for the jeep and ended up getting a top-of-the-line VRC47 radio installed with a matching antenna unit for free. Someone had sent it in for maintenance and never picked it up. Then we went to several other places looking for various freebees but struck out.

After a visit to the village, we headed home. When we got there, the Major was getting off of the work chopper with a whole Turkey in an ice chest. I was upset he sent me on a treacherous ride to end up bringing one back himself. Turns out he had been at a meeting where they gave the attendees a Turkey. I was appalled at how loose the supply system had been and how easy it was to basically steal property. I guess I got over that because I surely enjoyed the material and food we were able to get until the Cav went away. We missed them.

Figure 11.1 The C-7-Alpha was capable of using the dirt airstrips in the Jungles of Vietnam like the one at Dong Xoai. This picture was taken at the air field at Ben Hoa.

Things only got better after that. An operation which involved the Province Reconnaissance Unit (PRU) was planned by Province. Since MAT Teams were not allowed to work with the PRUs because they were mercenaries who were paid by body count, they sent a Regional Force

(RF) Company with the PRU and two advisors from MAT 111 with the RF Company. The RF company along with me, one of the MAT Team NCOs and SGT Yung, our interpreter were picked up at the Dong Xoai dirt airstrip by a fixed wing aircraft called a Caribou (C7Alpha in Army terms). The PRU were apparently transported differently to the drop point. We packed more soldiers on the aircraft than was allowed but were probably still under the weight limitation because all but two of us were Vietnamese. It was standing room only, and we were packed like sardines.

They flew us north past Song Be to at least the Cambodian border where there was a runway just large enough for us to land. We got off the plane, quickly assembled and joined up with the PRU just as they took off heading southeast from our drop point. This was the start of my first operation in country!

The PRU took off at an incredible pace sometimes running, almost always jogging when in open areas which were not really common on the operation. The area looked like it had been the target of a B52 strike because the bamboo was thrown all kinds of directions and was so tall yet tangled that often my NCO and I couldn't get through it without crawling or chopping away at it...meanwhile the smaller Vietnamese troops were charging on.

As I recall, because we had to use Caribou instead of helicopters for the insertion, they put us in at a point that was over 20KM from the objective for the mission. I had a map but no time to really look at it, but it felt like we may have been in Cambodia for a bit of time at the beginning.

I had an old football injury to my right knee and the faster we went and the more I had to drag myself through the bamboo, the sorer it got. They did take a break around noon, and we sat there trying to determine exact location while we ate. They convinced me of the location on the map, so I tried to follow our progress from there on.

The first night I had the problem with the whiz wheel (a device used to encode map coordinates, which would then be sent in the clear to be decoded by the recipient) and couldn't use it to call in defensive targets to the artillery unit that had been detailed to support us. I asked if anyone in the unit spoke Spanish. Someone did, so I ended up transmitting them in

Jim Roberts

Spanish.

I'm not sure if it was that night or not but one of the nights on the op, I was in my hammock between 2 trees, and I had the feeling someone was watching me. I slowly opened my eyes and saw a figure near the tree at my feet — a Vietnamese looking at me. I slowly reached for my weapon and he ducked under the ropes of the hammock said, "Chao, Dai Uy" ("Hello Captain" in Vietnamese) and moved further away. I asked Sgt. Yung who he was, so he spoke to the soldier and found out it was my body guard. According to Sgt. Yung, the guy was assigned to me to make sure I didn't get hurt or killed. If I was, he would die too!

On the second day my knee was so painful I could not walk without using my M16 as a crutch, so I left it on SAFE with the loaded magazine installed then put my hand on the muzzle and used the butt plate as the base of the crutch. The palm of my hand began to bruise and swell as well. The VN commander tried to call for a MEDIVAC for me but the Province S-3 would not approve it since I was not injured.

I believe it was supposed to be a four-day mission but by the start of day three, I was quite crippled and unable to keep up with the PRU. They went ahead to the objective and the plan was to send a platoon with them in order to support them if they came in contact. They did not make contact with the Viet Cong as either the objective was cleared because we were slow getting there or they just were never there.

We were extracted on the afternoon of day three by helicopter. I was barely able to walk but did walk into the S-3's office to give him a piece of my mind over the lack of planning and coordination for the OP! He didn't take it too well, and since he was a Major and I was a Captain, it never resulted in even an apology!

Story 12 - Air America

Air America was an arm of the CIA which operated an airline service that we frequently used. They flew a short takeoff and landing fixed wing Pilatus PC-6 Porter airplane that was capable of using dirt airstrips like the one at Dong Xoai. It had three or four rows of two seats behind the pilot; I don't remember exactly how many there were.

Figure 12.1 A Porter on the dirt airstrip at Dong Xoai. The plane is still in production today.

Leaving Dong Xoai, the plane would fly south to the Air America terminal at Ben Hoa. From there we could hop a chopper for a short ride to Saigon. If there were empty seats on the plane, it was not uncommon for the pilot to make stops at other bases and camps between Song Be and Ben Hoa. These side trips provided a good time for taking photographs.

The MAT Team Medic and I had business in Saigon. Having scheduled a pickup at Dong Xoai with Province, YB drove us to the airstrip in the team jeep, and we boarded when the plane landed. The pilot, a surprisingly older man, was the only other person on the plane. He asked us to sit in the last row of seats, probably to balance the load.

Figure12.2 Nui Ba Ra at Song Be.

The takeoff in a Porter is something to experience. Being a short takeoff and landing airplane, it gets to liftoff speed very quickly. Then the pilot climbs very steeply hoping to avoid any possible enemy fire. This time instead of heading almost due south towards Ben Hoa when the plane reached altitude, it tracked west towards Tay Ninh. The sister mountain of Nui Ba Ra at Song Be is Nui Ba Dinh in Tay Ninh. Both are the remains of extinct volcanic cones. Nui Ba Dinh is much bigger and higher so we could see it in the distance through the pilot's windshield.

The day was clear, the sky blue, and the flight was very smooth. Bac Si (Vietnamese for doctor — what we called the medic) and I passed the time talking above the din of the Porter's engine as we watched Nui Ba Dinh slowly grow bigger in the pilot's wind screen. Unlike previous flights that passed the cone above and to the eastern side, he was flying towards the western side and a bit below the top of the cone.

Bac Si asked me why he would be flying that route. I replied he probably had to make a pickup on the western side. As we continued to talk, the mountain continued to grow bigger. Now we were heading more

Figure 12.3.   Nui Ba Dinh in the distance.

towards it than to the western side of it and we were a little bit lower. Bac Si was beginning to get nervous. I assured him, "Hey, he works for the CIA. He knows what he is doing."

The plane continued on, now a bit lower and even more towards the mountain. Bac Si was beyond nervous. I told him to relax, and I moved forward past the intervening rows of seats and tapped the pilot on the shoulder. Much to my surprise, he jerked up violently, looked out his windscreen, pushed the throttle forward, and pulled the plane sharply up and to the right tossing me around in the row of seats behind him. Apparently, he had fallen asleep right after we reached altitude at Dong Xoai. Thank goodness Bac Si was the anxious type.

The pilot changed course and headed directly to Ben Hoa. Getting off the plane after we landed safely, the pilot said nothing. Catching a few minutes of sleep must have been business as usual in his line of work.

We hopped on a helicopter to Saigon and went our separate ways to take care of our business. When we met up later in the day as agreed, Bac Si told me that he found a convoy that would be passing through Dong Xoai tomorrow, and he was hitching a ride. He was not going to take a chance with Air America again. I told him that in all probability, the road to Dong Xoai would not be cleared of mines and booby traps before the convoy moves out, so it could be risky. He said he would rather take his chances with the Viet Cong than with Air America.

My Air America flight back to Dong Xoai was smooth and uneventful and I got some good pictures. The pilot called ahead, and YB met me at the airstrip to drive me back to the camp. Bac Si got back to Dong Xoai late the next afternoon; dusty, tired, and with a sore butt — apparently the road was very rough.

Story 13 - Thompson Sub-Machine Guns

In a War Zone, interesting decisions can be made by people whose pay grades are far above those of mere Sergeants, Lieutenants, and Captains. This does not always ensure that their decisions make sense.

Radio Watch returned from the helipad with the mail bag and a large wooden packing crate in the back of the jeep. He called for some help, and one of the NCOs helped him carry the crate into the team house. Some paperwork stapled to the crate said, "MAT 111 Dong Xoai." — an early Christmas present from an admirer? It was a military packing create, but it was too big for ammunition or grenades, and the crate would have been labeled accordingly.

Someone got a hammer and crowbar out of our conex (steel shipping/storage container) and pried off the lid. Inside were five World War 2 vintage Thompson Sub-Machine Guns (Tommy Guns) and magazines (not the round drums that the mob and Elliot Ness used during Prohibition) for the guns. We looked for ammunition and a Field Manual, but found neither. What in the world?

The Team Captain went down to the radio in the bunker and called Province "meeting them green" (scrambled) to find out what was going on. He came back up to the team house with a puzzled look on his face. Somewhere at MACV III Corp headquarters, someone had decided that issuing these weapons to the Hamlet Chiefs at Dong Xoai would be a good idea — sort of a status symbol of their position... Really? Hearing this, we gathered around the case and looked down on the five guns and had a collective head shake — not a good head shake.

Dong Xoai was the major village — in fact the only village — in Don Luan district. There were no rural populations anywhere in the province.

France's war followed by our war had seen to the end of that. Almost the entire district population lived in five hamlets around Dong Xoai for protection and the support services required in daily life.

Each of the five hamlets had its own PSDF; its Peoples Self Defense Force. The forces were composed of a few members — old men, women, older teenagers — who were issued weapons from WW2 like M1 rifles and carbines. They were trained to shoot and clean these weapons. Three members would share a single weapon and the weapon was supposed to be in someone's possession twenty-four hours a day. The working idea was that if the Viet Cong attempted to enter the village to collect taxes or "draft" someone for their squad, the PSDF would defend against the incursion. The gunfire would alert a nearby Popular Force platoon that would come to the rescue, followed by assistance from the Regional Force company[29]. The Hamlet Chief was the leader of the PSDF. The PSDF originated with the Special Forces A-Teams who worked in the hamlets and villages during the 1960s. The A-Teams provided the weapons, ammunition, and training for the PSDF.

By 1971, providing the PSDF with ammunition for their vintage weapons was becoming a problem. It was caused in part by Vietnamization, the process of turning over the full conduct of the war to the Vietnamese that was now in full swing. Supply of needed war materials was no longer the responsibility of the US. It was now in the hands of the Vietnamese, but these supply lines were essentially non-existent for the PSDF. Plus, the Vietnamese Army, the Regional Forces, and the Popular Forces did not use WW2 era weapons. For the PSDF to maintain any level of proficiency with their weapons, the MAT Team had to conduct periodic weapons training, so the members could practice firing their weapons; this meant that a fairly constant resupply of the vintage ammunition was needed. Even though the Thompsons used the same cartridges as the .45 automatic pistols many officers carried, adding the Thompson to the PSDF's weapons didn't help this problem.

---

[29] A Viet Cong strategy was to have a few VC attempt to enter a hamlet causing a PSDF response. The rest of the VC would be lying in ambush for the responding PF platoon.

Finding ammunition could wait because there was another problem — none of us were Korean War veterans. Among the nine men who made up the District Team and the MAT Team, I was the only one with any experience with the Thompson. 33 Tango had enlisted in late 1951 during the Korean War but never deployed to that war. Besides, he would have been a Private carrying an M1 rifle; Thompsons were carried by NCOs and Officers.

Part of my training at the Special Warfare Center at Ft. Bragg involved the weapons of WW2 and Korea. We fired and cleaned most of them. Having played War with my friends as a kid, that part of the training was a dream. Now it was time for the nightmare.

I removed a Thompson from the crate and checked the chamber to insure it was not loaded. Then I tried to remember how to disassemble the thing. With the rest of the MAT Team (except the medic) and our interpreter watching and with a lot of suggestions and advice, I broke down the weapon into its component parts. The weapon was fairly simple, so the process of taking it apart and reassembling it was not difficult. Everyone then took one, disassembled it and cleaned it.

One of the Sergeants retrieved a can of .45 caliber ammunition in the munitions bunker and we headed to the rifle range — a pile of dirt outside the perimeter where weapons could safely be fired. After figuring out how to best train the Hamlet Chiefs and having some fun, we returned to the team house and cleaned the weapons a second time. Knowing that we would not get ammunition from the Regional Force company, I called the S-4 shop (supply) at Province and made the request. The S-4 NCO replied that .45-caliber ammunition had recently become very difficult to acquire, so we added another item to our scrounging list. MAT Sergeants did a great deal of scrounging from American units, but American units were going home. It was becoming more and more difficult for our NCOs to find supplies of WW2 ammunition. After all, American units were not using those weapons. The team's NCOs would be traveling a lot in the coming days.

Another concern was language. The ethnicity of the five hamlets was not the same. Two were Vietnamese, two were Montagnard, and one was Cambodian - three different languages and our interpreter spoke

Vietnamese and English. Working with the Montagnards and Cambodians involved a lot of one-on-one pointing and demonstrating how to do something. A lot of head nodding was involved. And there was always an experienced hamlet member who was willing to help. The Thompson presented a completely new situation because there would be no experienced hamlet member to help.

The weapon itself was a concern; it is heavy and not easy to handle. Vietnamese and Montagnards are not big people. We were fairly sure that the Hamlet Chiefs would not be carrying this weapon around throughout the day.

We coordinated a training date with the District Advising Team and the District Chief, contacted the Hamlet Chiefs, and looked for ammunition. The morning of the training session we picked up the Chiefs at their hamlets with our jeeps (the Major's, the Intel Team's and the MAT's) and drove them to the range — first-class treatment to be driven by an American advisor. We were there to win their hearts and minds, so every bit helped. We broke them into three groups by language and did our best. The MAT Team leader and interpreter worked with the Vietnamese group. They had the easiest time because our interpreter had worked with the Thompson on that first day and knew what was going on. The team NCOs worked with the Montagnards and I worked with the Cambodian Hamlet Chief. We did ok, too.

After a dry fire session and a firing demonstration by the Team's Sergeants, each Chief took turns firing his weapon at targets leaning against the pile of dirt that served as the range backstop. I have often wondered if the Chiefs enjoyed firing the weapons or just tolerated it. After firing, we broke up into our three groups and cleaned the weapons. The "Graduation Ceremony" consisted of giving each Chief two loaded magazines, a case of Budweiser beer, and a chauffeured ride back to their villages. It was a good day, but I do not recall seeing the Thompsons again.

Story 14 - S P Packs, Poker, and Movies

The best morale boosters for us at Dong Xoai were mail and packages from home. Compared to other MAT Teams in Vietnam, we were very fortunate to receive mail almost daily. Other morale boosters were S P packs, poker, and movies.

S P stood for Sundry Package. This pack contained various non-combat related items that in theory would last one soldier 100 days or 100 soldiers one day. The MAT Team with five men was due one every twenty days. The District Team with four men was due one every twenty-five days. If both teams were lumped together, we were due one about every eleven days. Needless to say, the SP packs did not arrive anywhere near that level of frequency — once a month, maybe. Regardless of when they came in, they were appreciated.

Items in the S P pack included paper, envelopes, and ball point pens for writing letters home. Tooth brushes, toothpaste, soap, shaving cream, razors, and blades were also in the pack. There was a mixed collection of about 100 candy bars which is where we got the candy we passed out to the children in the hamlets. Hershey Bars were the children's favorites, though they did not do well in the heat. One Hershey bar that did hold up to the heat was the Tropical Chocolate Bar. Unlike the regular Hershey Bar, these came in white wrappers. They were thicker but not as wide or long, and had a very dense consistency that would not melt on the hottest day. And they were totally unwanted by the children. We could not give them away. Bit-of-Honey was almost as unpopular.

One of the most useful items in the pack were the boot laces. These were thin, extremely strong black nylon cords. We carried these laces on operations. Tying a poncho over your hammock on a rainy night in the field was one use. They were indispensable.

The S P pack also contained packages of different brands of small cigars, boxes of matches, and pouches of chewing tobacco. The cigars were taken by a few team members, but no one took the chewing tobacco, which I think went to the village. For the team members who

Figure 14.1 33 Tango enjoying a smoke.

did smoke, the most important items in the S P pack were the cigarettes.

The "Perfect" S P Pack had a mix of brands ranging from highly preferred (e.g., Pall Mall, Winston) to despised (e.g., Chesterfield); 10 cartons containing 100 packages of cigarettes. Not being a smoker, I do not remember how the smokers decided who got what brands, but I think the divvy of the cigarettes was a bit raucous. Woe unto the smoker who was not there for dinner on the day the work helicopter delivered the S P pack. He got his fair share number-wise, but it consisted of the brands no one wanted.

The term, "Perfect" S P pack was used above. By that I meant, "Unopened" S P pack. On some occasions the S P pack arrived in a resealed condition — it had been opened and re-taped. Someone, somewhere higher in the supply chain had opened the pack and removed the cartons of the desirable brands of cigarettes replacing them with cartons of the less desirable brands. This generated loud protests, but the smokers took the cigarettes anyway.

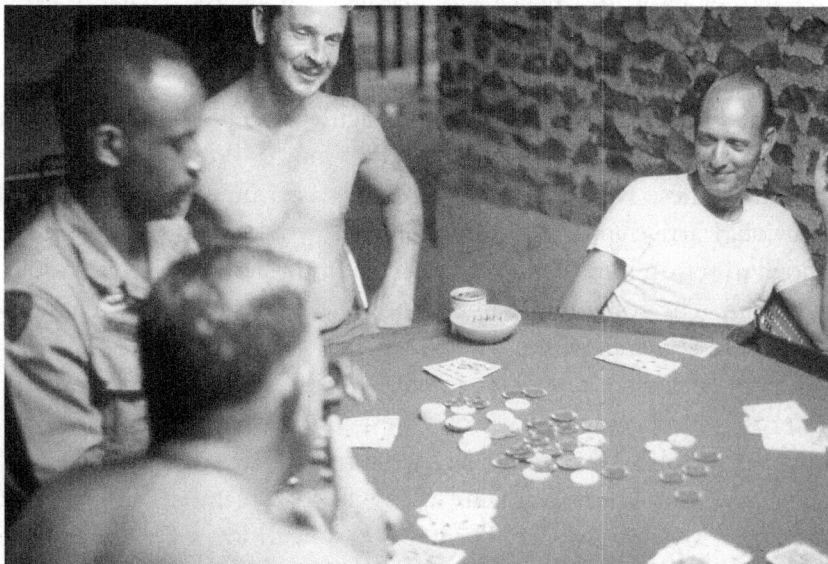

Figure 14.2   The friendly poker game.

Another activity for most members was poker. This was for real money though the amount, while not penny-ante was never up to paycheck level. After the "talking lizard" affair the first night I was at Dong Xoai, I was asked to join a game. I am not a gambler and certainly not much of a card player, but I do understand the rules for poker. For much of the night, I could not lose. My run of luck was incredible. My streak was the main reason that the game devolved to "3 card guts" where you are dealt two cards facing up and one card face down AND you could not look at the face down card. You bet based on what you saw on the table. I won more than I lost. It continued to get worse as it further devolved to "Indian Poker" where everyone was dealt one card face down. You picked it up and held it up to your forehead where everyone but you could see it and you bet based on what you saw on everyone's forehead. Again, I won more than I lost. When it was all said and done, I had a nice pile of "Monopoly money" — the Military Pay Certificates that was used by soldiers in Vietnam in lieu of actual US currency. I tucked this away in a tin box and managed to lose all of it in the next few months. I never had luck like that again — when it came to cards.

Movies added to the list of evening activities. The four District Teams and Province each had a projector. Every month Province would receive five films. These would be distributed one at a time to each locale. The film would arrive in the mail bag and we would keep it until Province radioed to return it in the next mail. Then the following day we would get a new film. The system was simple and it worked. Often, we invited some Vietnamese to watch with us; they seemed to like the films.

The movies were not deep, intellectual offerings; rather a mixture of westerns, murder mysteries, comedies, and from time to time a war movie. Any John Wayne movies, western or war were not liked. John Wayne was not liked. Watching a movie that featured him was liking watching, "Mystery Science Theater 3000" with lots of rude comments and sound effects made during the movie. That his movie, "Green Beret" used our camp as the setting for the major attack at the beginning of the film did not help. The attack did happen in 1965 with hundreds of casualties on both sides and two of the defenders earned Medals of Honor, but the movie event bore no resemblance to the attack beyond the camp name, "Dong Xoai."

A common interest with the movies was the wildly anticipated nude scenes, though such scenes rarely showed up. From a skin point of view, just as some tasty bit was about to be revealed, the movie would be spliced with the eagerly expected scene missing. The rumor was that someone up the supply chain was cutting up the films, removing the nude scenes, and editing them into one long skin parade. It was probably the same guy who was swapping out the cartons of cigarettes.

We had spare projector bulbs which was good. However, one evening the sound disappeared. Nothing we did fixed the problem that night; a mystery movie without dialog leaves a lot to be desired. The next day, after lunch when activity was at a lull, our medic got some of his instruments, and we operated on the projector hoping to fix the problem. After all, the entire team wanted to know who did it! Taking the cover off the projector, we discovered a second lamp. It was very small and had an odd type of base. The lamp was behind a small opening in the film's path. We blocked the bright light of the projector bulb and turned the projector on; the little light did not illuminate. Closer inspection showed that the filament was gone. We assumed that in some way the light was needed to generate the sound. First, we tested our theory. We got one of our flashlights, and removed the red lens. Then without replacing the projector cover, we threaded the film through the projector and, shining the flashlight as best as we could through the little opening, turned the projector on — SOUND. Our theory was correct. Now, how do we make a permanent fix.

The first strategy was to radio Province and ask if they had the little bulb. The S-4 shop (supply) said, "No" and in turn contacted Corp supply who replied, "What bulb?"

The second strategy was to improvise — something the Army is pretty good at. Whatever we did, it had to be small because the space for the lamp was not very big. We each had the standard issue flashlight plus a few extras. Using the entire flashlight was not practical so we pulled a bulb out of one. Now we needed a socket. We were able to wrap the bare end of a length of electrical wire around the metal cylinder of the lamp's base and twist it tight enough to make contact. Making a good contact on the tip end of the base was another problem.

Several attempts worked but were too big to fit into the space. Then our medic had an idea. He wrapped the bulb with one layer of adhesive tape covering the first wire leaving only the contact on the end of the bulb open. Next, he twisted a bare segment of wire into a little pad and placed it on the base and taped it to the bulb. Then he took his chewing gum, covered the entire base of the lamp, and pushed the bulb/gum blob into the small space where the burned-out light used to be. His idea was to use the gum as cement to hold the wire and tape in place and to hold the lamp in the right place in the projector.

We waited until after lunch the next day to try the fix. By that time the gum had hardened, and it seemed to be working. When the other ends of the wires were taped to two flashlight batteries, the lamp came on; so far so good. We replaced the projector cover and crossed our fingers that the gum would not soften from the heat of the projector lamp. Turning the projector on we had sound and the gum did not soften. That evening the team finished the film, and we learned who did it. But the gum did not solve the missing nude scenes.

Story 15 - Glowing Grass

It was another typical mission, if any mission in the jungles of Vietnam was ever typical. Captain Ky was leading a group of about 30 RF troops based out of Dong Xoai; 33 Tango and I were advising. Over the previous missions we had developed a good working rapport with Captain Ky and his troops. So much so that we each contributed a can of meat to the dinner pot and ate our evening meal with him and his small command group.

Earlier in the week several Montagnards had reported seeing signs of group movement in the jungle. The Green Berets who established the camp at Dong Xoai in 1965 had built a trusting relationship with the Montagnards, which the District and MAT Teams that replaced the Green Berets worked hard at maintaining. It paid off when they reported this type of information. The problem was that the Montagnards could not read maps. When they made such reports, they would point in a direction and say, "Three days walk." Since they moved faster through the jungle than we did and did not walk in a straight line, all we would do was make a best guess estimate of where the Montagnards were when they saw what they were reporting and request a reconnaissance. If we were lucky, we could arrange for an aircraft to pick one of us up and go take a look. The density of the jungle canopy made it very unlikely anything could be seen but the flight provided a general overview of the terrain through which we were going to be moving.

As we drove in a light morning fog northeast away from Dong Xoai in our usual four vehicle convoy, we had one trepidation; there would be no moonlight on this operation. It was the week of the new moon — the nights would be very dark. We dismounted, put on our packs, and headed north away from the road into the jungle moving in a single file column; flank security was not possible due to the thickness of the vegetation. On the morning of the second day, we found a small VC base camp, but its defensive structures were old. The wood they used to build their fighting positions was rotting. We did find some signs of recent occupation by a small force but nothing else.

During the morning of day two we also moved out of artillery and radio range from Dong Xoai — we were on our own. The Viet Cong knew the maximum range of the camp's two 105 mm howitzers (a bit more than six miles) so they moved just beyond that distance when they were in the area. Because of this, any hope of finding the movement the Montagnards reported necessitated that we operate beyond the limits of the camp's radios and artillery.

We found limited traces of movement; probably a small squad of Viet Cong. The movement was in a north/south direction, but we could not tell which way they were moving. Walking north for three days would take them into Cambodia and the heart of the Ho Chi Minh Trail. Walking south would move them towards War Zone D where they could have a base camp. Large Main Force Viet Cong units had been decimated during the Tet offensive in 1968 and were never reconstituted. Small squads still operated after 1968 but with little local support. Intelligence thought that the small squads might be acting as guides for the movement of supplies into caches for later use when a large-scale invasion would be launched. It was possible that this squad was moving north to pick up a supply train or to get needed supplies, but we could not be sure in which direction the squad was moving.

Attempting to follow the Viet Cong squad (5-7 men) presented an interesting situation. If our group of 30 caught up with the squad, it would be a one-sided fight in our favor. If the squad had actually met up with a VC company-sized unit and was now leading them back towards us and we met up face to face, it would be an even fight — one in which I would not want to engage. If the squad were leading a VC battalion — I would not be writing this story. We had no intelligence of company size or larger elements in the area so trying to follow was the right course of action. But which way to move; north or south? That decision was relatively simple — south. Moving north would take us even further from Dong Xoai towards Cambodia with no artillery or radio support; we had to move to the south. Later that afternoon we lost the trail, but we kept moving south hoping to pick it up again — no such luck.

On day three we moved into a region of open grass fields surrounded by much less dense jungle. Some of the open areas were the size of two football fields. The fields and the surrounding jungle looked unnatural — if they were abandoned farms, why hadn't the jungle reclaimed them? Maybe this was the result of Agent Orange applications. The grass was about three feet tall and our movement through the fields would have been very easy, but Captain Ky avoided them because we could have easily been observed by the Viet Cong. Instead, he moved the column around the fields in the jungle near the edges of the fields. He was concerned about being ambushed while we were in the open.

Very late in the afternoon we approached another field — as wide as it was long. Following our usual pattern for the end of the day, we stopped short of this field, ate dinner, and waited until it was close to dark. The topo map showed a small high ground just beyond the other side of the field that would be a good place for an NDP (Night Defensive Position). Captain Ky sent groups of two soldiers in three directions: one group to follow the left edge of the field, one to follow the right edge, and one across the middle of the field. They reported back that nothing suspicious was seen and that the high ground was defendable. We finished eating and moved out as the light dimmed. Since the scouts had seen no sign of the enemy, we moved through this grass field instead of around it. That left us with enough light to set up the perimeter and hang our hammocks. I walked the perimeter with Captain Ky checking each position and its firing lanes. The machine gun position had a good field of fire covering the field we had just crossed.

Night fell and the sky was cloudless. 33 Tango and I always alternated two-hour watches at night, and I took the first one. Sitting in my hammock leaning against a bush in total darkness, I was listening to the night sounds when I heard two clicks on the radio handset. I picked up the handset pushed the talk button twice in response. The reply came from Captain Ky who whispered, "Den day" (come here). He was only a few feet away but he apparently did not want to walk over in the dark — good thinking. I nudged 33 Tango with the butt of my rifle (never shake a sleeping combat veteran in the field — his reaction could be very painful for you) and roused him. He roused our interpreter. We crept over to Captain Ky's position who whispered, "Theo toi" (follow me), as we approached.

We moved to the perimeter position that overlooked the field and the sky was — indescribable. With no moon, no clouds and no horizon lights, the sky was a blanket of stars decorated by the Milky Way winding its way through its center. It was captivating until I looked down... Ever so dim, the field was glowing in the dark. It was a dim, grayish—greenish glow. You could see the edges of the field where the grass ended and the jungle began. It was a sea of uniform dim glow — **except where we walked**. Through the center of the field was a black line marking the path we walked moving to our position. It was like an arrow pointing and saying, "This way to the attack." This was very uncomfortable. We were not sure where the Viet Cong were and which way they were moving — they could be moving back towards us. Our movement was stealthy but they might know we were following them. In fact, they might be following us; we could not take any chances.

Captain Ky's soldiers were well trained but not for night movement. Trying to move in the pitch black would be a disaster. We were here for the night. Setting anti-personal mines in front of the perimeter would have been the next best thing but they were not available to the Regional Forces. Besides, any enemy moving through the dark path we created in the field would be invisible in the total darkness. The VC would be on top of us before we knew it.

33 Tango and I talked for a few minutes and presented a plan to Captain Ky. He agreed and we got busy. We returned to our hammocks to gather the needed items. While I dug two cans of C-Ration fruit cocktail and two boot laces out of my pack, 33 Tango cut two stiff branches off a plant and retrieved a small spool of trip wire (strong, thin wire painted green) from his pack. I handed him one can and we opened them quickly drinking the juice and almost drinking the fruit — no time to enjoy the taste. (Breakfast would be a bit thin tomorrow.) Using the boot laces, we bound the empty cans tightly to the sticks 33 Tango had cut. Then we moved back to the perimeter position where Captain Ky

and our interpreter were waiting. The four of us moved out of the perimeter, walking quietly in the dark on the path of non-glowing grass. We stopped when we were 50 meters out[30] and got to work. I pushed my stake into the soft ground until it was firmly anchored. 33 Tango spooled off some trip wire and handed one end to me. I wrapped this end around the base of the fuse assembly on a fragmentation grenade and slid the grenade into the can. While I held the grenade in the can, 33 Tango

Figure 15.1 The Grenade Trap with the pin pulled out of the grenade. The trip wire is barely visible in the picture.

---

[30] How did I know we were 50 meters out if it was totally dark? The answer is that I counted my steps. Part of land navigation is knowing how many steps it takes to move 100 meters. One month of the six months of Infantry Officer Candidate School (OCS) concentrated on land navigation. If you were not 100% sure of where you were in the field, you washed out of OCS.

moved to the other side of the path unspooling the wire as he moved. He shoved his stick into the ground. Then he put a grenade into the can on his stick. Pulling the wire as taut as possible, he carefully measured the wire's length and cut it with his knife. He wrapped the end around the base of the fuse assembly on a second grenade. When we were sure the grenades would remain in the cans, we pulled the pins that held the grenades' handles in place; they were armed. The cans kept the handles in place.

If a Viet Cong moved along the path and hit the wire, he would pull the grenades out of the cans releasing the handles. Five seconds later — no more Nguyen. Running would be of no avail because he would drag the grenades with him. Either way we would have a 50-meter warning if we were attacked. We returned to the perimeter and to our hammocks, but no one slept that night.

The next morning, 33 Tango shared his fruit cocktail with me for breakfast. Just before we moved out, 33 Tango and I went out to retrieve our booby trap. We walked 40 meters and then got on our knees searching for the wire; we did not want to trip our own trap.

33 Tango found the wire. Working in concert, we replaced the pins in the grenades while they were in the cans. Then we removed the wire which 33 Tango rewound on to the spool. I pulled some grass out of the ground and put it in a plastic bag so I could examine it when we got back to camp. We carried the cans back to the perimeter, cut the bottoms out, crushed them (so the Viet Cong could not use them in the same type of trap) and tossed them into the garbage hole Captain Ky's troops had dug.

We continued to move to the southeast finding no more traces of enemy movement. When we eventually reached the road at a point where we were back in radio range, Captain Ky called for pickup. The troops formed a perimeter and we waited for the vehicles.

That night, back a Dong Xoai I took the grass outside but there was no glow. I do not know what caused the glow — the grass, fungus on the grass, bacteria on the grass, some side effect of Agent Orange. I have no idea. Maybe someday I will find something on the web or someone reading this book will explain what we saw.

Story 16 - A Mission Too Long

Told by Jim Rice

The operation was jointly planned at Dong Xoai with the RF Group Commander, the Advisor staff of District Senior Advisor and the MAT 111 Leader (me). It was a large operation requiring helicopter insertion using US Air assets and as I recall 8 Hueys flying four lifts each.

Figure 16.1   Dai Uy Gao, the MAT team leader, directs the helicopters' landing for the air mobile assault.

Following my counterpart, the three of us went in with the second lift. As we were getting off the chopper in the drop zone, my interpreter was advised that there were 4 Vietnamese soldiers wounded by friendly fire during the first lift. The soldiers were trained to exit the choppers and immediately form a perimeter to protect the lift birds and the next lifts that came in. The RF troops spread out as the choppers were lifting off, and the door gunners on the choppers used M60 machine guns to fire into the surrounding jungle not knowing that our troops had already begun forming the perimeter. Their firing wounded the four RF soldiers. I called the lead pilot and asked him to land and pick up the wounded and he declined telling me to call a medivac unit. I told him his folks wounded them and to get someone down to pick them up. He said he had two more lifts to do and couldn't comply. I told him I couldn't continue my mission until these troops were extracted, and I was ready to call his unit to report the incident and ask them to order him to make the pick-up…he relinquished and sent a helicopter down to carry our wounded back to the rear.

Needless to say, this was a serious setback at the beginning of what was to be long operation and created a strained relationship that persisted for the duration of the operation.

As soon as the wounded were picked up and the other lifts were in, we headed through the jungle towards the first objective. We were in search of a Viet Cong .51 caliber air defense artillery machine gun and any other NVA or VC units in our area. We crossed several streams and moved in and out of overhead jungle cover for several hours. I tried to keep track of our location on my map but honestly, I lost track of where we were exactly. (GPS would have been a real asset, but it was 30 years too early for that technology!)

Soon the commander halted to eat and take their 2+ hour midday break. Every VN soldier and officer had a bag of cooked but then dried rice. I had a rucksack full of C rations, socks, and radio batteries for my NCO and me and my NCO carried the radio. I would say my ruck was between 45 and 50 pounds at the beginning. We sat with the Commander and his Lieutenants for lunch. They had filled their dry rice with water an hour or so earlier and the rice was now soft enough to eat although not hot. I opened cans of C's, and we shared their rice and our C-rations.

The commander asked me where I thought we were, and I pulled out my map and showed him a general area where I thought we might be. He had us at a little different location, and one of his Lieutenants had a different but close location. We tried to use surrounding terrain to more closely locate our position but it all looks alike so that didn't clear it up. Eventually we picked a spot in the middle of all 3 positions and called for an artillery marking round which was a White Phosphorous round fired so that it would detonate above the spot so we could see it and determine our exact location by measuring from that round. White phosphorous gives a bright white burst but then the fall out is burning white phosphorous which will even burn under water as it doesn't need oxygen. The round fired and when the artillery called "Splash" which meant the round would detonate in two-seconds, we all stood and looked in different locations to try to see the round. Unfortunately, it went off almost directly over our position dropping burning white phosphorous. Some troops got it on their uniforms but no one was hurt. Some of it hit my rucksack but I was able to smother it before it burned our supplies. The beginning of this long op was very problematic to say the least!

On day 2, we were traveling in a column when we came to a fairly wide and deep stream that we had to cross. The VN troops found a good place to ford and set up security for the company to cross. My NCO and I were positioned in the middle the company as it started to make the crossing.

When my NCO, interpreter and I began to cross, the RF commander had troops accompany us in front and rear. As we neared the middle of the stream, somehow, I stepped off of the ledge or whatever we were walking on. My rucksack, M16 and ammunition took me straight down; I was completely submerged. I was reaching to pull the quick releases on my pack so I could dump the weight and get my head above the water when a hand in front and one behind pulled me straight up out of the water and helped me get back on the higher ground. I was soaked as was everything I carried, cigarettes included, and I was embarrassed, but I didn't lose any supplies or drown, so it is a good memory.

The operation continued for the rest of the week with no contact and in fact, no indication of VC or NVA operations in the area. The commander wanted to continue the op for a second week in an effort to clear a larger area, but my NCO, interpreter, and I were short on C

Rations and other supplies. At midday the company stopped and set up a perimeter for lunch and the midday break. I decided to look for an LZ (helicopter landing zone) large enough to land a Huey, so we could get a resupply. My NCO and I did a recon around the perimeter to see if we could find one.

As we were walking around, we found a fairly large area that looked okay, but I wanted to walk across it to the far side and make sure it didn't have any booby traps or explosives that could take out the chopper. I had walked almost to the center of the area when the ground gave way under my feet, and I found myself falling in a hole. My mind immediately went to punji pits which were traps built by the VC where the earth gave way. As you fell into the pit, punji stakes (sharpened bamboo skewers often covered with feces that were driven into the bottom and walls of the pit) penetrated your body and immediately began infecting the wounds. Many soldiers were maimed or killed in punji pits, and I thought I was the next casualty.

My NCO saw me going down, and he ran toward me asking if I was okay. I told him I thought it was a punji pit but that I didn't feel like it had hurt me. He slowed to make sure he didn't fall in and finally crawled over and gave me his hand. Fortunately, I wasn't wearing my rucksack so I was lighter weight and between the 2 of us I was able to get out. I looked back in the hole and it was not a punji pit. It appeared to be either an abandoned underground headquarters or abandoned underground cache. Either way it was not deadly or occupied.

We were able to make radio contact and request a resupply. The Huey came in a while later with what we requested plus a small package containing a cold soda for my NCO, my interpreter, and me. Dong Xoai had not forgotten us. Frankly, I was ready to get on that chopper and get out of the jungle; I had had enough of this operation. But I stayed!

The operation went on another 4 or 5 days with still no enemy contact. The commander finally decided he was not going to find the VC unit he was chasing and decided to call for extraction. He told me through Sgt. Yung that he did not want US helicopters to lift us out because of the problems on insertion, and that he had made arrangements for Vietnamese Hueys to pick us up.

We found an LZ large enough to bring in the 4 or 5 helicopter lift, and it was on the edge of a rice paddy. The company formed a perimeter to secure the LZ and the commander called the choppers in. When they were close, the Vietnamese command and control helicopter contacted him. On board that chopper was a US advisor who was in contact with me.

When they turned in to the LZ, they began firing rockets and M60 machine guns over our heads and into the surrounding rice paddy and jungle. I yelled on the radio to the advisor to tell them to quit firing because we had the area secured and we could direct fire for them if there was any contact. I told him they were firing right over our heads. He said, "Wait, out!" He came back on and said, "All I can tell you is keep your head down." I couldn't believe my ears or eyes, but we kept our heads down as the firing continued. We went out on the second lift.

As was normal for Hueys doing this mission there were no seats in the chopper. We jumped in, and I sat with my feet hanging off the side and was leaning back on my rucksack. After nearly 2 weeks I was exhausted and closed my eyes. It was probably a 30 or 40 minute ride back to basecamp, so I thought I would rest. I opened my eyes to see how we were doing, and I saw the chopper next to us so close to us that his rotor blades were overlapping ours. Any amount of turbulence or pilot error could have created a collision of blades bringing both helicopters down. Suddenly I wasn't sleepy! I sat there staring at the other chopper the rest of the way back.

When we came in, we landed on the small airstrip close to the compound. As they flew down the strip, I was looking out the door toward the back and I saw the tail skid hit and scrape for about 50 yards before we slowed enough to hover to a stop. With my eyes probably popping out of my head, I grabbed my ruck and my weapon and jumped a few feet to the ground. The three of us ran to the jeep that the District Senior Advisor (the Major - my boss) had driven down to pick us up. We threw our stuff in the jeep and said get us the hell out of here. The Major asked why, and I told him I would tell him when we were far enough away to be clear of a crash if it occurred.

As soon as we got back to the team house, the Major wanted to "debrief" me on the operation. Standing there giving him a report was the last thing I wanted to do right now. I had been wearing the same set of jungle fatigues for two weeks. The closest thing to a shower I had during those two weeks was on the second day of the operation when I found myself exploring the bottom of the stream we were crossing. I had eaten nothing but C-Rations, I smelled, was very hungry and very tired. But he was the boss so I started telling him about it blow by blow, when he stopped me and said, "Stand downwind from me; you smell bad!" I thought I was pissed before but this broke the dam. "I'll brief you when I get cleaned up and get something to eat." With that, I turned and walked away. Definitely insubordinate, but this was more crap than I was in the mood for!

That was a terrible operation and was unsuccessful in finding or eliminating any enemy troops or supplies. Not our best effort on either side!

Story 17 - A Broken Water Pump and Chlorinator

Our camp was built by the Navy Seabees for Special Forces A-Team 342 in 1965. It was, by any standard for remote military camps, almost a resort, and we were fortunate to be based there. The Seabees had installed a deep well somewhere in the middle of the perimeter's barbed wire/mine field complete with a submersed electric pump giving us a dependable water supply. They mounted two water buffaloes (black water trailers) high on stilts and positioned them near the team house providing us with some water pressure and in the afternoon an almost warm shower. Even better, we had a flush toilet; extremely rare in this part of Vietnam. All of this drained to a septic tank somewhere else in the barbed wire around the perimeter.

Part of the water system was a swimming pool chlorinator to ensure the water was safe to drink. Every morning either the medic or I would go out and check the chlorine levels in the water. One morning when we turned the tap on at the pump control panel before making the test, there was no water. The pump was literally dead.

We pulled the cover off the pump control panel, and everything looked fine. There was power between the generator and the control panel, but pushing the start button for the pump had no effect on the flow of water. The water buffaloes held enough water for several days, but we had to fix this. It was our only source of good drinking water. The problem was that we did not know where the well was located, and the pump was submerged in the well.

The medic and I explained the problem to the rest of the team that morning. One of the NCOs recalled that a road grader had been working on the entrance road to the camp yesterday. The Vietnamese were trying to improve drainage that ran along the road which moved rain water downhill away from the camp during the heavy storms of the rainy season. We began our search there. It did not take long to find the problem — a thick black electrical cable that was apparently buried too shallow to be protected had been sliced into several pieces by the blade of the road grader.

Figure 17.1   The arrow above shows part of the two cables we used to make the repairs.

We went to the MAT Team's conex (a secure steel storage container) and looked for cable. Most MAT Teams had a conex for storing equipment and supplies used in our work with the Vietnamese. No weapons or explosives; just tools such as shovels, axes, a chainsaw, rope, chain, pulleys, farm jack, tool kit; anything that might be needed for building and maintaining an outpost like ours in the jungle. We found several epoxy-based cable splicing kits but no electrical cable.

Fate was with us today. We were scheduled for a visit by the chaplain. From time to time the chaplain would literally drop in. He would fly in on a small helicopter, set up an altar, usually a poncho over a stack of C ration boxes or ammunition crates and conduct a brief service. It wasn't Protestant, Catholic or Jewish — it was just a service. Then we would retire to the team house, have a beer, and talk for a while — an attempt for normalcy in a crazy place.

After the service but before the beer, we asked if we could borrow his helicopter, and he agreed not bothering to ask why. I talked with the pilot and crew chief explaining that we needed a spool of heavy-duty electrical cable and asked if they could help us locate one. The crew chief said that he knew where some cable might be found. I retrieved my flight helmet, climbed aboard, and we were off to someplace unknown to me. In a short while we were circling over a large supply dump. The pilot quickly located a number of spools of electrical cable and set the helicopter down near the spools. The pilot kept the blades spinning while the crew chief and I got out of the chopper and ran over to check the spools. The spools held two conductor wire but I needed three conductor, so we decided to take two spools. They were heavy so we carried them one at a time over to the chopper, loaded them, and took off not bothering to ask anyone if we could have them. Forgiveness is usually easier than permission, and why risk being told, "No!" That would have made us thieves.

When we got back to Dong Xoai, the crew chief helped me unload the spools setting them on the edge of the helipad. The helicopter crew and I joined the rest of the team and the chaplain who was still having his beer. Later, we walked the chaplain back to his helicopter where he saw the spools of cable sitting on the edge of the helipad. He looked at me and said, "Oh. I see your trip was successful." He climbed into his chopper, the blades sped up, and he was gone — off to his next service.

The story does not end there. We got the splicing kits from the conex; a collection of two-part molds, two-part epoxy, and instructions for making a water tight covering on a splice of an electrical cable. Several of us carried the spools and the splicing kits down to the road and repaired the cable using two wires in one cable and one wire in the other. We were fortunate to have the splicing kits or this would have failed the first time it rained. From there we went to the pump control panel and pushed the start button on the control panel. The indicator light came on and when we opened the tap, water began to flow. We were in business or so we thought — the green light on the chlorinator did not come on. We checked it out and there was nothing we could see that was wrong, so we surmised that when the blade cut the cable, there was a surge that blew the chlorinator before the fuse wire could melt. Another problem but it was one was for another day.

The medic or I chlorinated water manually for the next few days. One of us would climb up on the scaffolding and add a measure of the chemical powder to the tank and then test the water later in the day. One day the water tasted a little like bleach, but no one got sick.

The morning after the bleach flavor incident, the two MAT NCOs got into the jeep and drove out of camp not bothering to say where they were going. When they returned much later in the day, they handed the medic a cardboard box and said, "Don't ask." The medic found me and showed me the contents of the box. It was a swimming pool chlorinator; not exactly like the one we had but similar. It appeared to have been very quickly removed from its previous location. The electrical wires and the rubber tubing connecting the chlorinator to its original system had been roughly cut, and there were no instructions in the box. And the box was a C-Ration carton …

Working together, the medic and I jury-rigged this "new" chlorinator into our water system and it worked. No one got sick, and the water never tasted like bleach again. I often wondered which swimming pool at what rear area camp lost its chlorinator that day, but I never asked. Given the chance, I would have bet a lot of money that it came from an officers' swimming pool.

Story 18 - YB in Contact

YB was the Intelligence Team NCO. Part of his job was to support the combat activities of the Regional Force (RF) company and the allied MAT Team. Another part of his work was trying to identify Viet Cong sympathizers and spies living and working in the village. The nature of this work was classified and never discussed among the other members of the District Team or the MAT Team. Even though YB's position within the advising efforts in the district was that of a non-combatant, he earned a Purple Heart in the mortar attack in May (See Story 5 - First Contact).

The sensitive nature of the work of the Intelligence Team dictated that neither the Intelligence Captain or YB operate in the field. Should they be captured, they would suffer a terrible fate as their captors

Figure 18.1   Lt. Khan, YB, and the John Deere green Jeep.

attempted to extract what they knew. The realities of the work, however meant that YB was in the field. The factor that led to this was the advising practice of staying with your counterpart; a practice that would earn him another citation — the Army Commendation Medal with 'V' Device. The 'V' is for valor. How does a non-combatant Sergeant, who is not supposed to operate in the field manage to earn a "V" device?

Here is the story in YB's words:

The Intelligence Captain and I had a bad habit of driving in our jeep out to the airstrip every morning just to check things out. Our Jeep was manufactured by the Jeep Corporation, but it was not an Army Jeep. Somewhat similar, it was painted bright John Deere tractor green rather than a military olive drab color and stood out like a sore thumb saying, "Americans here!"

There was a small South Vietnamese outpost with a Popular Force (PF) platoon that guarded the airstrip. We would wave to them and check out the airstrip — just the two of us with no weapons. One morning we were about to head out to the airstrip in our jeep, when the Captain's counterpart, Lt. Khan asked us to have coffee with him to discuss something. While we were having coffee, Radio Watch called on the land line asking the Intel Captain to return to the team house to take a radio call. The Intel Captain decided it would be much quicker to walk back through the wire separating the District side of the camp from the RF side where the team house was located, so I remained with Lt. Khan, and would drive the jeep back to the team house when we were done. While we were having a second cup of coffee, a local PF soldier was walking on the side of the road out to the airstrip, and he noticed a mine aimed at the road. His presence caused the VC ambush unit to prematurely detonate the mine slightly wounding the PF soldier. I believe that the mine was meant for the Captain and me, as we had set a pattern and they were waiting for us. Based on our military's experience in Iraq and Afghanistan, today we would call that mine an IED (an improvised explosive device or roadside bomb). This incident occurred on 29 June, 1971.

Lt. Khan and I along with two RF soldiers got into our jeep, and we drove through the ambush site to the PF outpost. With a borrowed M-16, I got off a few rounds in the enemy's direction, and we fired artillery in the area of their retreat. Lt. Roberts was aloft in the work chopper, and he helped look for the enemy from the chopper, but they successfully made their escape. Lt. Roberts reminds me that I was the center of a decision dilemma for the Major (the District Senior Advisor or DSA) after the above incident. I remember the Major telling me that he did not know whether to court martial me for not having my M-16 or recommend me for a medal. We were not supposed to carry weapons because the village was supposed to be pacified, so I ended up getting the Army Commendation Metal with a 'V' device for valor.

While this was happening, I was in Song Be for a meeting. The S-3 (Operations) NCO entered the room, looked at me, and said, "Your buddies are in contact at Dong Xoai. The work chopper is waiting for you," and he handed me a portable field radio. I put on my web gear, picked up my M-16, and excused myself. It was a fast jeep ride to the air strip where the helicopter was spinning up. I hopped on board and we headed south to Dong Xoai; at top speed the trip took about 10 minutes. I called in, and Radio Watch told me to contact YB when I got closer. I called him, and he filled me in on what was happening. He gave me a direction from the PF outpost to where the VC were last seen moving away from the airstrip, and I directed the pilot to that area. Radio Watch told us that RF artillery was no longer firing and that it was safe to fly into the area. Radio Watch had obtained clearance from the RF company headquarters to fire into the suspected area and relayed it to me. I passed this on to the helicopter pilot, and the door gunners sprayed the area with M-60 machine gun fire though it is doubtful that they hit anyone or anything other than jungle growth and the ground. YB was ready to drive back to the team house, so the helicopter "escorted" his John Deere green jeep back to camp before returning me to Song Be.

When the helicopter got back to Song Be, the S-3 Major was waiting with his NCO at the air strip and wanted a full accounting of the situation. He said that the meeting had wrapped up, so I could return to Dong Xoai. I handed the radio to his NCO and got back on board the helicopter.

The Major discussed YB's fate with the MAT Team Captain — court martial or medal — I was not part of that. His medal was well deserved; he had driven through a Viet Cong ambush, organized the PF platoon to fire on the fleeing Viet Cong squad, directed artillery fire on the squad, and provided me with information for the chopper crew to use in trying to find the Viet Cong.

Also, in YB's defense for not having his M-16, it was the standard operating procedure (SOP) under the Province Senior Advisor (PSA) that Americans would not wear web gear or carry weapons in the village in order to show confidence in the ability of the local government and Regional Forces to maintain security in the area. Officially, Don Luan District and its main (and only) village, Dong Xoai were pacified. This SOP would soon lead to some other problems for us when a new PSA took over. But that is the next story.

Figure 18.2   Award Ceremony for YB, Lt. Khan and the two RF soldiers who were with them in the ambush.

Story 19 - A New PSA

1971 — Vietnam — Vietnamization was moving forward at top speed, and things were changing rapidly. One of those changes was a new Province Senior Advisor or PSA - a Colonel. The outgoing PSA was respected, and his standard operating procedures (SOPs) were well understood by those of us out in the villages and hamlets. When a new commander takes charge, some of these SOPs are bound to change. How the new commander implements those changes says a lot about the commander himself.

A helicopter pilot called to tell us he was five minutes out and had the new PSA on board. The members of the District Team and the MAT Team who were in camp walked to the helipad to meet and greet him. From there we would play everything by ear. The Major — the District Senior Advisor (DSA) would be in charge, and we would be there as needed.

The helicopter came into view, and someone threw a smoke grenade so the pilot could judge the wind direction and speed. The chopper settled on the "H" at the center of the helipad, and the PSA climbed out. We were standing off to the side away from the rotor's down draft in somewhat of a line loosely at attention. There was no saluting — saluting is frowned upon in a combat zone because it identifies a leader. The PSA walked over to us, and the Major put out his hand to welcome the PSA. The PSA, ignoring the extended hand said in a harsh tone, "Why aren't all of you wearing your web gear? And where are your weapons?"

No one spoke; the Major withdrew his hand. We just stared at the PSA.

"Well?"

The Major started his reply, "Sir, the SOP is to show confidence in the RF company, its Commander, and the district overall by not wearing our web gear and carrying our weapons in the camp or in the village so ..."

The PSA cut him off, "Major, this is a combat zone. Web gear will be worn and weapons carried whether you are in camp, in the village or on an operation."

The Major replied, "Yes Sir. What would you like to do first?"

"I want a tour of your village and this camp and then a briefing by you and your Intel officer." There was no mention of the MAT Team which was probably good. This was not going to be a comfortable command transition. Apparently, he saw us as a bunch of sloppy advisors who needed shaping up.

To this the Major said, "This way, Sir, to the team house. We will get our gear and weapons and drive through the village," as he pointed the way to the team house. The PSA turned and the Major led the way. The rest of us fell in behind in a "column by twos". I am not sure if we were mocking the PSA but we fell into step with him and marched quietly behind the two of them as if we were in a parade. Thank goodness one of the NCOs did not start calling cadence as we marched back to the team house. As we were moving, I was wondering what the Regional Force (RF) soldiers were thinking; they certainly were stopping and looking.

We went to our respective rooms to get our web gear and weapons. 33 Tango retrieved the M-60 machine gun and a belt of 100 rounds of ammunition from the bunker. Definite overkill but — what the heck? His DEROS (Date Eligible for Return from OverSeas) and retirement was only a few weeks away.

Someone asked the PSA if he wanted a cold drink while he waited, and he curtly declined. There would be no softening up this Colonel. Our jeeps were parked on the back side of the team house, so the PSA did not see them as we approached the house. When we exited the team house where the three jeeps were parked, the PSA asked, "Why aren't the tops up?" Jeeps had convertible tops that could easily be put up or down. Ours were down because the Regional Force (RF) Commander's and the District Chief's jeeps had their tops down, unless it was actually raining. With the top down, you can get into and out of the jeep by jumping over the back or sides. It is very difficult to get out of a jeep that has the top up if you are ambushed; you have to climb over the front seats to get out. And if the person in the front seat is dead or wounded, getting out is even more difficult.

The Major replied, "We follow the lead of our counterparts. When their tops are up, ours are too. This makes it more difficult for the Viet Cong to identify who the jeep is carrying."

Apparently ignoring the Major's comment, the PSA replied, "From now on tops will be up. Put those tops up!" We complied, raised the tops on the jeep and loaded up. The MAT Team Captain drove with 33 Tango beside him carrying the machine gun. The other MAT NCO, the medic and I squeezed into the two-person back seat.

Protocol for this level of command change and inspection, as I

Figure 19.1   The MAT Team jeep with the top up.

understood it from my training at Ft. Bragg, dictated that the new PSA first contacts the Vietnamese District Chief directly by radio, introducing himself, and asks permission to inspect the village, hamlets, and the RF camp. Upon arriving, he presents himself to the District Chief for a personal introduction, who then accompanies him on the tour. This adds to the District Chief's status with his people and his troops. What was happening right now was not following protocol and was disrespectful to the District Chief. Done properly, the District Chief would have time to inform the RF commander and Hamlet Chiefs that we would be driving through, and they could prepare to receive the two of them in a manner befitting of their positions.

DSAs and PSAs had specific training courses that gave them the background on the situation advisors face in the villages and what the advising protocols were. We were there to help the leadership improve economic and living conditions in the villages and hamlets and to improve the combat effectiveness of the RF companies, PF platoons and the PSDF. We were also there to coordinate with American assets when they were available. We were not in command. We could only advise and recommend. Apparently, this PSA missed the class where these topics were covered. According to the DSA's NCO who was riding in the back seat, as the Major drove through the village and hamlets, the PSA pointed out deficiencies he wanted remedied as if the Major could order the District Chief to do his bidding. On many levels this was not going to be a comfortable command transition. As our three-jeep convoy traveled through the village into and out of the hamlets with our tops up and the barrels of our weapons pointing outward, we presented a new and troubling sight for some of the villagers.

We drove into the District Chief's side of the compound, and no one came out to greet the PSA. If he was miffed, he said nothing. The same thing happened when we returned to our part of the compound and pulled up to the front of the RF headquarters — no one stepped out to meet the PSA. Again, he said nothing. I have often wondered if one of our interpreters informed the District Chief and the RF commander of what was happening and they snubbed him intentionally — possibly to show him he was not the boss.

Arriving back at the team house, the Major and the Intelligence Captain showed the PSA into the small briefing room and closed the door. The rest of us remained outside by the bunker to talk. Well, at least we thought we would talk but little was said. We just stood there with our web gear on and our weapons in our hands being stared at by the nearby RF soldiers.

After a while the PSA, Major, and the Intelligence Captain exited the team house and headed to the helipad. We fell in behind them in a "column by twos" and in step. 33 Tango still carried the machine gun with the belt of ammunition hanging over his shoulder. I have often wondered if I really did hear some muted Vietnamese laughter as we marched to the waiting helicopter.

As we came into view of the pilot, the rotor started to spin up. There were no handshakes before the PSA turned and moved toward the chopper. We stood there and watched it lift off, rotate and head north towards Song Be. We walked back to the team house — but not in a column and not in step.

After we returned our web gear and our weapons to our rooms, we met in the dining area for a debriefing on what just happened when the Major announced that he was buying the beer. The Major's NCO and 33 Tango headed towards the back door of the team house, and the Major asked, "Where are you two off to?" 33 Tango replied without looking back, "We're going to put the jeep tops down.

Story 20 - Eyeball 5

We had just finished lunch in the team house when Radio Watch called me over to the radio position, handed me the handset and said, "I have a call for 33 Quebec from Eyeball 5." 33 Quebec was my radio call sign. I put the handset to my ear and said, "Eyeball 5, this is 33 Quebec, over." The reply came immediately with an accent I did not recognize, "33 Quebec, I am inbound to your location. You and 33 Tango meet me at the airstrip in ten minutes. Eyeball 5, out." 33 Tango was the Sergeant with whom I operated when we were in the field with the Regional Force (RF) troops.

As I was thinking, "Who the hell is Eyeball 5?", Radio Watch handed me the SOI (Signals Operating Instructions) and said, "I can't find any Eyeball 5 call sign or frequency." I took the booklet and searched it a second time — definitely no Eyeball 5!

I found 33 Tango, and we drove to the airstrip on the edge of the road west of Dong Xoai. A few minutes later Eyeball 5 appeared on the horizon. Or rather, a Huey, a Loach, and two Cobras appeared on the horizon flying towards the airstrip. At an appropriate distance, 33 Tango threw a smoke grenade to the side of the airstrip, and I spoke into the radio, "Eyeball 5, 33 Quebec. Smoke out, over." The reply came back, "33 Quebec, Eyeball 5. Smoke is purple, over." Which was followed by my, "Roger. 33 Quebec. Out."

The Loach landed first, then the Huey. The cobras circled one time and landed behind the Huey. We waited at the jeep while the blades spun down to a stop. A figure jumped down from the Huey, took off his helmet, put it on the floor of the helicopter, and walked over to the jeep carrying a brown envelope. Saluting is not done in combat zones. It identifies the ranking person to anyone observing the scene, including a sniper. He offered his hand, and we introduced ourselves.

He spoke with an accent that 33 Tango thought was Greek. His

Figure 20.1   A Huey.

Figure 20.2   A Loach.

Figure 20.3. A Cobra.

fatigues had a camouflage pattern that I had never seen before, and the patches sewn on the shoulder and front pockets were unfamiliar to me. There was a patch where the name tag is usually sewn; the letters appeared to be Greek.

The conversation was one sided. He handed us the envelope and began to speak. He explained that the envelope contained maps, photographs, and a list of radio frequencies and call signs. There was a list of equipment we needed to carry and a set of instructions for tomorrow. We were to be at the helipad inside our compound at first light to be picked up by the Huey. We should be back by dark. We were to familiarize ourselves with the map and photos, memorize the frequencies, call signs, and instructions and pack the equipment on the list. And we were to bring the envelope and contents with us.

He went on to tell us all of the information was classified to be shared with no one on our team or at Province; the information was strictly need to know. He told us that there was a card with a radio frequency and call sign in the envelope; if anyone insisted on knowing what we were doing, have them make that contact. Then he asked us if we had any questions, which we did not. We just stood there in a bit of shock and wonder. Even for 33 Tango, with almost twenty years of service and on his third combat tour, this was something new.

Eyeball 5 went back to the Huey, and the four helicopters spun up and took off. 33 Tango and I drove back to the camp. Our team house had a small briefing room near the radio watch position that was off limits to our interpreters and most of the other Vietnamese in the camp. We decided to use that room for privacy. We entered it, closed the door, and opened the envelope to see exactly what the two of us had just "volunteered" for.

There were two copies of a topographic map that were somewhat different from the ones we used working out of Dong Xoai. Topographic features and vegetation covering colors were there along with the typical military grid system but there were no names on the map and the numbering on the grid system was *different*. There was a step-by-step list of what we were to do and a detailed list of equipment we were to carry. There was a list of several radio call signs and frequencies including the call signs we would use. Tomorrow we would not be 33 Tango and 33 Quebec.

We studied the map and compared it to the aerial photos that were included. We looked at the equipment list and talked about how to divide it into two sets. Weight was not the only or major concern. We had to make sure that items that worked in concert with each other were packed together. On "normal" operations we knew what each other carried and where it was in the other person's pack. This would be no different.

When we opened the door to leave the briefing room, the Major was waiting and asked what was going on. I replied that we had been op-conned (short for <u>op</u>erational <u>con</u>trol meaning that we were temporarily under someone else's command) and that the details were classified. He was less than pleased and pushed back asking us again what we were doing. Getting a nod from 33 Tango, I showed the Major the card from the envelope with the call sign and radio frequency and said, "We cannot talk about this. You can make this call for more information." The Major was not happy.

We gathered the required gear, separated it, and packed our rucksacks trying to remember where everything was. I was going to carry the radio and its accessories. Once things were settled, we tried to relax for the rest of the afternoon and had dinner with the team.

The next morning, we got up before everyone else. We reviewed the instructions and the maps while we ate breakfast. We checked our gear and weapons, and walked the short distance to the helipad. At first light the radio came to life, and we fired a star cluster to help the pilots find the helipad in the dim light. As the ship came into sight, we threw a smoke grenade so the pilot could check the wind direction. When the chopper touched down, we moved to the ship and climbed on board. Eyeball 5 was in the command seat with his helmet on. The chopper increased power and we lifted off.

As promised, we were back before dark. When the Huey sat down on the helipad, we jumped off and headed back to the team house. As we walked through the door before we could take our packs off, Radio Watch said that the Colonel (the PSA) wants to talk to us as soon as we returned. He wanted to "meet us green". This meant that he wanted us to use the radio scrambler so he could talk openly and freely.

33 Tango agreed to meet me at the radio in ten minutes and we took our gear to our respective rooms in the team house. We met in the bunker at the radio, and I called in to Song Be. I was told to "wait one," the usual reply when the person you were asking for was not present. The PSA came on and said to meet him green which we did. He immediately asked for a report on the operation. We replied that it was classified on a need-to-know basis, and we were not to discuss any aspects of the day. He, like the Major, insisted on knowing what we did, so we gave him the radio frequency and call sign provided by Eyeball 5 and instructed him to call that contact for information. He ordered us to give him the details of the mission; we politely refused referring him a second time to the call sign and frequency Eyeball 5 had provided. You do not make a Colonel very happy when you refuse a direct order. The

sign-off was not very pleasant; in fact, it was extremely unpleasant. We shut the green machine off and reset the radio to it normal state. We figured we would hear more about this tomorrow from the PSA and or the Major. Such is life in the army.

Tomorrow arrived on time, and the day proceeded normally. No one made any reference to the mission, but I am sure that my name ended up on a private list that the Colonel maintained for special missions. Put in polite terms, this list could be thought of as his "fecal roster."

Story 21 - Two Stories from Another MAT

My father retired as a Master Sergeant from the Air Force with 20 years of service. During WW2 he was an aircraft mechanic before being promoted to crew chief for a B-17. Being a crew chief meant it was, "His airplane." The flight crew checked it out like a library book for each bombing mission, and hopefully, they checked it back in flyable condition.

When he made crew chief, he named "his" plane after the woman who would become my mother, "Emma."

Figure 21.1 The WW2 B17 Bomber my father named after the woman who would become my mother.

My father died in 1981 and my mother in 1994. While we were sorting through things in her house, Linda (my wife) and I came across the picture in Figure 21.1 and a letter sent to my father by the wife of the pilot who was flying the "Emma" thanking him and his crew for keeping the "Emma" in good condition and safe to fly.

I was able to track down "Emma" through the 8th Air Force Museum records and learned that the plane survived WW2, was flown back to the states, and sold for scrap.

On the envelope with the letter from the pilot's wife was a return address. I did a Google search for this person and found nothing. I did "visit" the address using Google Earth, and the house from 1944 is still there. I sent scans of the letter to Todd DePastino who is a professor, historian, and founder of the Veterans Breakfast Club here in Western Pennsylvania, figuring he would be interested in the letter. Using much better search software than I have, Todd found information about the pilot who remained in the Air Force as a career pilot along with the names, addresses, and phone numbers of his two sons.

So, I called one of the sons, George. When he answered the phone, I introduced myself and asked, "Did your father fly B-17s in World War 2?" He replied, somewhat hesitantly, "Yes…" To which I said, "My father was the crew chief on the plane your father flew, the 'Emma,' and I have a letter your mother wrote to my father during the war. Would you like to have it?" This led to a long conversation, during which I learned that he was on a MAT team the same time I was at Dong Xoai.

American MAT team members shared common experiences under vastly different conditions in different locations. Dong Xoai physically was a good place to be stationed. There was only one village in my District and all the hamlets were around the village so even though we were "mobile," we never had to move. The Green Berets equipped the camp in ways that were incredible when compared to other MAT team locations.

George was on MAT 43 located in IV Corps — at Duc My in the Delta about 140 miles south-southwest of Dong Xoai. His team was located in places that had nothing resembling the amenities that we had in Dong Xoai, and his team had to move from village to village. Here are two stories from his tour. The first story is about an experience we both shared, but he tells his version so much better than I do.

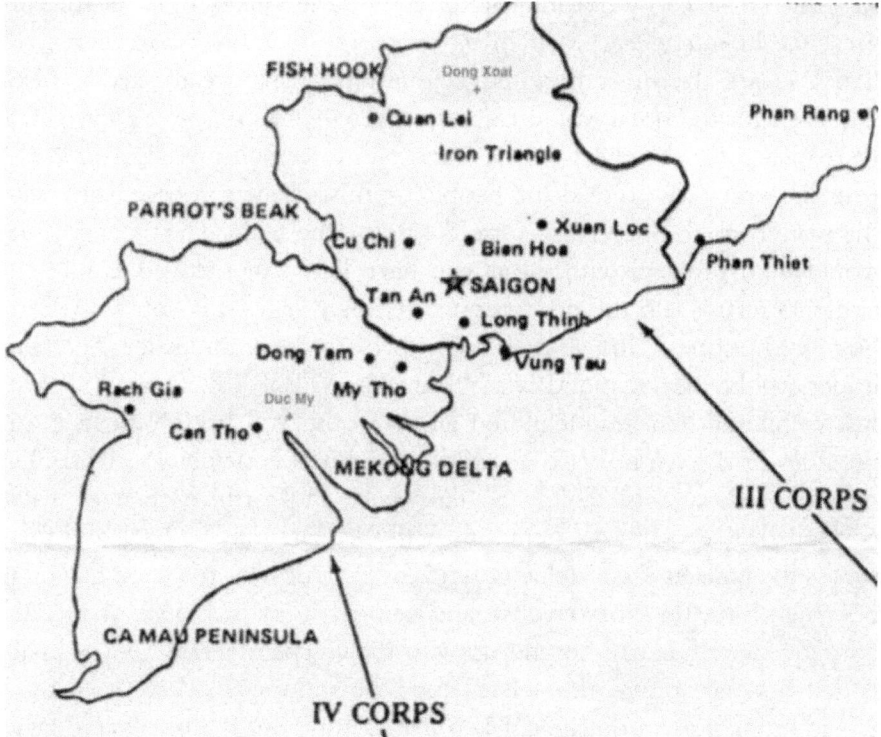

Figure 21.2   Map showing Dong Xoai and Duc My.

The Feast

Told by George Milman - MAT 43

The villages that I served in were always populated by ethnic Vietnamese peoples, and they still had their own flavor of welcome routine. With us it was in an invitation to have dinner at the Village Chief's residence, where he treated us to a meal of chicken, rice, and vegetables. As the meal progressed and the chicken was consumed, the only thing left were the chicken feet. The Village Chief would push the plate with the feet across the table to the team leader accompanied by a speech (translated by our interpreter as), "We are all so grateful for your presence in our village to help us overcome the threat to our way of life. You are the most honored at our table." The team leader, being familiar with the ritual would respond through the interpreter with, "It is you, Village Chief, who is to be honored more than myself, as you risk your life every day to lead the people of this village to peace," and slide the plate back to the Village Chief's side of the table. The Village Chief would then respond with, "But you have left your beloved family and come so far to help the poor people of this village. It is you who are to be more honored," and slide the plate back to the team leader. The team leader would then respond with "But you, Village Chief, have 3 wives, many children and grandchildren all of whom you bravely protect and provide for. I have no wife or children and it is certainly you who must be honored at this table" ... This back-and-forth exchange would continue for several more iterations with the plate moving back and forth across the table at each exchange, and the American at the table having to become more and more creative and verbose in his response or face the consequence of having to end up with the chicken feet. Whoever finally ended up accepting the plate and the honor that went with it would crunch down on the chicken feet spitting out the bones and claws over his shoulder for the ever-present family dog to scarf up.

This is 33 Quebec — In my story, we end up being the most honored... This ritual could also involve the head of the fish that was served as the main course. George's second story is an example of the close, personal experiences many MAT team members had with some of the Vietnamese people with whom they lived and worked.

The Watch

Told by George Milman - MAT 43

When I first arrived at my Mobile Advisory Team 43 (MAT) outpost in the village of Duc My, located on the banks of the Mekong River in Cang Long Province in IV Corps, South Vietnam, the adjustment to the pace of village life was a challenge. I had come directly from an in-country assignment with a towed-by-truck split (3 guns only instead of the usual 5) 155 mm howitzer battery in the First Air Cavalry Division, deployed just north of Saigon in Vinh Bin Province. Arriving the previous year, I had gotten used to the constant 24/7 activity starting with firing in support of air mobile infantry insertions in the morning, on to contact missions in the late morning and afternoon, then at night with firing-in defensive targets for platoons spending the night outside camp, and finally H&I (harassment and interdiction) fires all night long.

Of necessity, in the village, we had to adapt ourselves to activities around village life, which started at dawn with most of the village making their way out to the rice paddies and ended when darkness fell. The exception to all this activity occurred during the middle of the day starting about 1130 with lunch followed by a 2-3 hour rest period during the heat of the day. Old hands on the team quickly adjusted and took advantage of the mid-day respite to write letters, weekly reports or just nap. I had a hard time with this mid-day break. Activity in the village literally shut down... the village administrative offices closed their doors, and desks were converted to napping platforms; farmers came out of the fields to relax at home... foot traffic on the single dirt track through the village was quiet.

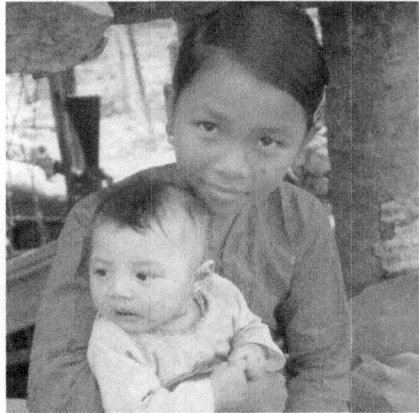

Figure 21.3   Loi and her brother.

The only ones out and about were the village children under the age of 10. They became my captive audience. They tried to teach me Vietnamese words with me reciprocating in English. One little 8-year-old girl named "Loi" was always the first to seek me out after lunch with the ulterior motive of trying to trade me out of my watch. For the time (early 70s), it was indeed a rather unique analog watch in that it had a chiming alarm that fascinated Loi. I had to demonstrate it for her each time we met. Several times each week she would show up with some purloined trade items, which she would offer to exchange for that watch. The most unique offer was a gunny sack of 8-10 spent smoke grenades which she was convinced would close the deal …but each time I turned her down.

It was well after the rice harvest time, and the rice paddies were hard, gray, cracked fallow ground waiting for the next cycle of the monsoon rain to bring them back to life. Our "base camp" was a small rectangular grouping of mud walled tin roofed huts along the dirt track, which separated the village and the river from the rice fields. One of the

Figure 21.4   The "Kite Gang."

boys in the group brought a homemade kite to me and explained through hand gestures that he could not get it to fly. The kite was skillfully made from thinly split pieces of bamboo for the frame and covered with a colorful pasted together patchwork of paper. The kite had been properly bowed with twine but lacked a tail for stability in the wind. Using another piece of twine, we fashioned a functional tail, and we set out for the rice paddies, as a group, to give the kite a try. The day was hot and humid with only a light wind. After several unsuccessful runs, the boy was still unable to get the kite to fly, and he handed the string to me suggesting through gestures that I give it a try.

Taking the string in hand, I started off across the rice paddy towards the distant tree line. My attention was focused over my shoulder on the reluctant kite and the gaggle of kids running with me shouting encouragement. The kite indeed started to fly, but I noticed that most of the kids, with the exception of Loi had stopped running with me. Loi continued to shout as I continued to run. The further I ran and the higher the kite got, the louder her cries became. She alone was running beside me and frantically pointing ahead of me, which I took to mean "keep running". The next thing I knew Loi threw herself in front of me, tripped me, and we both landed in a heap on the hard, gray ground of the rice paddy. I was pissed. She was hysterically crying with tears streaked down her dusty face. I was all ready to give her a good smack when I looked in the direction of her frantic pointing. There, not three steps in direct line of where I had been running was a live grenade trap stretched across the top of one of the paddy dikes. Had she waited just one more step to trip me, I would have fallen into the trap and we would have both been history. It took me a few minutes to center myself and flush away the "what-ifs" that had hold of me. When I came back to myself, I did my best to both thank and comfort her but without the words to adequately do so. So, I just took off the watch and put it on her wrist. I picked us both up and headed back toward our compound. I have no idea whatever happened to the kite.

The team finished our training duties in Duc My in another 3 months and departed for yet another village (that I do not remember the name of) to start all over again. I did not see Loi again. I often wonder where she is today and how she is getting along and if she remembers flying the kite. I remember her.

Story 22 - Who Lives?

There were only five Americans in camp. Those out of camp included the Major and the MAT Team Captain. Other than that, it started out to be an uneventful day in Dong Xoai but that began to change soon after breakfast.

The First Event: a call from Province saying that a Lieutenant Colonel from the Inspector General's (IG) office at III Corps in Ben Hoa was due by helicopter in the afternoon. What he wanted to inspect was unknown; we would find out when he landed. IG inspections were something to be dreaded.

The Second Event: we learned that a Vietnamese VIP was coming to Dong Xoai for a local governmental affair and he was traveling north from Ben Hoa by road. That meant that the Regional Force (RF) companies had to clear the road south from Dong Xoai to the province border. Clearing the road meant checking it for mines, booby traps, and ambushes and standing guard along the road so that the Viet Cong could not set up something after the road was cleared. The RF had a procedure to do this in an efficient and tactically sound manner. Soldiers with a lead vehicle check for mines, booby traps, and ambushes. Following the lead vehicle is a truck carrying more troops. At intervals, the truck stops and lets two troops off to stand guard over the segment of road that was just cleared. Ideally, they would be able to see the previous set of guards that had dismounted before them. When the last two troops on the truck dismount, the truck turns around and returns to Dong Xoai to pick up another load of soldiers. It retraces its route over the cleared road passing the previously deployed soldiers guarding the road to the position where it turned around. This continues until the Province border is reached. Ideally when the road is open, every pair of soldiers should be able to see the adjacent two pairs of soldiers.

Somehow, someway, either the lead vehicle missed a command detonated mine, or there was a gap between two pairs of soldiers that allowed the Viet Cong to set a mine up along the side of the road and camouflage it without being detected. When a truck carrying another full load of soldiers was making its return trip, the Viet Cong set off the mine as the truck passed blowing the rear axles off the truck and flipping the truck on its side. The mine was huge and gravel was packed in the explosives. Some troops were killed by the initial blast. Many others suffered bad head and upper body wounds.

Figure 22.1   The destroyed truck.

The Third Event: The call came in on the land line; RF headquarters notified us about the ambush and requested our aid. Our medic whom we called Bac Si (Vietnamese for doctor) found YB, me and our interpreter and briefed us. The four of us went to the medical bunker and loaded two litters with first aid supplies and plasma. The bunker was

built for the Green Berets and well stocked for use by their medics. YB
and I put a portable field radio on our litter. Then we placed a second
litter upside down on top of the first litter to hold the supplies in place
and, following Bac Si and the interpreter, moved to the RF aid station
near the helipad.

Figure 22.2   The Aid Station and the Helipad at Dong Xoai.

While we were doing this, the Intelligence Captain was radioing
Province requesting a Medivac helicopter. Province contacted nearby
American units, but no Medivacs were available, so Province dispatched
the work helicopter to help us in any way it could. The work chopper was
a Huey helicopter, the workhorse for the war. Medivac helicopters were
also Hueys equipped with a vertical sling system for stacking litters of
wounded above each other so more wounded could be carried and

treated by an on-board medic. In place of the sling system, the work chopper had an aluminum tube/nylon bench, but it was all we had to fly the wounded to the Vietnamese hospital at Song Be. These soldiers' wounds would probably exceed the level of care the hospital could provide, but we had to try.

Bac Si disappeared inside the aid station and several RF medics came out and carried the litters with the medical supplies into the station. Soon after, a truck that had been sent to bring in the wounded pulled up to the aid station. Working with the RF medics, YB and I helped unload the wounded. There were too many to take into the aid station, so we laid some of them on the litters that the RF medics had placed outside on the ground. When we ran out of litters, we laid them on the ground. By this time the families were beginning to arrive to see if their son or husband was among the wounded, and if so, how bad they were.

While Bac Si, our interpreter, and the RF senior medic moved among the wounded on the ground triaging them to determine which ones should be treated first and which ones would wait, other medics worked feverishly applying tourniquets, bandaging wounds and starting plasma IVs. YB and I helped where we could. Soldiers that had died were moved off their litters, placed on the ground, and covered with ponchos or whatever was available. Soldiers who were triaged to be mortally wounded were taken off of their litters, placed on the ground and marked somewhere on their forehead, chest or on a bandage with an X written in blood.

Bac Si took YB and me aside and said, "You two will have to organize the order in which the wounded would be loaded on the chopper because we have work to do here trying to stabilize them and keep them alive. Don't load anyone marked with an X, if others are still waiting. And don't transport any dead!" Things were moving fast and far beyond my first aid training.

The work helicopter radioed saying it was inbound. We threw a smoke grenade when we saw the ship. I directed its landing not on the usual circular pad but much closer to the aid station. We had talked on the radio with the pilot, so the crew knew what was expected. The moment the chopper landed, YB and I ran up to the ship and helped the crew detach and remove the bench, which we carried off to the side of the helipad out of the way.

YB and I ran back to the aid station to choose which two of the wounded to put on the helicopter. As we were doing this, wives and mothers were pleading with us to take their loved ones first. Difficult does not begin to describe the situation. Working with two RF medics, YB and I each picked up a litter that had a soldier with a plasma IV and carried them to the chopper. One door gunner took the plasma bags and looked for a place to hang them. The other helped us load them in. There was no sling system to stack them so we had to lay these first two on the floor.

When we returned to the aid station, Captain Ky, the RF company commander had arrived with several RF soldiers who were preventing the relatives from carrying their sons and husbands to the helicopter. Controlled chaos is probably the best description for the scene. YB and I chose two more litters and repeated the process. This time we had to lay these litters partially on top of the first two that we put on the floor trying not to put the full weight of this soldier on the first one. With that done, we stood back and signaled the pilot to take off. Turning away from the helicopter's rotor wash as it lifted off, I noticed that my hands felt sticky. Looking at them, they were red; covered with blood.

As we returned to the aid station, the Intelligence Team Captain was calling us on the radio. He said that the IG Lieutenant Colonel's helicopter was inbound; that we needed to contact the ship, and he gave us the helicopter's call sign. I called the pilot, explained what we needed, and he agreed. Apparently, the IG Lt. Col. was not wearing a flight helmet, so he was unaware of what was transpiring at Dong Xoai.

We threw another smoke grenade as the chopper came into view and I directed the pilot to land close to the aid station. When the IG Lt. Col.'s helicopter touched down, he stepped off, probably expecting to be met in a manner appropriate for his position and the gravity of his visit, only to see YB and me dart past him without even a nod. He turned back towards the helicopter to see us yank the bench out of the helicopter. YB and I ran past him again back to the aid station, and trying to ignore the pleas of relatives, chose two litters. With the RF medics we carried them to the helicopter. These two door gunners were not as helpful as the work chopper's gunners — they just sat in their nooks where their guns were mounted and watched. YB and his medic got there first and set one end of the litter down on the floor and slid it into the cabin. When my medic and I got there, we did the same.

Back to the aid station for two more litters. Ignore — or try to — the pleas of mothers and wives. Out to the chopper. One at a time YB and I had to climb up into the cabin and back through carrying our end of the litter so we could put it down, being careful of the soldier on the floor.

As I jumped down from the cabin, I signaled to the pilot to take off, and the bird lifted, turned, and headed north to Song Be.

Still ignoring the IG Lt. Col., we went back to the aid station to decide which four would go in the next trip. While we waited for what seems like an hour, we helped Bac Si and the medics where we could. In reality the wait was only a few minutes.

The radio came to life with a call from the work ship pilot. He was inbound. YB and I chose four more litters and with our RF medics, repeated the process.

At some point during all of this the IG Lt. Col. disappeared.

The IG Lt. Col.'s helicopter called to say they were inbound. It landed, and once again, the door gunners continued to act as observers. YB, I, and our two RF medics had two litters waiting. When the ship settled on the helipad, I moved out first and slid my end of the litter into the cabin. YB did the same. We returned to the aid station to get two more wounded. Back at the helicopter, I climbed up into the helicopter with my end of the litter trying not to walk on the soldiers lying on the cabin floor. I slipped on the slick layer of blood that covered part of the cabin floor and almost dropped my end of the litter on the solder laying on the floor.

As the pilot lifted off, we went back to the aid station, where Bac Si was waiting to tell us that we were done. The remaining wounded were being transported to Song Be by ambulance or had died.

YB and I walked back to the edge of the helipad to wait for the helicopters to return. This was our first down time since it began. Both of us were soaking wet with sweat and mentally more than a bit "fried."

Choosing who was put on the helicopter amid the begging of the family members had been difficult. The effects of everything we experienced were beginning to surface. As we stood there silently, our two house maids walked up. Each was carrying two buckets of hot water and a cold can of soda. The Intelligence Team Captain told our cook to heat some water when all of this started. The cold cans of soda were our cook's idea.

When the work chopper landed, each maid took one of their buckets out to the chopper and poured the water onto the cabin to flush out the blood. The water ran red as it drained from the floor. YB and I carried the bench to the chopper and helped the door gunners reattached it. I signaled the pilot to take off and he did. Back at the aid station, YB called him on the radio and thanked him and the crew for their help.

A short time later we received a call from the IG Lt. Col.'s helicopter pilot saying he was on the way in. YB answered that there was no more wounded. When he landed, the maids repeated the flushing of the blood, and we sat the bench in the cabin not bothering to help re-attach it; the door gunners/observers could do that. We went back to the aid station and YB called the pilot and thanked him. We left it to him to thank the crew.

As Bac Si, our interpreter, YB and I walked back to the team house, the IG Lt. Col. passed us heading back to his helicopter. Not smiling, he said something that neither Bac Si, YB or I could make out — it was probably not a compliment. I am not sure what the other three did but I took a long cold shower. We had sent sixteen soldiers to Dong Xoai and I wondered how any would survive. I never did find out.

Three things remain with me about that day. One is the pleas of wives and mothers to choose their loved one as the next one to be put on the helicopter. Another is the picture of the red mixture of blood and water draining out of the cabins when the maids poured their buckets of hot water on the floors of the helicopters. The third is that blood can be both sticky and slick; it was sticky on my hands and the handles of the litters, while it made the cabin floor of the helicopters slick.

Story 23 - Donut Dollies

One morning Radio Watch received a call from a helicopter. The pilot said his chopper was inbound to our location and asked for smoke, so he could judge wind direction and speed for landing. Radio Watch checked the SOI (Signals Operating Instructions) for the radio call sign used by the pilot and could not find it. 33 Tango who was standing nearby looked at me as if to ask if this was going to be another "Eyeball 5" visit?

Worriedly, he and I accompanied Radio Watch out to the helipad. After a few minutes we heard the ship approaching — just one; no gunships or observation chopper this time — just a Huey. When it started to circle the camp, Radio Watch pulled the pin on the smoke grenade and tossed it to the side of the asphalt that was the landing pad. The pilot maneuvered the helicopter towards the pad, flared his descent and settled gently on the white "H" painted on the pad.

Not sure what to expect, we stood our ground as the rotor blades gradually stopped spinning. A jungle fatigue clad figure climbed down out of the cabin. Even from our distance we could see that his fatigues were almost their original green color, neat, pressed and possibly starched. He was not a "bush" soldier. As he turned to help another person to climb out — then a second person, someone muttered, "What the #$%?" These two people were not wearing green jungle fatigues; they wore light blue — dresses — and had blond hair? They were round eyes![31] — Donut Dollies! — And they had just landed at our camp! What was going on?

During World War 2, a group of very brave and adventurous women volunteered to work in the European Theater of Operations in positions

---

[31] G I slang for American women.

that came to be known as Donut Dollies. Working in teams of two, they were assigned to a mobile kitchen. Their job was to wake up in the middle of the night, go to the kitchen and make hundreds of donuts and gallons of coffee. Then they would drive to someplace in the rear area just behind the front lines and serve coffee, donuts, and conversations to the GIs who were resting before moving back up to the front and the fighting. This served as a major morale booster for the war weary troops. The Dollies served again in Korea, and over 600 of them found their way to Vietnam during the war. Since there were no frontlines in Vietnam, instead of driving mobile kitchens, they traveled by helicopter. This meant that there were no donuts — just the Dollies.

Dong Xoai was at an important intersection of roads running north from Ben Hoa to the Cambodian border and east From Tay Ninh. The village had five hamlets and a former Special Forces Camp that was now the home of the District Advisory Team of four men and MAT 111 composed of five men. Because of its location, Dong Xoai was militarily significant but, unfortunately, it would never rate a visit by the Donut Dollies. With only nine Americans based there of which two or three were usually not in camp, there were not enough soldiers to warrant a visit. There were larger concentrations of troops in other locations better served by the too few dollies.

But there they were; walking towards us. The jungle fatigue clad figure, a Lieutenant who was not wearing Infantry insignia on his collar put out his hand to shake ours. We really did not see him; we were transfixed by the two women walking next to him. They looked at us and one said, "Hello, I hope we are not interrupting anything." The sound of an American woman's voice… I'm not sure what the reply was or if it was even coherent. We shook hands all around and the Lieutenant, their escort[32], explained that the three of them were heading to a fire base to visit the soldiers when the helicopter developed some sort of mechanical problem. The pilot decided to land at the nearest camp (ours) and leave the three of them while they returned to base to either have the problem fixed or get another helicopter. If the ship did go down on the way back

---

[32] His was a tough assignment but someone had to do it…

to base, the crew did not want to endanger the passengers. 33 Tango walked over to the chopper and asked if they needed to use our latrine or wanted a cup of coffee but they declined. As we turned to walk back to our team house, the blades spun up and the helicopter lifted off heading to the South.

We talked as we walked back to the team house. After giving them a brief tour, we sat at the table in the dining area and talked some more — to be totally honest I do not remember what we talked about. I just remember listening to their voices. Their speech did not have the sing-song tonal accents of the Vietnamese language. It was so different, so

Figure 23.1   The Donut Dollies who visited us.

pleasant — and so memorable. They stayed long enough to eat lunch with us — nothing special — just whatever our cook prepared.

Eventually, we received a call from their returning helicopter once again asking for smoke. We all walked as a group back to the landing pad and waited for the ship to land. We shook hands and watched them walk to the waiting chopper. They boarded and the pilot lifted off — and they were gone. I don't think anyone talked as we walked back to the team house.

The story continues forty-nine years later here in Pittsburgh, Pennsylvania. The H. J. Heinz History Center put together a Vietnam War Retrospective complete with about 90% of a Huey among the displays. The American Red Cross Overseas Association (ARCOA) — the Donut Dollies – was having its annual meeting in Pittsburgh during the Retrospective. The Veterans Breakfast Club arranged for the Dollies to meet at the Heinz Center and talk to the public about their experiences in Vietnam.

I sent the two pictures in Figure 23.1 to the President of their association and asked her if she could find out who the two women were and if they would be attending the meeting. I attended the session at the Heinz Center, where she showed the two pictures and asked if they were in the audience or if anyone knew who they were. One Dolly thought she knew who one of the women was. They asked me why I wanted to contact them and I replied that, "I just wanted to thank them for their visit and for turning just another day in Vietnam into something to remember." Unfortunately, the possible lead to the one Dolly did not pan out, and I have never learned their names. And I will never get to thank them.

Story 24 - No Light at the End of the Tunnel

I must not have been sleeping well because I think I heard the whisper clearly, "L T." It was our Team Medic outside my door. Groggily, I replied, "What do you need, Bac Si?" (Vietnamese for doctor) He said that we were needed at the Regional Force (RF) aid station just outside of our perimeter gate. I rolled out of my bunk and opened the door to the hallway where Bac Si was waking our interpreter. As we crossed to the other team house where the medical bunker was, he explained that one of the RF soldiers had overdosed. He needed my help carrying medical supplies to the aid station.

Our medical bunker was built for Green Beret medics who had extensive training beyond that of regular Army medics. The medical bunker was stocked with plasma IVs, instruments for surgery on wounded soldiers and other supplies for treating various tropical illness. Bac Si gathered up the items he thought would be useful, put them in two bags, and handed one to me. We left the bunker, exited the team house where our interpreter was waiting, and quickly walked to the RF aid station.

Captain Ky, the RF company commander was standing in the doorway when we arrived. Inside the aid station, lit by several kerosene lanterns, the RF medics were working on the unconscious soldier. I asked Bac Si if I should go start the generator and supply electricity to the building. He replied, "No, the lanterns were sufficient." Besides the aid station had no electrical equipment.

I stepped inside the aid station to get a better look at the soldier — I knew him. Bac Si knew this, and it was why he woke me. The soldier was a young platoon leader in the company; the reason for Captain Ky's presence. He was a bright, talented, smart young man who wanted to go to school and become a teacher, but that was not possible in this war. He joined the RF company, qualified for officer training and returned as an aspirant — sort of a third Lieutenant. He earned the respect of Captain Ky and was promoted to Lieutenant. He was a good officer, well-liked by the men he led. Somehow, I had gotten to know him. We would meet every week or so after lunch and help each other with our language skills. I helped him with his pronunciation, and he helped me with mine. I could understand a decent bit of Vietnamese if it were spoken slowly. My problem was speaking. Vietnamese is a tonal language. Each word can be said with five different tonalities or inflections and have five different meanings. For example, the two words "bon" and "toi" spoken with one set of inflections mean, "I'm a friend." Change the inflections and the words mean, "Shoot me."

Seeing him lying there, I realized that his attitude and outlook had been slowly changing. Recently he had begun to ask me if I thought the war would ever end. My language skills were not strong enough to clearly explain my thoughts. I encouraged him to keep doing the good job he was doing for his men; that it would help keep them alive.

Bac Si walked over and explained that the young Lieutenant, whose name is lost to me, had bought a bottle of whiskey and a jar of pills at the local chemist (pharmacy) and had himself a one-man party. There was nothing anyone could do. He was gone. We didn't have the medicine, equipment, or the knowledge to keep him alive.

The three of us walked silently back to the team house. Our interpreter returned to his room while Bac Si and I took the equipment and unused supplies back to the medical bunker. Dawn was just two hours away. Bac Si looked at me and said, "We need a drink." I am not much of a drinker. I saved my beer drinking in Vietnam for village social occasions, and I stayed away from the hard stuff, but right now his offer sounded reasonable. While most of the team liked their beer, Bac Si preferred whiskey, and he had a bottle in his room. We walked to his room, entered, and I sat in the chair. Bac Si poured two fingers of whiskey into two coffee mugs, handed one to me, and sat down on his bunk.

Looking down at the whiskey, I thought I could understand how the young Lieutenant, seeing that there was no light at the end of this tunnel of war, was able to extinguish his own and slip quietly into the darkness.

I drank the whiskey.

I cried.

I should have done more.

Story 25 - C B U

The things we remember most vividly may be the happenings in our lives that made us extremely angry and the things we did that were unspeakably stupid. The CBU story falls into both categories.

This operation was called by Province. The Province S-2 (Intelligence) wanted a specific area of Don Luan District checked out. That was it. Province did not say what we were looking for, just that we had to explore the area and report anything interesting that we found — a "walk in the woods" type of operation. The Province S-3 (Operations), working with the S-2 and his Vietnamese counterpart laid out the mission specifics. We would be transported by truck to a launch point. From there we would proceed west to a specific coordinate, turn south and move along a designated line of march back to the road. Total time: three days for this, "Walk in the woods," — we'll see... The dismount would be beyond radio and artillery range, but the southern march on day three should bring us back into range of both, depending on the terrain and the vegetation. Everything associated with this operation was based at Dong Xoai except planning and command.

Captain Ky aided by his executive officer (XO — second in command) finished supervising the loading of about twenty Regional Force (RF) soldiers into two trucks and climbed into the lead jeep. Unlike some commanders he drove and I sat next to him. His radio operator (RTO) and my interpreter were in the back seat. 33 Tango was riding with Captain Ky's XO and our RTO in the other jeep at the end of the four-vehicle convoy.

The dirt road was a major Vietnamese route running northeast from Dong Xoai but it was in bad shape; full of ruts and holes, and more importantly, uncleared, meaning that it had not been swept for mines and booby traps. Ambushes were always a possibility so Captain Ky led the convoy at a very fast speed — much faster than the road conditions dictated.

The dismount point was about 12 kilometers (about 7 miles) from the camp so the travel time was short. We dismounted, and as the four vehicles turned around for their return trip, we formed up and headed west into the jungle. The vegetation was too thick to put out flank security, so we moved as a single file column; two soldiers on point moving carefully looking for booby traps and ambushes. Following them were Captain KY, his RTO, me, my interpreter, and the rest of the RF soldiers. 33 Tango was at the rear of the column with our usual RF RTO and the company's XO. 33 Tango always moved at the rear with our RTO in case we triggered an ambush. Being at the rear, he would probably be outside the kill zone of the ambush with a working radio to call for help and to work with the XO to counter the ambush.

The movement west was slow due to the jungle growth but relatively uneventful. At one point on the first day's march, we were moving through what looked like an overgrown, unattended orchard when I noticed that the two soldiers on point stopped to climb trees. Captain Ky kept walking — he and I were now the point element of the column. Using the best of my limited Vietnamese speaking ability, I asked, "Tai sao chung ta di bo diem?" — "Why are we walking point?". He stopped, chuckled, and with a wry smile pointed upward at the trees overhead. They were bearing something that looked like a citrus fruit. "Qua co VC khong" — "Fruit here, no VC". I looked back to see a few other troops climbing up the trees, picking the fruit and dropping them down. I learned two things: one— a way to know if Viet Cong were in the area and two — what we were having for dinner.

The rest of the day was uneventful. We followed Captain Ky's usual pattern of eating in late afternoon, arriving at a night defensive position (NDP) at just before dark and alternating two-hour radio watches with 33 Tango through the night.

The next morning, we ate, packed up and continued to move to the west. We were to continue moving west for one more day before turning south to continue to explore the area Province wanted checked. Barring incident we should intersect the road late afternoon of day three. Day two went the same as day one but without any citrus fruit. We were still out of radio range. We could hear Dong Xoai but our transmissions went unanswered. We should move within range tomorrow morning.

The morning of the third day, we turned south and began our march along the line Province wanted us to take — essentially a moderately wide valley with slightly less dense low vegetation but much more overhead growth from small trees. We had been moving about thirty minutes when the point element stopped and signaled for Captain Ky to come forward. Very quietly he moved up followed closely by me and my interpreter. The two soldiers were kneeling down looking at a gray metal sphere about the size of a tennis ball. Nearby was another strange looking device that looked like it had wings.

I did not even think about using my limited Vietnamese language skills. I told my interpreter to tell Captain Ky to pull everyone back. He did and we followed. I had been briefed on this object at Ft. Bragg's Center for Special Warfare. The door to the briefing auditorium had been labeled, "SECRET BRIEFING IN PROGRESS" and there were armed guards at the doors to the auditorium. The information provided by the officer during the briefing was cursory, but the field experience that afternoon conducted by a Green Beret NCO was eye opening. He went into great detail on how these gray metal spheres about the size of a tennis ball worked and disassembled one as part of his demonstration before having another one detonated at a safe distance. He closed by saying that, if at all possible, never operate in an area where these had been deployed. It was too risky.

He was talking about a relatively new type of secret[33] munitions called cluster munitions or cluster bombs. This was a CBU - a Cluster Bomb Unit or a bomblet. When dropped by aircraft, the cluster munition housing opens at a predetermined altitude and spreads upwards of 200 CBUs over a wide area. The 155 mm Howitzer fires a similar device that could deploy 40 CBUs. The winged unit aids the dispersal and orients the explosive sphere during the fall, so it explodes on contact with the ground. These are essentially air-dropped grenades but with no delay

---

[33] Why it was a secret is not clear. Once it is used against an enemy, they know about it, so it is no longer a secret.

before exploding. There are problems with this ordinance. Not all of them explode on contact. They can go off when disturbed by someone on the ground. A second problem in a jungle is that some of them can hang up in the vegetation and fall to the ground when a passing solder jostles the tree or vine holding the CBU.

I was not aware of the use of cluster munitions in any area in this district or, for that fact, in the province. This finding of the CBU by the point element was extremely fortunate and very troubling. I moved back to the sphere and took a very close look. It appeared that the fusing device had been triggered but failed to work. My thinking was that this one was never going to explode.

33 Tango, our RTO, and the company XO had moved to the front of the column when it stopped, joining Captain Ky and our interpreter. I returned and explained to the Captain and the XO through the interpreter what the CBU was and asked him to have his troops look carefully where they were without moving very much to see if they could find any other CBUs and to not touch them. Another one was reported near the front of the column.

I asked Captain KY if I could call Dong Xoai and have them contact Province with a request to alter our line of march because of the CBUs. He readily agreed. While I was doing this, 33 Tango had removed his pack, pulled out the collapsible ten-foot-long radio antenna and mounted it on our field radio. Captain KY passed the word down the column for everyone to freeze in position. I thought we might be close enough to contact Dong Xoai with this long antenna, and we were just barely able to make contact. Radio Watch reported that our signal was weak but understandable. I asked Radio Watch to relay my request to alter our line of march to Province. The reply was, "Wait one, out". So, we waited.

Radio Watch called back in a few minutes with a simple reply, "Negative on your request." I replied telling Radio Watch to write down my exact words and relay them to Province, "Encountered cluster munitions. Unexploded Charlie Bravo Uniforms[34] encountered on ground. Cannot move forward. Must reroute." Radio Watch replied, "Roger, Wilco" meaning, "I understand and I will comply."

We waited longer this time. When Radio Watch did call, his message, also written word for word was, "Specified ordnance never used this Alpha Oscar (AO - Area of Operation). Advise counterpart to proceed on original line of march."

While 33 Tango had been mounting the long antenna on our radio, Captain KY was switching his radio over to the MAT frequency so he could listen in. At this distance he could receive communications from Dong Xoai but not successfully transmit with the short antenna that we used when we were moving. My interpreter joined him and translated the conversations so he knew what was being said.

He looked at me and said through the interpreter that he would not follow that advice. I replied through our interpreter, "Captain, my advice is to reverse course and move on a different line of march to the road." He smiled, nodded his head, and spoke to his XO telling him to return to the rear and move the column back to the overnight position. 33 Tango and our interpreter accompanied him, and I waited for our end of the column to begin to move.

I had just made two extremely serious errors; I had mentioned classified information in the open on the radio and I was disobeying a direct order. Thinking about this a for a minute, I returned to the CBU the point element had found and took a much closer look. From what the Special Forces (SF) Sergeant had shown us, this unit was never going to explode on its own. I was angry — VERY ANGRY at being told I did not know what I was talking about by someone who was sitting in an air-conditioned office at Song Be and at being given incorrect information that could kill someone — maybe me. I picked the sphere up, placed it in the winged delivery unit and put them in my pack hoping the SF Sergeant knew what he was talking about — which he did or I would not be writing this story.

---

[34] "Charlie Bravo Uniform": The Army's phonetic alphabet replacements for the letters, C B U.

We moved quickly as possible to the previous night's position. Captain Ky chose a new route, and we continued to move as fast as possible so we would get to the road for pickup and return to camp before dark. By noon both radios were close enough to Dong Xoai to make contact, so Captain Ky radioed new coordinates for our pickup and a new time. We ate a quick lunch and moved out. The trucks arrived a few minutes after we got to the road. The trip back to camp proved to be very uneventful. Tomorrow would prove to be anything but uneventful.

When 33 Tango and I walked into the team house, Radio Watch was waiting, "What on earth did you do, L T? Province wants you on the work chopper tomorrow. It is going to stop in the morning on its way up to Song Be just to pick you up. The Colonel (the Province Senior Advisor) wants you in his office as soon as you get there." The MAT Team Captain along with the Major were standing beside Radio Watch. After Radio Watch delivered the message, the Major told me to clean up and talk to them when I was done. After a quick shower I explained to the Captain and the Major what had happened leaving out the part about bringing the CBU back to camp. Carrying unexploded ordinance around is a court martial offense — that's three mistakes now.

The next morning, 33 Tango asked if he should go with me, and I said that would not be necessary, besides I had proof of what happened. He almost exploded when he learned that I had carried the CBU back with me. He reminded me of my promise to get him to his DEROS and in his mind that came very close to breaking the promise. With everyone out of the team house after breakfast, I took pictures of the unit while I was waiting for the chopper to call on its way in to Dong Xoai. Figure 25.1 is one of those pictures.

The chopper stopped to pick me up and there was a jeep waiting at the airstrip when we landed at Song Be. The Colonel's clerk was driving, "What did you do, L T?" My reply, "Why? What's going on?"

"The S-2 and S-3 are in the old man's office waiting for you. It looks like you stepped into some deep shit." The clerk was right on both counts; all three were there. This was going to be memorable; memorable in possibly a very bad way.

I knocked on the door frame and the Colonel barked, "Come in." I walked in, stood at attention in front of his desk, and said, "Sir, Lieutenant Roberts reporting as ordered, Sir" falling back to my OCS formality. I did not salute — that was not done in a combat zone. The S-2 and S-3 were sitting to one side.

"Lieutenant, you sent classified information over an open radio frequency, is that correct?"

"Sir, yes sir."

"Your counterpart did not follow the prescribed line of march for the operation and changed the pick-up point. Is that correct?"

"Sir, yes sir."

"Do you have any idea why he did not follow your advice?"

"Sir, he followed the advice I gave him."

Figure 25.1   The CBU delivery device and the explosive unit.

"Do you have anything else to say before being dismissed?"

"Sir, we were to gather intel on the operation and we encountered something none of us had ever seen in the district. Being told that cluster munitions were never deployed in the AO, and not knowing what we had encountered, I thought it would be best if I brought the item back so the S-2 could have it analyzed in case the VC are deploying something new and unknown to us." With that said, I pulled the delivery unit out of the bag I was carrying and placed it on the Colonel's desk. He sat up a bit straighter. I continued, "And there is this," placing the explosive sphere on the desk beside the delivery unit. Before he could speak, I said, "It's inert, sir. I removed the firing mechanism and the explosive charge last night at Dong Xoai. I was thoroughly briefed on this munition at Ft. Bragg, so I knew what I was doing." Staring down at the two devices on his desk, the Colonel said without looking at me, "That will be all Lieutenant."

I did an about face and marched out of his office, not looking over at the S-2 and S-3, though it was all I could do to keep facing forward.

I heard no more about this, there was no court martial, and I was still a First Lieutenant when I DEROSed.

I learned more about this from YB who was proofreading these stories as they were being written. We had a 155 MM Howitzer battery at Dong Xoai for several weeks, and YB remembers that they fired the cluster munitions into the area. YB was the Intelligence NCO at Dong Xoai. The intel work they were doing was secret and not shared directly with the MAT team. The 155 has a range of 15 KM, and we were 11 KM out, and the 105 Howitzer did not have a cluster munition.

There were a number of changes in Province staff during this time. The PSA was recently new and the S-2 and S-3 were relatively new. It is possible that the new S-2 and S-3 did not know the munitions were used but they should have. I would have liked to have been the "fly on the wall" in that office after I left.

Story 26 - Animal Life

In this story animal refers to any life form that is not a plant or fungus. The talking lizard (actually a gecko) has been discussed — enough said about that critter.

Animal life in and around Dong Xoai and Phuoc Long was typical of what you might expect in a jungle setting if you really knew what to expect in a jungle setting — in the middle of a war... First qualifier — refrigeration was not widely available in Dong Xoai because there was no electricity. We (the advisors) generated 10,000 watts of electricity for 18 hours each day. This was distributed to our two team houses, the District Chief's headquarters and offices, and the RF Command headquarters and offices. This meant that the market in the village was a "live market". The protein being sold there was either living or freshly killed.

Before the war there were elephants and tigers in the area. It was rumored that elephants were still being used by the Viet Cong in some areas to move heavy equipment. I had seen elephants up close in Africa, but I did not encounter tigers or elephants in the jungles of Vietnam. Before I arrived at Dong Xoai, there was an elephant as described below by the MAT Team Captain:

"There was an elephant killed by an air strike. Everyone in the hamlets went out and stripped the carcass but since they had no refrigeration, everyone cooked it in one or 2 days. The stench was horrendous! I remember standing on the bunker with one of the MAT NCOs and almost gagging from the smell."

The largest animals commonly found in our area were the water buffalo used by the farmers for various tasks. The rumors were that these beasts were docile around the Vietnamese but very dangerous for

Figure 26.1   Water buffalo.

Americans. I saw water buffalos pulling carts on the roads and plows in the water on the villagers' fields. I never came close to one for which I am thankful. The MAT team Captain describes one close encounter:

"I stumbled on a Montagnard wedding one night, having joined the District Chief on a Peoples Self Defense Force (PSDF) inspection in one of the hamlets. We heard eerie music so we investigated to see what was going on at 2300 hrs. What we ran into was a water buffalo staked out with all 4 legs spread apart and wide eyes. Sgt. Yung, our interpreter wasn't very good at translating Montagnard but between him and the District Chief we learned that there was a wedding going on, and the water buffalo was to be sacrificed to guarantee a great marriage. I ended up being invited into the hooch by the father of the bride, as my presence was a sign to him of good luck for the couple. There is a long story of drinking before we left the celebration, but that is for another time. (Refer back to Story #1.) We did not stick around for the sacrifice!"

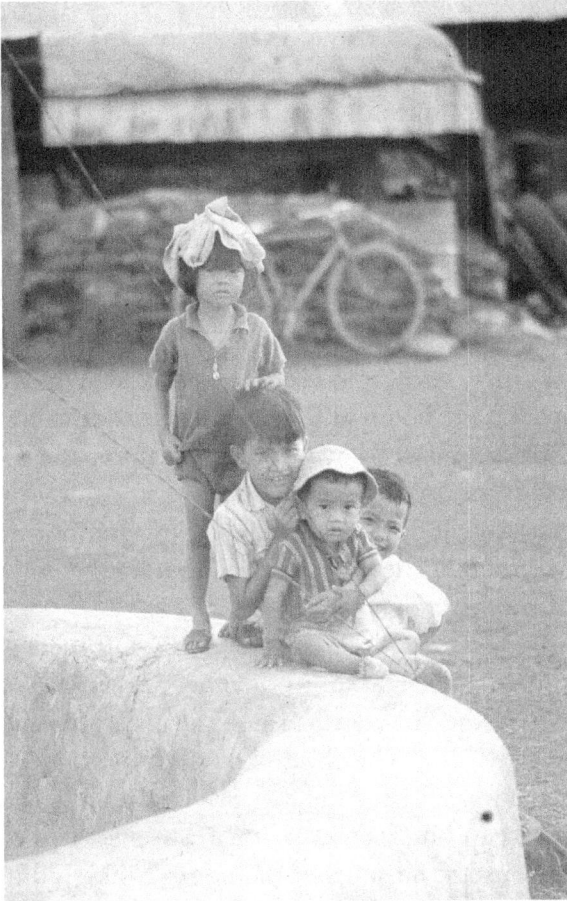

Figure 26.2   RF soldiers' children in the camp at Dong Xoai.

The children of the RF soldiers were a form of life that had a positive effect on the team members. It was always enjoyable to see them marching off to school in the morning. They seemed like they wanted to go to school, and their school house was probably the nicest building in the village. It was certainly the newest.

Everyone in the village shut down for about two hours each day after lunch to nap through the heat of the day. Many American soldiers referred to this time as, "Pot Time." The children returned home from school to eat; for the younger ones, school was over. The older children would return after pot time for several more hours of schooling. The younger children were the only Vietnamese you would see out and about during pot time. Three of them used to take the family hog out of the compound to a swampy area between the barbed wire and the road each day during pot time so the hog could do whatever a hog does in a swampy pool. These were young children. One child would lead the hog with a rope that was attached to the ring in the hog's nose. The other two each had switches that they would use to encourage the hog to move and keep it on the path. The hog was a willing participant in this noon time parade following the lead child with little resistance; the switches were rarely used. They seemed to be a happy foursome.

Coming back was a bit different. The hog came but not as willingly on its return trip, and the switches were needed to keep the hog moving. Still the four of them seemed to get along.

One day this parade was different — VERY DIFFERENT! First, it was happening in the morning; not pot time. Second, the hog was not cooperating. Two of the children had hold of the rope and were doing their best to drag the hog. The third child had the switch but was not using it. Instead, he was shoving the hog from the rear. They managed to move the hog along but it was a total struggle. All of this was accompanied by constant noise from the hog — loud, pitiful grunts and other sounds. It was a very different parade.

As we were watching this, our cook, having heard the noise, joined us outside. One of us asked her why the pig was not cooperating with the children, and the cook said two words, "Di market." The Vietnamese word, "Di" means "go" or "go to". Sometime later the children returned with the rope but no hog.

Dogs were easy. We usually had two or three hanging around. We did not walk them because they had the run of the camp. Our dogs seemed to know where to go. We put food and water out for them and gave them a bath from time to time when they had fleas or had gotten into something rotten. They did not accompany us on missions. They were company and provided a bit of comfort during the all-night radio watches that each of us pulled.

There were a couple of "dog incidents" before I arrived. The MAT Team Captain remembers two of them this way:

"We had a puppy named DEROS. One day he tried to follow me when I went to District Chief's office for a meeting. I stopped and tried to send him back several times. I finally carried him back and put him in the team house. Later, when I returned from the meeting, I couldn't find DEROS, so I asked if anyone knew where he was. Someone said they thought he followed me, so I called the District Chief on the land line and described the pup asking if the Chief had seen him. He said he would investigate. When he asked his soldiers about the puppy, one acknowledged that they had eaten him. I was pretty torn up about it because I am sort of a dog whisperer. I like dogs more than I like most people! But either during that week or early the next we got a new pup for DEROS as a replacement gift from the District Chief...the obvious choice for a name was Hot Dog because this was during the "Hot Dog" incident. Unfortunately, he got very sick and with no vet in the District, one of the NCOs had to take him out in the jungle and euthanize him. "

Figure 26.3   Deros. Courtesy of Jim Rice

I remember two dogs, Bitch who was named by the prior members of the team and one of her pups, Lady (possibly our team's naming effort to make up for the mother's rather dubious name). The memory of their origin is very different. The MAT Team Captain remembers them as being there when he arrived. My memory is that Bitch came with our replacement NCOs and had her pups shortly after they arrived.

Either way, Bitch and Lady interacted with another common form of animal life at Dong Xoai — rats. Rats were common. Bitch was the champion rat killer. She would catch, kill them, and be done with it. As Lady got older, she developed a habit of playing with a rat instead of killing it outright. One evening, Lady was playing with one when Bitch took it away from her, killed it, and literally gave it back to her.

There were other incidents with rats. My first encounter with them is described in Story #3, Radio Watch. Here are two rat encounters as told by the MAT Team Captain:

The rats would get into my room, and they loved the life savers we got in SP packs. I got one of the huge rat traps with about 3/16-inch wire. It would break a finger if you got it caught while you were setting it. I tied a life saver to the trigger lever, set the trap then put it on the table I used for a desk. In the middle of the night the trap slammed closed and it woke me up. I quietly smiled knowing I had killed the sucker. Then I heard scratching and a crash. The thing was still alive and had pulled itself and the trap off the desk onto the metal folding chair by the desk. Then it was scratching and pulled itself onto the floor. By that time, I had my flashlight and I was able to see its back was broken but it was using its front legs and feet and was trying to get away. As I picked it up by its tail, it was trying to bend around and bite me. I carried it out back to a trash can and managed to kill it by bashing it on the side of the can. It was huge; probably 3-4 pounds, and it was mean.

Every night I wrote a letter to Linda (both L T's wife and my wife are named Linda). I would often lay on my bunk while writing, but I would take off my watch and put it in a fold in the top of the mosquito netting over my bunk, so I could watch it to make sure I was finished by the time the generators were turned off. One night, I went to sleep before I retrieved my watch. In the middle of the night, I rolled over and something hit me in the back. I remembered that huge rat, and I was sure that it was another rat, so I rolled out of bed taking sheets and mosquito net with me. I jumped up and down on the sheets for quite a while; then found my flashlight to see if I had killed the critter. As I pulled the sheets and net apart, I realized I was trying to kill my watch. It had rolled out of the fold in the netting and fallen onto my back!

I do not have any rat stories. One reason is that I never brought food to my quarters except for the Hershey's Tropical Chocolate Bars that were in the E&E pack — the candy the village children would not eat — and neither apparently did the rats. I did have one carnivorous visitor that became my adopted pet. I only glimpsed this pet a couple of times. It was a very large centipede; large in terms 6 or so inches long. It was the centipede's size that allowed it to remain in my room because it was too heavy to climb up into my bunk. The mosquito netting we had over

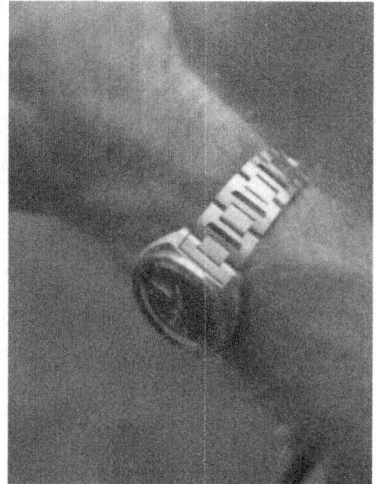

Figure 26.4   The MAT Team Captain's "rat."

our bunks took care of the flying bugs, and if you tucked it in carefully, it kept the spiders out. I have awakened when the generators were started in the morning, looking up to see a spider on the netting above me. It is an interesting way to begin the day. When I arrived at Dong Xoai I had a different defense for crawling creatures. To keep them out of my bunk, I put each leg of the bunk in the middle of a C-Ration can. The can was partially filled with water and oil literally making a mini-moat around each leg of the bunk. I thought this would be the perfect defense. Then I "met" the centipede. Centipedes are carnivores — they eat insects. And this is what my new friend did on a regular basis. It literally ate anything (insect that is) that wondered across the floor of my room. More than once I was awakened in the night by the quiet sound of crunching. The next morning, I would find some insect legs and a few other parts in the area from which the crunching was heard. This centipede was my buddy and I probably did not need the four mini-moats around the legs of my bunk but I kept them anyway.

159

Snakes were endemic to Vietnam. We avoided poking into dark places because they were good places for Jake the Snake or Charlie No-Shoulders to live. Finding an underground bunker on an operation was not something to cheer. Someone (not an advisor) had to explore the area inside the bunker. In addition to possibly being booby trapped, snakes were a very real threat to the soldier who entered the bunker. A small block of C4 with a short fuse was frequently used to clear the bunker first.

We had a series of communication trenches just inside the inner perimeter at the camp. "Communication" in this context refers to movement from place to place. These are zig-zag ditches that provide a place from which to fire your rifle at the invading forces along with cover if you need to move to another position. They are zig-zagged so an attacking soldier cannot take a position at one end and fire down a long straight ditch where defenders are fighting or moving.

The month before I arrived, the District Team's NCO recruited YB to help him clean out the communication trench behind our team house. It had become overgrown with weeds and had been partially filled in by sediment from the heavy monsoon rains over the past two years. He hired two older boys from the village to help him and YB with the project. Here is YB's memory of that project:

The four of us had been working about an hour. The villagers went first using a machete to cut the plant growth, and we followed with shovels. We heard a vicious scream and looked up to see one of the boys, still screaming, running towards the District Team NCO with his machete held high over his head. We both immediately thought, "Viet Cong!" The NCO held his shovel up for defense, but for some reason did not swing at the machete wielding boy which was a very fortunate decision. The boy swung his machete, not at the NCO but at a large snake that was only about a foot away from the Sergeant's leg, cutting its head off. American soldiers referred to this snake as Charlie-Two-Step because the rumor was that once bitten, you were dead before you took two steps. The snake's venom is not that quick, but there is no doubt that we could not have evacuated the Sergeant in time to save his life.

The District Team NCO decided right then and there that the communication trench was just fine and could be used as it existed. He paid the two villagers two days wages and sent them home.

Mosquitoes were one form of animal life that we could have done without. For one reason, they carried malaria. The strain of malaria in our area was treatable, and we took Chloroquine prophylactically — one pill each week administered by our medic. Every Monday he would actually hand the pill to each of us, one at a time and watch us take it. One side effect of Chloroquine was diarrhea, which hit most of us. So, the medic followed up Monday's malaria medicine with Tuesday morning's dose of Lomotil to shut down the diarrhea. And that set us up for a pill called the Brown Bomber which the medic would offer us on Saturday night. The unofficial name of this pill indicates it purpose — a quick acting laxative to counter the effect of the Lomotil.

As a closing note to this collection of memories and stories about animals, protein is vitally important to the human diet. Getting that protein can be problematic for populations who are under stress, such as that of a war time environment. The live markets that may have spawned the virus that is causing Covid19 provide a serious question, "Why?" to most of us in the West, but for some people who do not have the luxury of electricity and refrigeration, keeping protein in a market from spoiling usually means keeping the protein source alive. Another thing is the protein that different societies eat. Food that is a delicacy for one group is unthinkable for another. Think about escargot as one simple example. Some societies find and use as protein, animal life that is easy to raise and matures very quickly. It was not uncommon to see rats being turned on a spit over a cooking fire in some of the hamlets. As an advisor I ate many different forms of protein, trying to make sure it was always thoroughly cooked. Listing all of the protein sources we ate in the hamlets and on missions would undoubtedly disturb most readers of these stories, but it was part of our job to share the food the Vietnamese and Montagnards ate. And on operations with no chance of resupply, it allowed us to eat enough to be able to carry out the mission.

Story 27 - The Song Be River

Vietnamization was in full swing. Both MAT team NCOs had DEROSed and were not replaced. MAT 111 now consisted of the Team's Captain, its medic and me. Having no MAT 111 NCO, I was assigned to work with different NCOs from the other districts and Province HQ — all strangers to me — on operations with Regional Force (RF) units from other districts with whom I had no experience, rapport, or knowledge about their combat effectiveness. For me as well as the various NCOs with whom I worked, it was an interesting time — in the sense of the old Chinese curse.

I woke up with a knot still in my stomach. It had been there since yesterday. Physically in Vietnam, you never really felt good. There was always something nagging at you, keeping you just a bit out of whack. I was always very careful about what I ate and drank, but sometimes something got through. However, this felt different. I skipped breakfast again, and the Team Medic gave me another shot of Compazine to settle my stomach. It gave me some relief. Diarrhea had not showed up so far, and I was hoping it would stay away.

Midmorning, the radio call came; the S-3 Major (Operations) at Province asked for 33 Quebec (me). Radio Watch found me in my bunk, and I got on the radio. The S-3 said he was sending the chopper for me this afternoon, and he wanted me in Song Be with full field gear for a briefing on a five-day operation. I told him that I was sick and that he needed to assign the mission to someone else. If he wanted me to, I could put our medic on to confirm my condition. The S-3 replied that, "There is no one else, **LIEUTENANT**, and what I want is you on that chopper. **OUT**!" ending the transmission. It was against radio security to use my rank in an open radio transmission. Had I addressed him as Major instead of using his call sign, the Colonel would, to use a phrase from that time, "Have my butt in a sling!" The S-3 was really mad!

My rucksack was always packed with a basic set of "stuff" and ready to go, but what mission specific gear would I need? I'm not sure why but I decided to take a radio with my gear. It added 16 more pounds to the weight than I usually carried, but it seemed like a good idea.

The S-3 clerk was waiting at the helipad when I arrived and drove me to Province headquarters. The S-3 NCO met me and introduced me to the Sergeant with whom I would work on the operation. He was a Sergeant E-5, younger than me but on his second tour in Vietnam. He had extensive experience in his first tour on a LRRP unit (Long Range Recon Patrol), one of the most dangerous infantry assignments in Vietnam. This would be his first operation as an advisor working with a Regional Force (RF) unit. US soldiers often had very dim opinions of the combat abilities of the ARVN (Army of the Republic or Vietnam — the regular army) and even worse opinions about the Regional and Popular Forces. I wondered about his opinion since we were going to be operating with an RF company.

The S-3 came in to brief us on the operation. We were going to be accompanying a reinforced RF company commanded by an RF Major. We would be east of Song Be where the terrain was steep and the vegetation was fairly dense at ground level. There was a double canopy of growth (one layer or canopy close to the ground and a second layer above that consisting of trees). Movement would not be easy, and the range of our radios would be reduced, plus the availability of landing zones (LZ) would be limited. We were looking for what could be a major infiltration trail that was reported by Montagnards who had recently passed through the area. The trail ran north-south so, we would start the mission west of the suspected trail location and move eastward hoping to find the trail when we crossed it. We would be inserted by a US helicopter flight of eight ships. It would take four lifts (trips) to the LZ to get everyone on the ground. The first lift would be at 0800 hours (8:00 AM) tomorrow. There would be helicopter gunships in support for the insertion. The LZ was out of artillery and radio range with Song Be, but the S-3 and his counterpart would be overhead during the insertion. The S-3 would also be overhead once each day for a situation report. Pickup on day 5 was uncertain at this time, but it was being worked out. Beyond that, we would be on our own. Advisor presence was required to coordinate the insertion and pickup with the American helicopter crews, gunship sweeps against enemy positions, medical evacuations if needed, and to advise the RF company commander.

I asked about the RF company and why a Major was leading the company when the leader is usually a Captain or senior First Lieutenant. The S-3 said very little about the company, but he did say that the Major had just returned from a "retraining assignment," and we would also be evaluating him and the company; a detailed report was expected when we returned. I asked if we could meet the RF Major later today. The S-3 replied that we would meet him on the air strip tomorrow morning before the first lift.

I asked about an intelligence briefing by the S-2 (the Intelligence Major) or his NCO to get a picture of the enemy presence in the area. The S-3 replied that they were not available. With that he dismissed us, and we left his office. The S-4 (Supply) clerk directed us to a room where we could sleep tonight. We dropped our rucksacks there, and I gave the Sergeant a tour of the compound in an effort to get acquainted with him. I explained how my former Sergeant and I had operated with me up front near the company commander and the Sergeant at the rear with the company Executive Officer and the radio. I told him that for this operation his call sign would be 33 Tango. He was OK with all of this. I told him that I brought a field radio (he was glad to hear that) but that we might not get a soldier from the RF company to carry it. He said that he would carry it — since we did not know anything about the company, it would better if we did carry it. I would carry the replacement batteries[35] and the accessory pack. Then we studied the topo map for the area and wondered if the RF Major had reconned the LZ for the insertion and the planned LZ for the extraction. Either way, without an intel briefing, a recon of the area, and a meeting with the RF Major prior to the insertion, we were going into this operation deaf, mute, and blind. The

----

[35] Normally 5 radio batteries would be needed for a 5-day operation but we were out of radio range so our radio would be off much of the time. For this operation I would carry two extra batteries.

one good point was that we would not have to cross the Song Be River, which was running through the area of operations, to get to the extraction point. The knot in my stomach was worse; either because of the bug or the anxiety I had about this operation... or possibly both.

Operation Day 1

We got up early, and I forced down some breakfast in the small mess hall because I had no appetite. We put on our packs and walked to the air strip just to get some exercise. We wanted to be there before the RF troops and the Major arrived to introduce ourselves and discuss the mission. It was rainy season, so it was going to be a hot, humid day. When we got to the airstrip, we dropped our rucksacks, sat on them, and waited; it was 0730, and the first lift was due at 0800.

At 0830, we were still sitting there; the heat and the humidity were already building. One feature of an air strip is that there is no shade, no trees, no buildings — nothing to get in the way of an airplane or a helicopter using the field. There were also no RF troops and no helicopters either. I radioed Province and asked to speak to the S-3. "Wait one," was the reply. So, we waited — more than "one." Eventually the S-3 called and told us that the ships had been delayed. I asked about the RF company's status and got a very fuzzy reply. I thought about returning to the compound but that was really not an option; we needed to meet the RF Major who should be here soon. So, we continued to sit in the sun, the heat, and the humidity.

Sometime later the S-3 radioed that the American helicopter unit had been reassigned to a different mission, and they were working on getting a Vietnamese helicopter unit for the lift. So much for an early insertion. There were physical and tactical problems with the delay. The physical concern was that the high temperatures and humidity in the afternoon reduces the lift capability of a helicopter. A chopper that could carry twelve troops in the morning might be limited to ten in the afternoon heat. The tactical concern was the insertion itself. Thirty-two (4 round trips by 8 helicopters) landings and takeoffs from a small landing zone is not exactly a stealthy operation. Anyone (e.g., Viet Cong) in the area knows where you are, so you want to move as far away from the LZ as possible before setting up for the night. I asked if a jeep could be sent for us so we could come in, refill our canteens and get something to eat. We were both carrying two one-quart canteens and a 2 1/2-quart canteen even though it was rainy season; good water could be difficult to get where we were heading. The reply came back, "No. Stay put. The RF company should be there soon. OUT"

A little while later 33 Tango suggested that he take our canteens and jog back to the compound, fill them, and try to bring something back to eat. I told him to eat there if there was nothing suitable to bring back. My stomach was still not good and I did not have an appetite. The heat and humidity were not helping. Thirty or so minutes later he returned with two full canteens and two sandwiches.

Eventually a convoy of trucks pulled up alongside of the air strip, and troops began to unload and mill around in a very non-military manner, but there was no jeep or obvious command vehicle. The radio was silent, and we did not call in. We figured that when we needed to know something, the S-3 would call. Maybe if we were lucky, the operation would be canceled. Hey, we could hope.

A jeep finally pulled up by the first truck, and a soldier got out and walked over to us. He introduced himself, saying he was going to be our interpreter. We put on our packs and followed the interpreter back to the jeep to meet the Major. As we approached, the Major looked at us and asked the interpreter, "Dai uy o dau"[36] (Vietnamese: "Where is the Captain?") The interpreter replied "Trung uy la co van" (Vietnamese: "The Lieutenant is the advisor.") At this point the Major appeared to get very angry and he turned his back on us. I only heard part of what he said, but I was sure the interpreter was untruthful in his translation when he turned and said that the Major was very busy right now. We would talk later. It seems the Major was insulted to have a mere Lieutenant and a

---

[36] My language training at the Defense Language Institute gave me an advantage of being able to compare what I heard to what the interpreter told me. I trusted Sgt. Yung, my MAT interpreter at Dong Xoai but this one was an unknown and would have to earn my trust. So far, he is failing.

Sergeant with only three stripes as his advisors. He felt that he deserved at least a Captain, if not a Major and a senior NCO. It was clear there would be no meeting or consultation between us before the operation began, and it was also clear that the interpreter was going to be unreliable.

We were going into this operation in a way that was far beyond deaf, mute, and blind, and my stomach was strongly disagreeing with the sandwich the Sergeant had brought back. These were indeed interesting times and they were about to become even more so...

Soon, helicopters could be heard and eventually appeared. They circled the airstrip and sat down in a line. There were eight troop ships and two gunships. These helicopters were being flown by Vietnamese crews, so there was no one with whom we, as advisors would coordinate during the insertion. Typically, I would board the first ship in the first lift with my counterpart, while 33 Tango boards the last ship in the last lift with his counterpart — the XO. Since we had not talked with the Major, we did not know who the second in command — the Executive Officer or XO — was, and it was not clear at this point that the Major wanted me on his helicopter. So 33 Tango, the interpreter, and I moved to a position lateral to the second helicopter. An order was passed along and the troops began to board, but the Major did not move towards a helicopter. His command group remained in place.

33 Tango and I looked at each other and decided to wait for the Major and his command group to move. The eight helicopters returned for the second lift, and once again the Major and his command group remained in place. Same for the third lift. The Major boarded the first ship on the last lift, so 33 Tango, our interpreter, and I got on the second bird. Through all of this our radio was silent. Where was the S-3?

The helicopters flew close to the top of the trees to limit the amount of time anyone on the ground would have to aim and shoot at them. Normally, it is an exhilarating ride, but my stomach was not appreciating the motion of the helicopter as it pitched up and down following the terrain.

The helicopters settled down into a clearing, but we could not immediately exit the chopper. We had to wait until the Major exited his ship before we moved. When he moved, we jumped out following the group to the company's rather dismal perimeter. The Major paid no attention to us; our radio was silent; the S-3 was not overhead, which was puzzling. Looking around, the company exhibited very little training for an air mobile operation. Instead of troops exiting the helicopters from both sides and setting up a defensive perimeter around the landing zone, the entire company had apparently exited to one side of the LZ. What should have been a circular perimeter at the edges of the clearing was in reality a single line of troops. And they were just sitting around like they were at the airstrip waiting for pickup. It appeared that the entire company should have been sent back for retraining along with their Major.

We moved closer to the command group, but we were still ignored. The Sergeant and I talked while waiting for the company to mount up and move out. We decided to remain together and stay near the command group for now. The Major was not talking or listening to us, so we would be useless to him if we stumbled into a firefight. We would have a better chance if we could find a platoon in the company with a decent leader and some level of competence.

During this time, we tried to contact the S-3, who should have been in a helicopter overhead with his counterpart during the insertion. The radio remained silent; no one replied to our calls; where was the S-3?

That the LZ had been cold (no enemy fire) was a blessing, but it was late in the afternoon. The Major had very little time to find a defendable position for the night. Eventually the soldiers formed up into a column and moved out. But we did not move that long or that far before the column stopped and troops began to set up for the night. Unlike Captain Ky at Dong Xoai, we were not going to eat first and then move to a night defensive position (NDP). If we were being watched, this could be a problem.

The position the Major selected for the night was indefensible. We were in a narrow valley with a stream flowing through it. The water was good, but the high ground on either side was not. We could be attacked from both sides, and the attacking force could bring effective fire down on us without the danger of hitting their own troops on the other side.

There was no perimeter — the troops spread along both sides of the stream in a long two-sided line. We had hammocks but the vegetation would not support them so we had to sleep on the ground. It was rainy season so leeches were going to be a problem.

We cleaned our rifles, ate our rations (at least I tried to eat something). Then we walked over to the command group but there was no interaction; our presence continued to be ignored. As advisors it was our place to remain close by until our counterpart called us. It was not our place to interject or comment first. Doing this could cause the leader to lose face with his troops. This is how I operated with Captain Ky at Dong Xoai. It was how I wanted to operate here. But Captain Ky never ignored me or 33 Tango; we were always part of the command group. That was not true for this Major.

It was still light when 33 Tango, our interpreter, and I walked the line (instead of a perimeter) of the troops, and the only good thing we saw was a small perimeter at one end of the line of troops. These troops appeared to have a level of discipline and training that the others did not exhibit. We found their Lieutenant and talked with him. He was the leader of the first platoon, which always led the way. The Major would show the Lieutenant where he wanted to go on the map. The route was not discussed; just the destination. Apparently, this Lieutenant was very good at reading a topo map, so he led the company to the position. He presented himself as a good leader. There may be a glimmer of hope.

On the way back to our position, we decided to move with the first platoon tomorrow. That would mean that if we stumbled into anything, we would be in the thick of it, but we would know what was happening, and we would be with a good (relatively speaking) unit. The command group would be following right behind the first platoon, so we could drop back to their position if we had to. Tomorrow the interpreter and I would move with the platoon leader near the front of the column, and the Sergeant would be at the rear of the platoon near the command group. The interpreter was listening and argued that this was too dangerous; we should move with the command group and not the first platoon. He seemed to be very afraid of moving at the front of the column. We set up our ponchos on the ground and arranged them as well as we could to try to keep the leeches away. We smeared the Army issued leech repellant on the tops of our boots and trouser legs where they were tucked in and on our wrists, followed by a coating of mosquito repellant on exposed skin. Then we alternated two-hour watches through the night, and I took the first watch. In reality I could have pulled all of the watches because my stomach was not in the mood to let me sleep.

Operation Day 2

The next morning things were not good for me — I felt worse. This stomach bug was now a point of major concern. Thankfully, we did not move very far yesterday, but this would be a full day's march. We would be moving up and down steep pitches, and it would be hot and humid making it physically taxing for someone in good health — which I was not. I had this dread of not being able to make the march when falling out was not an option. I was becoming a liability to our two-man advisory team — a strong negative and putting the Sergeant at risk. I needed energy to make the march but I had no desire to eat. Even worse I was not sure I could keep any food down...

I ate some c-ration fruit cocktail and drank the juice hoping that the sugar would give me some energy and that the fruit would sit better in my stomach. We packed up our gear and walked over to the command group for another episode of being ignored. Then the three of us moved to the first platoon and through our interpreter told the Lieutenant that we wanted to move with him. He smiled, apparently pleased at our confidence in him. The interpreter took me aside and said that this was a very dangerous thing to do — we should be with the command group. I ignored this and told him in a firm voice to stay right behind me. The platoon leader pointed to his map indicating the place where we would stop at midday to eat and the route he would take. This was the first real information we had since our briefing with the S-3 two days ago. It was the first time we actually knew what was going to happen, if only for half of a day. It gave 33 Tango and me a bit of hope.

Finally, we mounted up and headed out. Movement was slow (which was good for me) otherwise the column would have been scattered in a very long line. The first platoon Lieutenant had a decent grasp on what was needed for security and his troop followed his instructions. Where possible he put troops out to the flank for security. We stopped several times before arriving at our destination for lunch. Each time 33 Tango came forward to check his map against mine and to see how I was holding up. He insisted I keep drinking water. Fortunately, it was rainy season so the streams were running, and good water was available.

We had stopped for lunch and I was not having much success trying to eat, plus I was now a bit light headed. Following the topo map was becoming impossible — my eyes would not focus on the terrain markings. About this time, we heard our call sign on the radio — the first time we had heard anything on the radio since before we were picked up by the helicopters for insertion. The S-3 was overhead somewhere, and he wanted to know where we were and how the mission was proceeding. We encrypted our position and transmitted it. I gave him a full report, pulling no punches on what we had seen and how we were proceeding. His only reply was to. "Carry on." I replied, "33 Quebec (me) is very sick and not capable of continuing. He is endangering the mission and 33 Tango. We need immediate extraction. Over."

There! The words almost stuck in my throat. I had done it. I pulled the plug. I had quit. I was putting 33 Tango in tremendous danger. He had to look after the mission and me. If we got into trouble, I would be next to useless, and his chances of making it were seriously diminished. There was a very long silence. Then the reply came back in a terse voice, "Negative. Extraction is not possible. Carry on. OUT!" As the sound of the helicopter faded in the distance, I reached out and turned the radio off in disgust. I was not sure what the Sergeant was thinking, and I did not look him in the eye. I had just admitted defeat in front of him — not the type of impression you want to make on someone when you are supposed to be in charge.

A soldier from the first platoon walked up to the Lieutenant and then over to our interpreter and spoke to him. The interpreter turned and said that this soldier was a medic, and the Green Berets had trained him; he wanted to give me a shot. Then the medic said in his best attempt at English, "Trung Uy (my rank in Vietnamese) need shot. Feel numbah one." The Vietnamese Lieutenant had moved closer and was nodding his head, "Yes." I looked at the medic and said, "No morphine" and the medic replied, "No Morphine." Nodding my head, I held out my arm.

It was hot and humid; the slope was steep. We picked up our packs, put them on, and took up the march. Thank God the column was moving at an extremely slow pace and for the medic's shot.

The afternoon passed like the morning and the night like the one before. During the day we found no trace of any movement or trail. Everything appeared untrampled and completely natural.

Operation Day 3

The next morning, I felt no worse — maybe I was getting better or maybe it was the shot masking what was wrong. Regardless, I did not care because I did feel a bit better. I ate my last can of fruit cocktail for breakfast. As we were packing our gear, the medic approached and talked to our interpreter who looked at me, "He wants to know how you are this morning." I nodded and said, "Numbah one" and pointed my thumb up. The medic spoke again and the interpreter said, "He wants to know if you want another shot?" Why not? I offered him my arm. As the medic was leaving, I said to him, "Cam on." (Vietnamese for "thank you") and gave him another thumbs up. He smiled, returned the thumbs up and moved away as the first platoon Lieutenant was returning to the perimeter.

He had just met with the Major and had his map in his hand. We moved closer to find out what the line of march would be for the morning. The route he indicated on the map could not be true. It was to the northeast but that would move us away from out extraction point; we should begin moving southeast. We were a two-day march from the extraction point and did not have the time to move northeast. Besides, continuing northeast, we would have to cross the Song Be River which would still be running high from the heavy rains of the wet season, and we would have to recross it to get back to the extraction point. And we would be one day late for our helicopter extraction. As I said earlier, an advisor was not supposed to question his counterpart in front of his troops, lest he cause his counterpart to lose face.

Sorry about that!

33 Tango and our interpreter followed me as I walked over to the command group. Holding my map in front of the Major, I told the interpreter to ask the Major why we were moving away from the pickup LZ. The interpreter's body language showed that he did not want to interrogate the Major like this. Angrily, I said, "Go on. Ask him!" The interpreter asked a different question as the Major looked at the map. Then he actually looked at us while he spoke to the interpreter. The translation, "Pick up tomorrow — here" pointing to the same place the first platoon leader pointed to. This is not what the S-3 told us. I was trying to figure out what to say next when 33 Tango stepped in and told the interpreter to ask the Major if the extraction had been changed. The Major's reply through our interpreter was, "No. This original plan." This left both of us at a loss for words.

I do not remember why, maybe it was because the Major was actually willing to talk with us, but we decided it would be better to remain with the command group for today's march. However, 33 Tango and I would stay together. The Army at all phases: basic training, AIT, OCS, has expressions to describe the situation in which 33 Tango and I found ourselves but they are by far too obscene to print here. Talk to any Vietnam veteran if you really want to know to what I am referring. 33 Tango and I knew where we were on the ground in Vietnam but as of now, we had no idea what we were doing or why we were doing it. At least the medic's shot seemed to be settling my stomach…

We put on our rucks and joined the day's march. We moved along the valley for a while and then turned to move up the side of the ridge that separated us from the Song Be River. The stream valley would have taken us to the river eventually but it is tactically ill-advised to move in a valley with high ground on both sides. It makes an inviting place for any enemy to spring an ambush. We did not move directly to the crest of the ridge but in a line that made the climb longer but much less steep. The first platoon Lieutenant was good. We found no evidence of any trail or path or movement by anyone. The medic's shots were working. I was not great, but I was able to keep up, and my stomach was no longer talking to me on a regular basis. We made it to the military crest of the ridge[37] and broke for lunch.

Soon after stopping we heard our call sign on the radio; I answered back. The S-3 was in the chopper and asking for our location. We encrypted the coordinates and transmitted them to the S-3. After a pause the reply came back, "You can't be there. Are you sure your coordinates are correct? You are off the line of march." 33 Tango took his compass and shot a direction towards the sound of the helicopter, and I encrypted his reading and read it to the S-3. The reply came back that continuing on this line would cause us to miss our pickup time. 33 Tango was giving me a Whisky Tango Foxtrot look.[38] I replied that we were moving to a different LZ for a pickup tomorrow. There was a very long silence on the radio. I spoke into the handset, "What does your counterpart say about this? Over." Again, silence. Finally, the reply, "I will get back to you on that. Out." I returned the Whisky Tango Foxtrot look to 33 Tango, as the sound of the helicopter faded.

As we were finishing our rations, 33 Tango, on his first operation as an advisor, asked me what all of that meant. I explained that every advisor had a Vietnamese counterpart. The Province Senior Advisor (PSA) worked with the Province Chief. The District Senior Advisors worked with the District Chiefs. On this operation my counterpart was the Major and 33 Tango's was the company XO - whoever he was. The American S-3 worked directly with the Province S-3. In every operation organized by Province that I had been on, the American S-3 was always in the chopper with his counterpart and an interpreter. If our S-3 was alone in the chopper and if our S-3 did not know about the change for the day of the extraction day and its location, something very strange was

---

[37] The military crest is a line below the actual top of the ridge. You do not want to walk along the actual ridge top because you can be easily seen silhouetted against the sky making a good target for an enemy. We moved along a ridge below the top at a level that kept us low enough to avoid being silhouetted.

[38] This is the Army's phonetic alphabet and the three words stand for the letters, W, T, and F - ask a veteran...

Figure 27.1   The Song Be River.

going on, very strange indeed… Thanks to the medic's shot, I was able to eat for a change, did not feel too bad, and was able to read the map.

We moved out, crested the ridge and started down the other side towards the river. We took a winding route down reducing the slope, and giving us better footing. We could hear the river before we saw it, meaning that it was running high and fast. When we got to the banks of the river, the company situation degraded even more than it had the previous two days. It was late and we would finish the crossing just before dark. This meant that we would spend the night on the other bank in another indefensible location.

The tactically sound method for a river crossing is to put a few troops upriver and downriver for security. A third group should be placed on the slope behind and above us, also for security. A small team is sent across first to scout the other side and provide security. Once these four units are in place, the bulk of company crosses. When the main element has finished crossing the river, the security elements follow. The Song Be

River was too deep to wade, so small rafts of bamboo would be needed to float the soldiers' packs while they swam across the river.

The Major sent no one anywhere for security. Everyone began to cut bamboo and fashion rafts, as if it were a race to see who could cross the river first. At this point we would have been better off to have remained with the first platoon, but we were committed to the command group. I carried a machete, so I helped cut bamboo for the command group's raft, and 33 Tango helped lace the lengths together with vines. We pulled our boots and socks off, stuffed the socks into the boots and tied them to our rucksacks. Then we tied our web gear to the rucksack Finally we pulled off our shirts and put them in the rucksacks and placed the rucks in the center of the raft. We would swim the raft across the river, carrying only our M-16s. I did have a sheath knife on my trousers belt, for what good it might be. There were four in the command group and three of us. 33 Tango moved to the leading edge of the raft to help pull it across the river. I would be on the trailing edge kicking to help move the raft. The command group moved to the sides of the raft. We were positioned at the upstream end of the pool, so we should have enough time to cross before being swept past the point where the Major wanted to land. At least the Major's thinking was sound on this point.

Our interpreter was useless through all of this. He stood there frozen; apparently terrified of the water. He silently watched our preparations, making no effort to help. I slung my M-16 over my shoulder and chest with the stock up and the barrel down to keep as much of the rifle out of the water as possible and waded over to him. I lifted his pack from his back and took it back to the raft and placed it near the center. I turned and grabbed his arm to pull him to the raft. As I turned back toward the raft and stepped into the water, the Major who was now leaning on the back of the raft put his foot in the center of my chest when I got close to the raft and shoved me backwards causing me to fall into the water landing on my butt. He said in very bad English, "Too heavy; sink raft," as he pushed off the river bottom and kicked the raft out into the current. When the raft started to move, 33 Tango began pulling the raft and looking towards the other shore; he did not see any of this. Had he, there was nothing he could have done — absolutely nothing.

There I was sitting on my butt on the muddy bottom of the Song Be River watching the raft move away. The interpreter was standing in the water near me, frozen in place — terrified. Worst of all, the muzzle of my rifle now buried in the river bottom was packed with mud and — like my interpreter, totally useless.

It was not time to feel sorry for myself — it was getting late in the day and there was a river to cross. The only question in my mind was should I leave my interpreter behind or drown him on the crossing...

Looking around I saw a group of five soldiers standing on the river bank near the lower end of the pool doing nothing; just standing there apparently talking to each other in some stage of panic. Grabbing the interpreter by the arm I dragged him down river to the group. They stopped talking and stood to attention — sort of — when they saw us approach. Except one — he was wearing a field radio and frantically blowing into the hand set. Some Vietnamese thought they had to blow into the handset to wake the spirits who carried the words to the other radio — really. After blowing, he would speak into the mike but the radio remained silent. Either no one was answering, or something was broken.

I shook the interpreter and told him to tell the two that had machetes to cut bamboo and tell the other three to gather vines so we could build a raft and do it quickly. It was getting late, and we would be losing the light soon. The interpreter translated my words in a weak raspy voice. Four of the five started to move into action, but the fifth soldier who was carrying the radio slung his M-16 over his shoulder, stepped into the water, and started to swim for the other shore — carrying 16 pounds of radio, 7 1/2 pounds of M-16, plus his web gear. The six of us could do nothing; we just stared. Someone shouted something but it was too fast for me to understand — probably, "Come back." He did ok for a while, making good progress, but about one-third of the way across he started to struggle. Then he quit swimming and just tried to keep his head above the water. Soon his head dropped below the surface... He was gone.

I told the interpreter to tell the other four to get busy. He did and they did. We tied bamboo into a rickety raft, loaded their packs in the middle and pushed off just as light was failing. I am not a strong swimmer; I can take care of myself, but this was going to be at or beyond my ability. I don't think any of them could swim. Their efforts seemed more like a lot of thrashing around. Once again, the interpreter was useless; just hanging on — no kicking or arm motion or even thrashing. Having started near the downstream end on the pool, the current swept us past the point on shore where the company had gotten out of the river, around a bend and down river out of sight of the company. We managed to kick, thrash, and finally drift into a gravel bank on the opposite side that was formed where a stream joined the river. Exhausted, we struggled to shore just as it was getting dark. We gathered our breath for a few minutes. Just as I was starting to tell the interpreter to tell the others that we would move upstream along the shore to find the company, the other four started moving inland at a quick pace away from the river following the stream.

Shaking my head, I grabbed the interpreter by the arm and pushing him in front of me, we moved to catch up. The rocks were volcanic in origin, very sharp, and I was barefoot. I could feel them cutting my feet, but there was nothing I could do but keep moving up the stream. We caught up when the four stopped. I started to speak to the interpreter when he turned and "shushed" me and whispered, "Be quiet. VC". The other four started moving up the stream bed again. It was now dark. This sequence of catching up, trying to talk, getting shushed by my interpreter, happened two more times. The fourth time the group stopped, the dim light of a fire could be seen at a distance through the foliage on our right. The sound of the water flowing in the stream hid any sound we had made. This fire was not at the company's location. I had studied the topo map carefully when we got to the river. The next two streams that flowed into the river came from a southerly direction away from the area where the company should be. A fire at the company was unthinkable, but if they had one, it would be on our left. The dimness of the fire's light meant it was probably a small fire and possibly made by Montagnards. But it could be Viet Cong.

I was beyond angry with my interpreter and these four soldiers. I was not going to be shushed again. Fearing that the four would move out of the stream bed towards the fire, I stepped up close behind my interpreter, pulled my sheath knife off my belt and grabbed my interpreter from behind putting my free hand over his mouth and the knife blade lightly

179

against his throat. I whispered in his ear, "Toi noi tieng Viet" (I speak Vietnamese) and pressed the blade ever so slightly into his skin. He stiffened — either from the knife or from the realization that I had been understanding his translations. "Ban di chuyen, ban noi chuyen, ban chet" (You move, you talk, you die). The knife pressed a bit harder. I removed my hand from his mouth.

"Tell them the fire is VC". Weakly he whispered the translated words.

"Tell them we go back to the river."

"Tell them now." The words whispered out.

Remarkably, the four soldiers listened and moved past the two of us and started downstream very quietly. Before removing my knife from the interpreter's throat, I took his rifle out of his hands and pushed him towards the other four. I was not about to be shot by my interpreter.

We returned to the river quietly and quickly with no pauses. Once we got to the river, we headed upstream walking in the water at the river's edge because of the dense foliage at the edge of the river. The rocks here, even though worn by years of moving water were still very sharp.

When 33 Tango dragged himself on to the opposite shore, he turned and realized that I was not with the raft. He looked across the river and could see me on the other side with the interpreter. There was nothing he could do, but at least he knew I had not drowned. The Major said nothing and offered him no help moving my gear. He had to carry two heavy rucksacks, two sets of web gear and his rifle several hundred meters up the steep bank to the center of the area where the company was setting up for the night. He could not leave one pack on the bank while carrying the other one up the bank because the soldiers would probably steal it or steal much of what was in the pack while he was gone. The packs were too heavy to carry both at the same time. So, he moved one pack about ten meters, dropped it and returned for the other one. He carried it ten meters past the first pack and repeated this process until he was near the Major's position in what the company had formed as a perimeter for the night. He sat down, caught his breath, and wondered where I was. He tried contacting anyone on the radio, but no one picked up his call. Without an interpreter, all he could do was clean his weapon, eat, and wait.

As we were moving quietly upriver towards the company, I thought that we might walk into an ambush set up by one of the squads in the company or be shot by some of the troops on the perimeter of the company — nah! Not much chance of that with this outfit. In fact, we walked directly into the center of whatever made up the company's perimeter without being challenged by anyone. Plus, we were guided by a large fire[39]. It was not the one we saw from the creek bed.

The light of the fire showed me where 33 Tango was. I moved to his location, and 33 Tango stood up as I approached. "Where the hell have you been?" he said extending a welcoming hand. I took it, replying, "It's good to see you too." We both laughed a sick laugh. I sat down and pulled my shirt out of my pack and put it on for a bit of warmth. Then I pulled my cleaning kit out of my pack and started to clean and dry my rifle. The first chore was clearing the plug of mud in the muzzle. As I was jamming the cleaning rod through the chamber into the barrel trying to push out the mud, 33 Tango looked at me and asked, "How did you manage to do that?" My reply was simple, "You don't want to know". Once my rifle was clean, I looked after my feet. The red light from my flashlight showed that they were cut up from the sharp rocks, but none of the cuts were too deep. Most of the bleeding had stopped. We had walked back upstream in the water, which had apparently cleaned the cuts. The walk from the riverbank up to the company was on vegetation, so my feet were not dirty. I pulled out my spare socks and put more of the Army issue foot powder laced with fungicide in them and put them on. Then I put on my boots — painful now and tomorrow's march would be worse. Hopefully the fungicide would stop or slow any infection until I got back to Song Be.

Picking at a cold C-ration (my stomach was better but not that good), I went over what had happened. When I finished the story, 33 Tango remarked, "I wondered why you were carrying two M-16s." The

---

[39] A fire on a combat operation in disputed territory — would the S-3 believe that in my report? I am not sure I would.

interpreter's weapon was still lying there. I said that if he did not retrieve it by tomorrow morning, I would throw it in the river. I asked 33 Tango about the fire. He said that the Major was cold and wanted to dry his clothes so he had his command group build the fire. I told him how we walked into the center of the company without being challenged. Neither of us slept much that night.

I took the first two-hour watch; I was too keyed up from my walk in the woods to sleep. But I was sound asleep the next morning when 33 Tango nudged me with the butt of his rifle while keeping a safe distance away.

Operation Day 4

It was early, and we were the first to stir. I pulled out the block of C-4 I was carrying and handed it to the Sergeant. He broke off a piece and returned it to me. I did the same. We lit the C-4 with his Zippo lighter and poured water into our canteen cups. The C-4 burns very hot, so it took only a few minutes for each of us make a cup of C-Ration instant coffee. Lousy coffee but when it's all you got, it's pretty good. My stomach was almost back to normal, which was good, so I had some canned cheese and crackers for breakfast — the fruit cocktail was gone. Walking was not fun but doable. I wondered how far the pickup point was and when we had to be there. Eventually, I picked up the interpreter's rifle and started towards the river. 33 Tango reached out and stopped me. So, I removed the magazine and emptied the round in the chamber before I carried it over to the command group and handed it to one of the Major's toadies. The Major did not look at me and said nothing. I returned the favor and went back to our position. We packed up our gear and waited. 33 Tango moved down to the river and filled our canteens. He returned and we waited some more.

Finally, the troops began to form up, so we put on our packs and moved up to the first platoon. Their Lieutenant greeted us and looked for our interpreter, saying, "Trung si dau" (Where is the Sergeant?). I replied, "Toi noi duoc mot chut tieng Viet" (I speak a little Vietnamese). He replied, "Numbah 1". We moved out away from the river through the middle of another open area — not around its edge. We climbed a little higher through vegetation and entered another open area. This time we moved along one side of the open area. When the first platoon got to the end of the area, they moved into the vegetation and dropped their packs. It was only mid-morning, so I looked at the Lieutenant and asked, "Tai sao" (Why?) He pointed to the center of the open area and said, "L Z" — this was the pickup up point? I asked him, "Khi nao" (When?) and he shook his head — he did not know. It was going to be another hot humid day but, at least we had some shade.

So, we sat. Noon came, but the S-3 did not. The radio was silent. We ate some lunch and drank some water. Sitting and doing nothing is one of the most difficult things on an operation. Time seems to run backwards. There was nothing to talk about. Whittling shavings from a piece of bamboo with your knife holds your attention for only so long. We moved away from the first platoon and walked the edge of the open area where the troops were positioned. Once again, there was no perimeter. Just a line on one side of the field. We returned to the first platoon and sat down on our packs in the shade. 33 Tango got up and walked over to the Lieutenant and pointed to his watch and whirled his hand over his head literally asking when the helicopters were coming. The Lieutenant shook his head, "No." We sat some more, and the radio remained silent.

It was well into the afternoon, and I was beginning to wonder if we were actually going to be lifted out today. It was one day early. The S-3's briefing said five days, and this was day four. Unlike the previous three nights, there was no stream close by, so we slowed down on drinking our water. Both of us began the day carrying 4 1/2 quarts but if we were going to spend the night here, we needed to conserve water for tomorrow. At least my stomach was no longer bothering me, and we were not moving, so my feet were ok.

We heard them first. Eventually six helicopters appeared low in the south. The two lead ships circled the LZ twice. They were gunships looking for potential trouble. The remaining four were troop transports. I wondered if four more were coming because there were eight helicopters on the insertion. With only four, the extraction would take more than four hours to complete.

One gunship sprayed the ground on the opposite side of the open area with a door mounted mini gun firing 2000 bullets per minute. It didn't make a series of separate bangs like an M-60 machine gun; it made a loud buzz. The troops began to move, putting on their packs. We did likewise. A smoke grenade was thrown, so the pilots could see which direction the wind was blowing. The four troop ships circled and set up to approach from the south for landing. We moved to the northern end of the clearing where the first ship would set down. Under "normal" conditions 33 Tango would be on the first or second ship of the first lift so he could coordinate things at the airstrip. I would be on the last ship in the last lift to coordinate things here. But there was no one to talk to. Vietnamese were flying the choppers, the S-3 was not on the radio, and the Major was giving us the silent treatment again. We decided to follow the Major. He should be on the last ship of the last lift, but we doubted that would be the case. When the first ship set down, he and his command group moved out to board. We jumped in front of the group heading to the second ship and boarded.

The flight back was better than the flight out. My stomach did not care about the pitching up and down as we followed the terrain. Sitting on the edge of the floor with my feet hanging down towards the skid, it was a beautiful trip back to Song Be. The ships circled the airstrip at Song Be and sat down. We jumped off and walked over to the waiting trucks. The Major and his group got into a jeep and drove away, never looking back at us. We never existed. There was no jeep waiting for us, so 33 Tango called in and asked for a ride to the compound. And we waited some more...

Eventually a jeep arrived and drove us back to the Province HQ compound. It was good to be back. I told 33 Tango that I needed to check in with the S-3. I told him that I would be filing a report with the S-3 and the Colonel (the Province Senior Advisor), and it would reflect very highly on him. I tried to reassure him that my short comings on this mission would not reflect on him in any way. I held out my hand and he took it. We went our separate ways, and I never saw him again. I cannot find his name in the dark maze that is my memory of that time — which is my loss.

I walked over to the S-3 shop and asked the clerk if the S-3 or his NCO were available. Shaking his head, the clerk said that they had been out all day. I said that I would be back tomorrow morning, and he made a note to tell the S-3. As I turned to leave, the clerk said, "Lieutenant, no offense sir, but you stink. You might want to take a shower." That took a lot of guts. I thanked him and headed to the S-4 shop to see if the work chopper was still here. I needed a ride to Dong Xoai.

The S-4 NCO was at his desk and grimaced when I walked up. I guess I really did stink. I asked about a ride to Dong Xoai and he said that the chopper had already departed for Ben Hoa — going home for the day. I did not bring a change of clothes or toiletries with me when I flew up to Province five days ago, so I asked the Sergeant if he had a set of jungle fatigues he could loan me. He said no but that he could find a towel and a bar of soap. Given the state of my feet, I asked if he had a pair of socks, as he got up from his desk. He came back with a towel, soap, and a pair of socks, plus an olive drab tee shirt, and a razor.

From there I took a chance of finding a medic in the aid station and was lucky again — he was there — the same medic I pulled the MedCap with on my first day in Province. I explained what I needed, and he told me to take off my boots and socks. As he examined them, he asked, "Exactly how did you do this?" "I took a barefoot walk on a path of sharp rocks." He just shook his head, "The cuts are not too deep and only one is still seeping some blood. There is no sign of infection but I will give you some stuff to smear on your feet after you shower. If they begin to hurt more than they are now or seem to get warm, have your medic send you down to Ben Hoa for treatment of an infection, but I think you will be ok." With that, he put some greenish black ointment in a small paper cup and handed it and a pair of green slippers to me, "Wear these when you are inside; they will be easier on your feet than your boots. And keep using the foot powder."

I returned to the bunk room, stripped and took a shower. The water was cold and there was not much pressure but it felt good. When I was done, I scraped as much beard off as possible. I was clean, but my jungle fatigues were not. The pants had been laundered to a degree when I crossed the river, but my shirt was in the pack and stayed dry. Salt stains encrusted the back, and it smelled heavily of body odor from five hot, humid days in the jungle. I put on my dirty trousers and the clean tee shirt the S-4 had (thankfully) given me. I smeared the greenish black stuff on the bottom of my feet before putting on the socks from the S-4 and the slippers from the medic.

I walked over to the small mess hall and had a nice warm meal and a glass of something called milk. The carton said, "Filled Milk" — not instant or powdered but "Filled." Anyway, it was cold and tasted good.

Walking back to the bunk room, I ran into the S-3. He seemed surprised to see me. Apparently, he had not been to his office since I returned. He said, "Lieutenant, what are you doing here? Your pickup is tomorrow."

"I told you yesterday that the pickup was today at a different LZ, Sir."

"I thought you were wrong. I'll need to see you tomorrow morning… And the next time I see you, Lieutenant, you better be in full uniform including boots!"

"Sir, Yes Sir," was my reflexive OCS reply. I went back to the bunk room and smelled my jungle fatigue shirt. "If you want me in full uniform, that's fine with me." I rolled up the shirt and stuffed into my rucksack. I did not want it to air out to any degree.

Post Operation

The next morning, I took a chance and went to the mess hall wearing the tee shirt and the slippers. The S-3 was not there and did not come in while I was eating. I ate quickly and returned to my bunk. I removed my fatigue shirt from my pack and put it on — it was rank, but orders were orders. I put my jungle boots on and limped over to the S-3 shop. The once again grimacing clerk told me to come back in about two hours. My feet were hurting, so I returned to the bunk room, took off my shirt and boots and laid down.

Two hours later I returned to the S-3 shop. The clerk asked me to wait outside if I didn't mind. Sure — why should he suffer? The S-3 walked up and looked at me — no words, no smile — and just passed by. A few minutes later the clerk came out and said the S-3 would see me now. I entered his office and thought about saluting, but we did not do that in a combat zone. I knew this was going to be an uncomfortable meeting, so I saw no reason to add to that discomfort. Who would have ever thought that a salute in the military could be taken as something negative?

Even though he seemed to notice my pungent aroma, he did not comment on the smell or ask me to sit down when I stood in front of him. He asked me to go over the mission which I did in detail. He said nothing while I was speaking. When I finished, he asked about my dealings with the interpreter. My first comment was that his translations were untrustworthy. The S-3 questioned this remark, "How would you know that?"

I replied, "Toi noi tieng Viet. Khong ban?" (I speak Vietnamese, Don't you?). That stopped him. I went on to explain that I had spent three months studying the language at the Defense Language Institute. Apparently, he had not read my 201 File (my personnel file) and was not aware of my training prior to arriving in Vietnam. I was just another OCS grunt Lieutenant to him.

Then he asked about what happened after the river crossing. After a repeat of my previous explanation, he asked, "Did you really put your knife to your interpreter's throat?" So, he had talked with someone on the Vietnamese side of the operation,

"Yes Sir."

"Did you say to him that if he spoke or moved, you would kill him?"

"Yes Sir."

"Would you have really done that?"

He looked me in the eye as I replied, "Definitely, Sir. I would have slit his throat and left him lying in that stream." I don't think the S-3 liked what he heard in my voice or what he saw in my eyes when I spoke those words. With that, he said, "That will be all, Lieutenant." I did a formal about-face and left his office.

This S-3 and I had some history. He was the same S-3 that had told me no cluster munitions were deployed in my area when I was looking at one on the ground in front of me. What I wanted to do was ask the S-3 some questions: What was the real purpose of this mission? Was it a training mission to see how competent the commander was? Was there really intelligence about an infiltration trail? What was the real threat to us in that area? Was there ever an American unit scheduled to insert us? Why weren't you overhead during the insertion? Why wasn't your counterpart in the helicopter on Day 3 when I told you the day and location of the extraction was changed? Did you ever ask your counterpart if my information about the extraction change was correct? Why weren't you overhead on day 4 during the extraction? Why didn't you read my 201 files so you would know what my qualifications were before assigning me to this or any mission?

Lieutenants do not question a superior officer. A good NCO will teach a new Lieutenant when and how to work around the orders of a bad superior. The operative word is "when" — sometimes you can't work around them. All you can do, as we said in OCS is, "Salute and carry on."

When I got back to Dong Xoai that afternoon, the Major met me at the helipad with a jeep. Driving the short distance back to the team house, he told me to clean up before we talk. I showered and put on fresh fatigues and found the Major. He offered me a cold soda, and we talked about the operation. The Colonel had called the Major that morning and asked if I was physically fit because I had requested extraction during the operation. The Major said that he told the Colonel that I ran almost every day in the heat after lunch, and that I lifted weights several days a week. The Major went on to say he told the Colonel that our medic reported I had been sick for two days when I flew to Song Be for the mission. He also told the Colonel that my counterpart, Captain Ky spoke highly of me as his counterpart. I thanked the Major for the information and the support. Then he asked me if I would have really killed the interpreter…

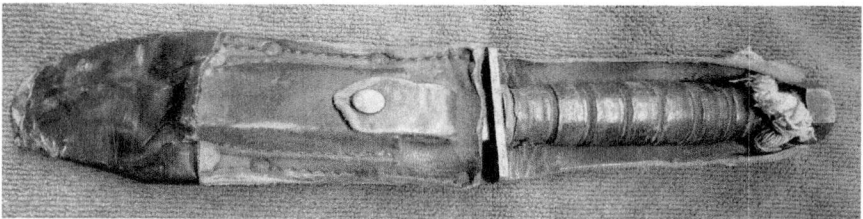

Figure 27.2   My sheath knife.

Story 28 — Letters

Receiving letters was always a great morale boost, but even if the special people back "in the world" wrote every day, their letters did not arrive every day. They would arrive in batches after some length of time when no letters were received. One error my wife and I made in our letter writing strategy was not numbering each letter as well as dating them. If we had numbered them, then we would know if any letters were lost. A case in point: A letter arrived and Linda (my wife) wrote somewhere in the body of the letter, "The mechanic said the damage was not too bad and the car would pass inspection, so I don't have to have it repaired right now." DAMAGE! WHAT DAMAGE? WHAT HAPPENED? WERE YOU HURT? HOW ARE YOU?

Of course, this generates an immediate reply from me which is one week there and her reply takes one week back — at best — so I have at least two weeks of wondering what happened. Being an optimist (it really helps to be an optimist in a combat zone), I assumed that since she was somewhat cavalier with the comment, she was fine, and she was concerned more about her studies than the car. At least I hoped that was the case.

Then there is the letter to West Virginia University about my college loans. In the 1960s there was a little-known federal loan program for Land Grant Universities, such as West Virginia University, that allowed me to go to college. The $300 ($2,500 today) they awarded me each semester paid for my tuition and books. Without that loan, I would have been in Vietnam five years sooner. The loan program allowed me to suspend the loan repayments while I was in the Army, but the paperwork required the signature of a commanding officer, so I filed it when I was in Basic Training. In the fall of 1971, I was hoping for an "Early Out"[40]

---

[40] See the Chapter 38 — "Why Are You Here?" for details on early outs.

for Christmas, so I wrote to the university asking for the paperwork needed to restart the repayment cycle for the loan. I received a nasty letter (which I have lost) telling me that they had no paperwork for me, my entire loan was past due, and without some form of immediate remediation, they would start foreclosure on my parent's house because they had co-signed the loan. Thank you very much, WVU, for such thoughtful consideration of an alumnus serving in Vietnam.

One of three things were possible:

- The original form I mailed to the university was lost in the mail (highly unlikely)

- WVU lost the forms (possible)

- Private Roberts and Lieutenant Roberts could not possibly be the same person even though the Social Security numbers (the official student number at that time) were the same (very probable in my opinion).

Included in the envelope with this letter was a form to request the suspension of my loan repayment. Wait a minute, this gets better. I filled the form out and it required my commanding officer's signature. I talked this over with my Team Captain, and we decided that in order to avoid another nasty letter and since the District Senior Advisor, a Major had just left for a two-week R&R[41], it would be better to have the Province Senior Advisor (PSA), a Colonel sign the form; he was our overall commander. I got on the work helicopter and flew to Province Headquarters at Song Be to get the form signed. The PSA was out of Province for the week so I met with the assistant PSA. Showing him the letter that accompanied the form, he agreed to sign it so I could put it in the outgoing mail that day. The assistant PSA was not military; he was a State Department professional with a rank of GS-14, which is equivalent to Lieutenant Colonel. So, he signed his name followed by his rank on the form. This probably would have been satisfactory to most people but not the people dealing with student loans at WVU. Several weeks later

---

[41] R&R: Rest and Recuperation - a two weeks leave almost anywhere in the world but the continental United States. Thailand, Australia, Guam, and Hawaii were popular destinations.

this mail arrived along with another form to fill out.

The scan of the letter (Figure 28.1) was from a fuzzy copy so here is part of the contents:

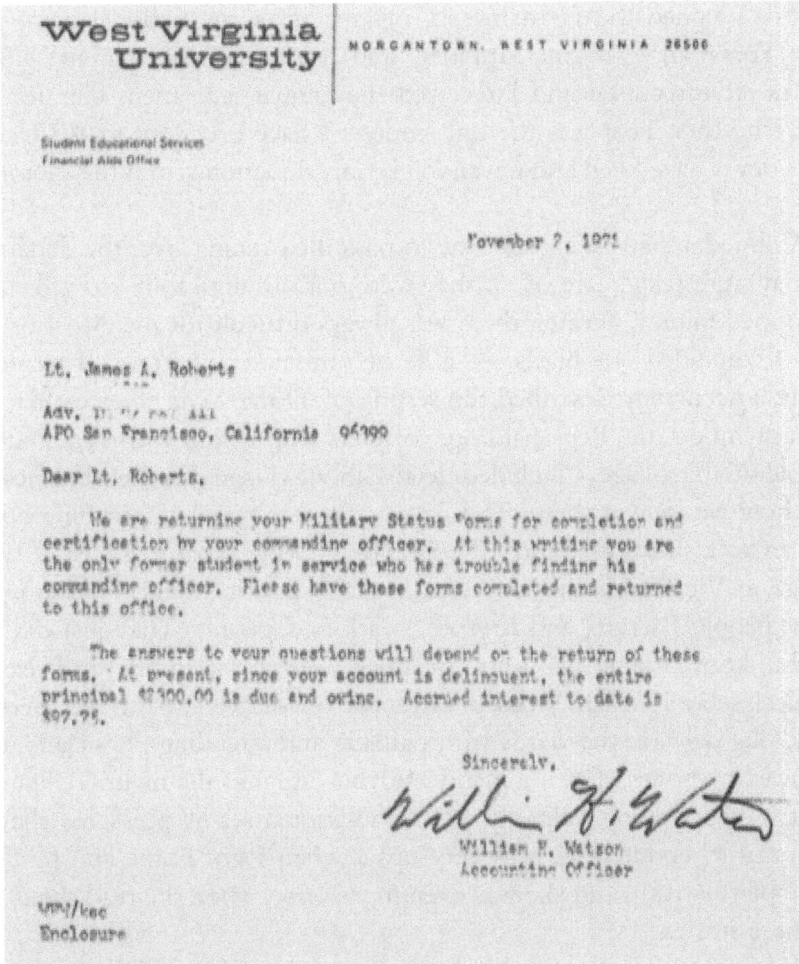

Figure 28.1   The letter.

We are returning your Military Status Forms for completion and certification by your commanding officer. At this writing you are the only former student who has trouble finding his commanding officer. Please have these forms completed and returned to this office.

The answers to your questions will depend on the return of these forms. At present, since your account is delinquent, the entire principal $2300.00 is due and owing.

So, I signed the form myself, making up some fictional name like John Yossarian[42], Colonel, Infantry and returned it. My parent's house was never foreclosed and I received the annual repayment bills for the next ten years. That was the only money I have ever sent to WVU, and there never have been and never will be any donations from this alumnus.

Writing letters was a good way to pass the evening after the details of the day were taken care of, or they were put off until tomorrow, or until it stopped raining. Writing them was always difficult for me. Most of my letters contained one big lie — a lie of omission, even those I wrote to Linda. I accurately described the setting of Dong Xoai, the weather, the team members, the Regional Force officers with whom I worked, and the people of the village. I included details about village life, their businesses, and how we helped them. The lie was the omission of anything about our tactical situation. Linda thought that Dong Xoai was just a small village in Vietnam with little actual military activity. Same for the many other people I wrote, and I wrote to a lot of people. They just did not need to know. I kept this from Linda because she was in her third year of medical school which focused on actual medical care for real people. Very long days on the wards with patients and attending physicians were followed by hours of reading and studying late into the night. Telling her what we were doing militarily was an additional set of pressures she did not need to endure. She was very upset when I got home and told her some of the truth, and she was even more upset when she read the drafts of these stories.

Because I tried to write Linda almost every night, preparation for an operation included the writing of a letter for each day I would be in the field. I dated these and gave them to our medic so he could mail one each day to make it appear that I was at Dong Xoai. I also wrote one letter

---

[42] John Yossarian was the main character in the book, "Catch 22".

that he never had to mail. Even though it was essentially the same every time, I wrote a new one for each mission. When I returned from the field, he would meet me, hand me the letter, and I would tear it to pieces.

That letter began something like this, *"If you are reading this, then you know I won't be coming back. I am sorry I broke my promise but…"* To this day, I am so very sorry I lied in those letters, but I would do it again.

I made cassette tapes, usually in the middle of the night when I was on radio watch. It was one way to pass some of that interminable time in the dark waiting for that Viet Cong with the explosive backpack to rush through the team house door. The tapes I made had the same "lies of omission" that the letters had for the same reasons.

There was one tape I made that was never mailed. This tape was in an envelope marked, "Doomsday," that was tucked behind some electrical wires next to the door of my room in the small team house. The MAT team knew about this tape and when it was to be mailed. As the name indicates, its fate was tied intimately to mine. Fortunately, it remained there for my entire tour. I destroyed the tape while I was at Tan Son

Figure 28.2   33 Quebec writing a letter.

Jim Roberts

Nhut airport in Saigon waiting for my flight back to the World.

Story 29 - The Doctor

Phuoc Long Province[43] was an extremely rural province. Air Force pilots based at the province capital of Song Be, who were doing bomb damage assessments (BDA) of B-52 strikes on the Cambodian border in the late 60s called the province the "Siberia of Vietnam" because there were no large cities and no night life. There was one hospital in the province, and it was at Song Be. The doctor at the province hospital provided care for the people in the immediate area. For the residents of the other villages and hamlets, the primary source of health care was usually the medics on the MAT teams.

Part of the MAT team's job was to visit the hamlets performing MedCaps (Medical Civic Action Patrols) to check on the health of the people. One or two of us and our interpreter would accompany our medic on a visit to a hamlet where he would conduct a clinic to care for anyone who showed up. If a villager needed more acute care, we would call Province and ask to have the work helicopter fly in to transport the person to the hospital at Song Be.

There was a volunteer doctor program during my tour. I have never been able to find any reference to this program in my reading, so this is what I remember — which is suspect at best. The program brought civilian doctors to the province for a tour of some specific length — possibly ninety days.

The doctor that I remember was a major pain in the backside for Province but in an interesting way. He was an older doctor (from our point of view then — today the memory is that he was not that old) who had a habit of grabbing his black bag and hopping on the work chopper regardless of where it was going and getting off at the first stop — unannounced. If no one (American) was there to greet him, he wandered

---

[43]Today it is named Binh Phuoc Province courtesy of North Vietnam.

around and found some place to set up shop. Speaking no Vietnamese and with no interpreter, he would hold a clinic.

Usually, the chopper pilot would call us and say that they were inbound with a passenger. Radio Watch would either walk or drive to the helipad to greet the passenger. When the passenger was the doctor, Radio Watch would bring him back to the team house, give him a cool drink and contact us. Unless we were doing maintenance on weapons or defensive positions at the team house or on an operation, we were out in the village. Radio watch would call us and let us know the doctor was in camp. Discussing this among ourselves over the radio, the medic and one of the other MAT team members would return to the team house and help the doctor get ready for a visit to a hamlet. The medic and the doctor would gather needed items from our medical bunker and the other MAT team member would pull some candy out of our stash from the SP packs.

Radio Watch would try to notify the District Chief's office and the RF (Regional Force) Commander's headquarters that we were going to a hamlet for the clinic, so the Hamlet Chief would know we were coming and could tell his people. If the Chief announced our arrival, it would appear that he had arranged for our visit adding to his standing in the hamlet. Arriving unannounced at a hamlet could be seen by the Chief as an affront. We had three interpreters working with the District Team and the MAT team. If none of them were available, this notification could be difficult. One time a MAT team member and the doctor walked over to the RF headquarters to try to explain what was happening. Using hand gestures, the doctor's stethoscope, and pointing to the hamlet on the map, the personnel at the RF headquarters got the idea and made the call.

The three (possibly four if we had our interpreter) of us would drive to the hamlet, where the Hamlet Chief would be waiting for us. He had announced our coming and sent messengers to those in the fields around the hamlet to come in if they needed to be seen. When we arrived, I held up a box and the children rushed me. They knew from past visits that the box had candy. While I passed it out to eager hands, the doctor and the medic laid a poncho out on the jeep's hood and set up their clinic. When the children had their candy, I returned to the driver's seat in the jeep and watched the clinic. Except for helping apply a bandage on a cut or scrape, my job was done.

When everyone was seen, we would say goodbye and return to the team house for either lunch or a beer (soda for me). [44]

While this was happening, Province would be calling everyone on the radio asking a simple question, "Have you seen the doctor?" There was always an exasperated sound to this call because it was almost a daily occurrence. Had the doctor been in the Army, the Colonel would have court martialed him. Radio Watch, not wanting to lie to Province would desperately try to find someone else who had not actually seen the doctor to answer the radio so an honest denial could be made. Eventually his location would be determined and a message left for him to return on the work ship before it returned to Ben Hoa. We liked the doctor.

---

[44] Montagnard hamlets could be a different story as told in the Story #1.

Story 30 - Rubber

The rubber plantation, Thuan Loi has a special place in the history of the Vietnam War. In 1965 the camp at Dong Xoai was being fortified by Navy SeaBees for the Special Forces A Team 342. While work was

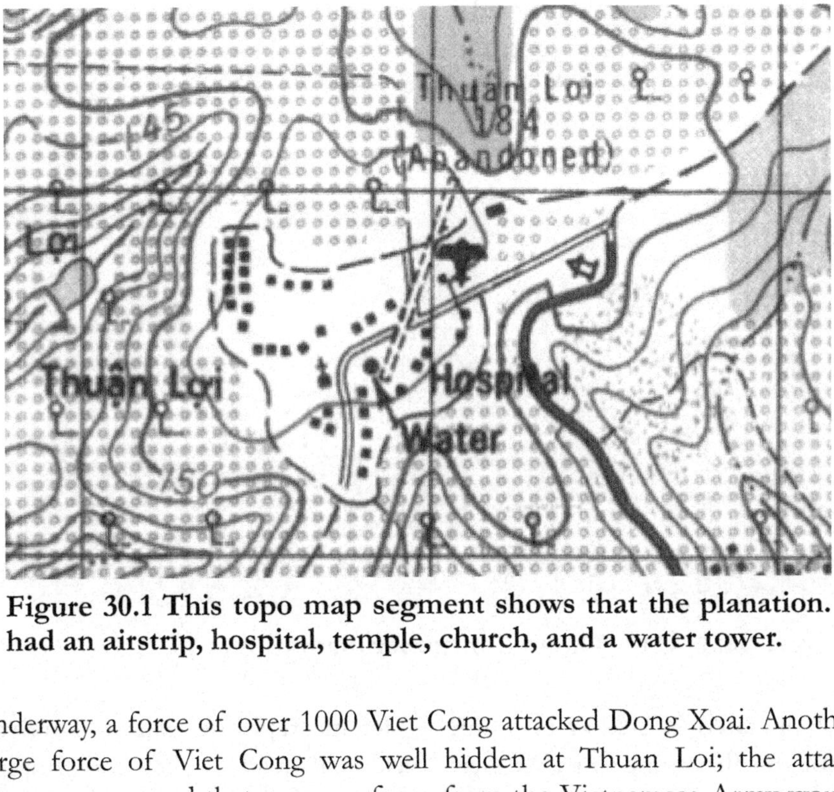

Figure 30.1 This topo map segment shows that the planation. had an airstrip, hospital, temple, church, and a water tower.

underway, a force of over 1000 Viet Cong attacked Dong Xoai. Another large force of Viet Cong was well hidden at Thuan Loi; the attack planners reasoned that a rescue force from the Vietnamese Army would land there to relieve Dong Xoai. They were right. When most of the rescue force landed, the Viet Cong opened fire on the helicopters as they settled down to discharge the last lift of troops. By the time the fighting was over at Thuan Loi, the Vietnamese lost over 300 soldiers along with 2 American advisors, several helicopters, and their crews. The water tower marked on the Thuan Loi map (Figure 30.1) was the position of a hidden .51 caliber heavy machine gun that wreaked havoc on the helicopters.

Each of the Districts in Phuoc Long Province had a village with a collection of hamlets. The French and American wars had driven most of the population from the rural areas to these villages for safety and protection. Our topographic maps marked most of the rural settlements as "Abandoned" or "Destroyed," as shown on the cover and in Figure 30.1 showing the Thuan Loi rubber plantation. Thuan Loi was owned by the French corporation, Michelin; it was about 6 KM (3.5 miles) north of Dong Xoai.

Figure 30.2   The Thuan Loi rubber plantation.

I operated in rubber one time — let me rephrase that — I moved through rubber one time. We were tracking a squad of Viet Cong hoping to find an overnight camp and some supply caches. Tracking the Viet Cong could be risky. The Regional Force (RF) Captain felt the squad was at least a day ahead of us, meaning that we would not catch up to them. If the squad was only an hour or so ahead of us and they determined that we were following them, they might decide to ambush us. The rubber plantation would offer an ideal location for such an ambush. That was our thinking when their trail took us into a rubber plantation that was considered "old" rubber — the plants were too old to be financially worth harvesting the latex sap that is used to make rubber products. Because it was old rubber, the trees had not been thinned, and the under growth was not cut back. Once we entered the trees, it was DARK. Worse yet, it was like a house of mirrors but there were no mirrors.

Rubber is planted in a pattern the Army would call, "Dress Right and Cover Down" meaning that the trees were aligned in perfectly straight rows and columns like a formation of soldiers marching in a parade. Inside this pattern of rubber trees, there was no forward or back or right or left. Diagonals looked no different from rows. Looking in one direction was exactly like looking in any direction. If you got separated from the column of moving soldiers, finding it could be difficult, if not impossible. Since we were not following a straight line of trees, a compass was our best friend. Radio transmission was limited due to the dense growth. It was the perfect place for an ambush. We moved carefully but quickly through the rubber trees looking for an ambush or booby traps with an urgent need to get back into the daylight as soon as possible. We weren't ambushed, encountered no booby traps, and never caught up with the Viet Cong. Eventually, we did find daylight along with a cache of rice.

Michelin had long been rumored to be paying the Viet Cong a "tax" to be left alone. The company had begun a project at Thuan Loi to restart rubber production. A French national was on site as the manager and was directing Vietnamese workers in the reconstruction.

The Major decided that someone needed to visit the work site at Thuan Loi each week as part of the preparation of his weekly report to Province on economic development in the District. He wanted the plantation visited every Thursday morning so the progress could be included in his report that was due on Friday. A little more than six kilometers north of Dong Xoai, it seemed like a simple task. But simple tasks in a combat zone are frequently not so simple; patterns and routine can get you killed. One of the things the Special Forces NCOs at Ft. Bragg stressed repeatedly during training was to avoid setting patterns. We heard more than once, *"Assume you are being carefully watched, even when you are in camp. Charlie (GI slang for the Viet Cong) knows how many steps it is from the wire to your bunk. He can find it blindfolded. He will watch you and search for a pattern. If he finds one, he will use it to kill you."* The easiest pattern is to always do something at the same time on the same day of the week. That is exactly what "checking Thuan Loi every Thursday morning" was — a pattern which had been followed for 3 weeks.

There was another problem with this weekly inspection plan. The Major chose the Intelligence Team to do the checking. The Intel Team was supposed to avoid unnecessary risk of capture because they knew what the RF Vietnamese Intelligence Team knew about the hidden Viet Cong assets in the village, as well as knowledge of any agents we might have working inside the Viet Cong. Avoiding the risk of capture meant that they should not be traveling without security to and from Thuan Loi.

Added to the errors of setting a pattern and the uncalled-for risk of capture, another rule was being broken: "Do not stand out as an American — try to blend in as much as possible." Granted it is difficult for 6' Americans to blend in while standing in the middle of a group of 5' Vietnamese but we tried. The District Intel Team stood out in another obvious way — they did not have an Army issue Jeep. They had a civilian version built by Jeep that vaguely resembled the Army Jeep but was painted a bright John Deere tractor green, which did not exactly blend in with the olive drab green jeeps the Vietnamese and the MAT team drove.

For some reason the battery on the Intel jeep was dead on Thursday morning of week #4. We do not drive at night and if we did, we would not have used our lights, so they were not left on. Maybe someone left the radio on — but there was no radio in the Intel vehicle… Instead of jump-starting their vehicle, the District Team NCO put a charger on it, so the inspection trip had to wait. Jump starting the vehicle would not guarantee that the battery would have enough charge to restart the jeep for the return trip to camp.

The battery charge was not quite finished when we heard a muffled

Figure 30.3   The Army Jeep (top) and the Intel Jeep.

bang — an explosion? Radio Watch took his position with our interpreter and waited for a call on the radio or the land line from the RF command with information and letting us know what they needed us to do.

Silence.

No scurrying troops.

No vehicles moving out of the camp loaded with armed soldiers.

Maybe an animal stepped on a mine on the edge of the perimeter?

Finally, the radio came to life — Province called asking to "meet us Green" — use the scrambler — so they could talk openly. The Major went to the bunker to take the message. He returned with the story. The explosion was apparently a command detonated mine that was used to attack a civilian automobile on the road to Thuan Loi. There were two probable dead: a French National who was a Vice President of the Michelin Rubber Corporation and his driver. They were traveling to Thuan Loi to inspect the recovery work that was ongoing at the plantation. Worse yet — the Vice President was a member of the Michelin family. Since the victims were French Nationals, the Vietnamese were not responding in any way to the deaths. They were leaving that to the French Embassy, and evidently, this was causing somewhat of a diplomatic flap in Saigon. Apparently, a flap that had quickly worked its way down to Province. Province instructed us to take two body bags to the site and recover the bodies. We were to return them to camp where the work helicopter would pick the bodies up for transport to Saigon, so they could be transferred to French Embassy officials. We were to provide two officers to act as diplomatic escorts for the transfer in Saigon. And the two officers should "dress appropriately." Great! Now exactly what day in the Team Captain's ROTC or my OCS training did they cover how to be Diplomatic Escorts for the dead? Not everything was in the manual. So, we figured we would play it by ear. As for dressing appropriately, clean jungle fatigues would have to do.

We hooked up the trailer to the MAT team jeep, and four of us: the MAT Team Captain, the Team Medic, our interpreter, and me along with two body bags left camp heading north towards Thuan Loi. It was a short drive to the ambush site.

A black Citroen was sitting in the road, and Popular Force (PF) platoon members from the nearby outpost were in the bush checking both sides of the roads. There were no bodies to be seen. We inspected the car finding a few shrapnel holes on the rear passenger side door and the rear fender and fresh blood on the rear seat.

There was a blast location on the side of the road. The device appeared to have been similar to, if not an actual, US Claymore mine — a device that explosively fires about 700 steel ball bearings at a high velocity like a large shotgun shell. These are detonated by a person using a battery of some sort. Apparently, the Viet Cong were a bit late in triggering the device because only a few of the pieces of shrapnel hit the car. The PF solders' movement through the brush eliminated any chance of finding the position from which the mine was triggered.

Through our interpreter, we learned from a PF Sergeant that the casualty was in the rear seat. The driver was not wounded. Furthermore, a French National, possibly the Michelin manager at Thuan Loi, had rushed to the site, picked up the body, and was transporting it and the driver to Saigon. We were too late. We returned to camp and reported to the Major who reported to Province; we heard nothing further.

I wondered if Michelin asked the Viet Cong for a tax refund that year or at least a credit from the Viet Cong for next year. I also wondered why the Intel Team jeep battery just happened to be dead. Had it not been dead one or both of the Intel Team could have been. Patterns can kill you. And I never got to add Diplomatic Escort to my resume… sigh…

Story 31 - Visiting Saigon

The job of advising for MAT Teams operated on many levels and at many places. One of the places was Saigon. Dong Xoai was a short flight via Air America to Ben Hoa followed by a helicopter ride to Saigon. We went there to straighten out pay issues, personnel matters, medical conditions beyond the Team Medic's skills, and to guide villagers through the process of receiving a grant that had been awarded to them. Our presence helped them avoid having to pay "extra fees" during the process.

Figure   31.1 Businesses at Dong Xoai.

The trips with the villagers were one day trips since they did not have a place to stay overnight. For some of them, it was their first trip in an airplane and on a "may bay whop whop" — the Vietnamese slang for helicopter[45]. Sometimes the grant was for money to set up or improve a small business, and other times it was for paperwork to take delivery of

---

[45] Helicopter translates in Vietnamese as, "may bay truc thang."

some serious machinery.

There was an element of enjoyment sitting at an official's desk with the villager as the paperwork was being processed and hearing something about money owed right now to finish the process. At that point I would butt in with a simple comment such as, "Tien noa?" — "What money?" When the startled official looked at me, I would continue, "Toi noi ting Viet." — "I speak Vietnamese," and then watch the blood drain from the official's face. This ended any extortion right then and there. The villager would return home with everything to which he or she was entitled.

Saigon trips without a villager were usually good for one or two overnights whether it was necessary or not. Once the actual reason for the trip was satisfied, the remainder of the time was a chance to visit the PX for items needed back at Dong Xoai[46], maybe an "American" hair cut

Figure 31.2   Bunk room at MACV Annex.

---

[46] The PX sold liquor which I could not buy through the general store, so I usually had a shopping list for liquor from the other team members.

though the barbers were still Vietnamese and to run other errands.

It was also a chance to try to call home. The USO had a place in Saigon where this was possible but rather unpleasant. Call time was strictly limited to three minutes. The procedure was straightforward: Wait your turn. When you're up, you enter the phone booth but leave the door open. It remains open until the party on the other end accepts your collect call. At that point, you close the door, and the next soldier in the line starts timing you on the clock next to the booth. When your three minutes are up, he knocks on the door and you are obligated to hang up right then. There is no, "Wait a minute," or "Just a bit more, please." You hang up. If you have the time, you can go back to the end of the line and repeat the process, but the line was always long — day or night.

A Saigon trip early in my tour took me to the US hospital next to the MACV (Military Advisory Command Vietnam) Annex. I was being checked by two different doctors. When Doctor-1 was done, his assistant showed me to a lounge because it would be a while before I would be seen by Doctor-2. It was a comfortable room; air conditioned with nice furniture. I was the only one in the room, so I nosed around. There was a phone on an end table with a paper under it. Among other things it said, "Long Distance Operator, dial 32" … Why not?

It was Saturday morning[47] here and eleven hours behind or Friday evening in Philadelphia where my wife, Linda was going to medical school. I picked up the receiver and dialed 32. A female voice came on and said, "What is the number you want to call?" I gave her Linda's phone number and in short while a phone started ringing; it was picked up and Linda said, "Hello." That's it! No waiting line, no time limit, and apparently no collect call charges. And no one came in while I was talking. We spent a good bit of time on that call — a real treat that was quite unexpected. I made a note of the location of this room in the hospital for use on future trips to Saigon. Sometime later Doctor-2 sent for me, and I was done by noon.

Most of the offices that I had to visit were in the MACV Annex.

---

[47] Many services throughout Vietnam ran 24 hours a day; 7 days a week. Weekends did not exist in Vietnam.

Among other facilities, the annex had a bunk room for company grade MACV officers[48] where I could always get a bed, bedding, and a locker to secure my stuff. This was used by officers who were just arriving in Vietnam, preparing to leave Vietnam, and over-nighters like me. Accommodations were spartan but they were clean, there were no rats, no mosquitoes or other bugs, and it was air conditioned. AND the showers had HOT water.

Mixing new arrivals with seasoned advisors had some interesting effects. A Tactical Officer from my OCS[49] company was bunking there before he DEROSed, when a number of us from the same OCS company came into country heading to MAT teams. He had just finished eleven months on a MAT team and had some good advice to offer along with a realistic image of what an assignment on a MAT team entailed.

Another reason to spend some extra time at the Annex was the food at the cafeteria. It was outstanding — at least outstanding when compared to what we were eating at Dong Xoai. Don't get me wrong. Tei Lai, our cook was very good, and we ate well but it was not American food. Even food we purchased through our supply channel was prepared by our Vietnamese cook in a Vietnamese manner. And we could not buy enough food for one month through our supply system. Much of what we ate was purchased in the village markets by our medic and cook. The cafeteria had real milk which was a delight. It also had ice cream — another delight.

Eating at the cafeteria, I stood apart from almost all of the other soldiers. It was a visual difference that was striking. The standard uniform for most soldiers was jungle fatigues whether they were in the jungle or in a staff job in a rear area. Only a few soldiers in certain jobs wore khaki uniforms. Most of the soldiers in the cafeteria wore very clean and nicely pressed jungle fatigues that looked almost new. Some appeared to have

---

[48] Captains and Lieutenants.

[49] A Tactical Officer or TAC is the Officer Candidate School equivalent of a Basic Training Drill Sergeant only much tougher — this one was the toughest of the six "Tacs" in my OCS company.

been starched. Mine were clean but very faded with dark permanent stains and were definitely not ironed. At Dong Xoai we wore a fresh set of fatigues every day unless we were out on an operation. Our house maids would scrub our fatigues by hand with a stiff brush on a washboard. It only took a few weeks of this washing for a pair of jungle fatigues to take on a well-used patina.

Figure 31.3   Notice the white US ARMY strip over the pocket and under my CIB on my shirt in the picture above. It used to have the same dark green color of the new jungle fatigues when it was issued.

There were no clothes lines on which they could hang our clothes to dry, so they used what was available — barbed wire. The barbed wire occasionally made small triangular tears in the fatigues which enhanced the appearance of heavy use. Combine the faded light green color, the wrinkled material, a few permanent stains, the small triangular tears, and, in my case a Combat Infantry Badge over the faded US ARMY tag on the shirt and I looked very different when compared to almost every other soldier eating there.

Usually, I ended up at a table by myself. The only men that I can remember joining me were wearing fatigues that looked like mine. I have always wondered if I should have seen this separation from the others as a point of honor. Or were the others thinking, "Except for a different toss of the dice at the Army Personnel Office in Washington, that could be me…"

Figure 31.4.   Barbed wire — our clothes line. The figure in sky in the upper left corner of the picture is a Sky Crane helicopter carrying a 155 mm Howitzer from Dong Xoai back to Ben Hoa. The American artillery unit was being deactivated on the day this photograph was taken and its equipment was being turned over to a Vietnamese unit.

Story 32 - Outnumbered 10 to 1

The Army prefers lopsided battles as long as the lop is on the side of the Army. 10 to 1 is a good ratio. You should be able to win the fight with minimal casualties and equipment loss. 1:1 is going to be a tough fight and the outcome is not clear. The skill of the leadership, the quality of the soldiers' training, and more importantly, the hearts of the soldiers will determine the outcome. But this is not a fight a good leader seeks out. Ego is paid for in lives.

Dong Xoai was in the south of the province. The province capital, Song Be was to the north and east. The area west of Dong Xoai was very swampy. The area east of Song Be had dense jungle and steep slopes — the beginning of the foot hills of the Central Highlands. If you want to set up an infiltration route running from the Ho Chi Minh "highway" in Cambodia south to an area called War Zone D, taking a line that runs west of Song Be and east of Dong Xoai was your best route of travel. The black line on the map in Figure 32.1 shows a favored route. Cambodia is near the top of the map. The circles at the top right are centered at Song Be. The circles at the bottom left are centered at Dong Xoai. The larger circles were the maximum ranges for American artillery units that were no longer in Vietnam. The smaller circle around Dong Xoai was the maximum range for the two Regional Force (RF) 105 MM howitzers and our field radios.

That area provided somewhat easier movement. Some of the land had been cultivated for rubber plantations by companies such as Michelin when the area was part of French Indochina. Agent Orange spraying had thinned other areas. The French and American wars had destroyed many of the rural hamlets and the infrastructure of the rubber plantations. The only humans in these areas were a few Vietnamese lumbermen, Montagnards collecting rattan, and the Viet Cong.

The District Intelligence Team working with their Vietnamese

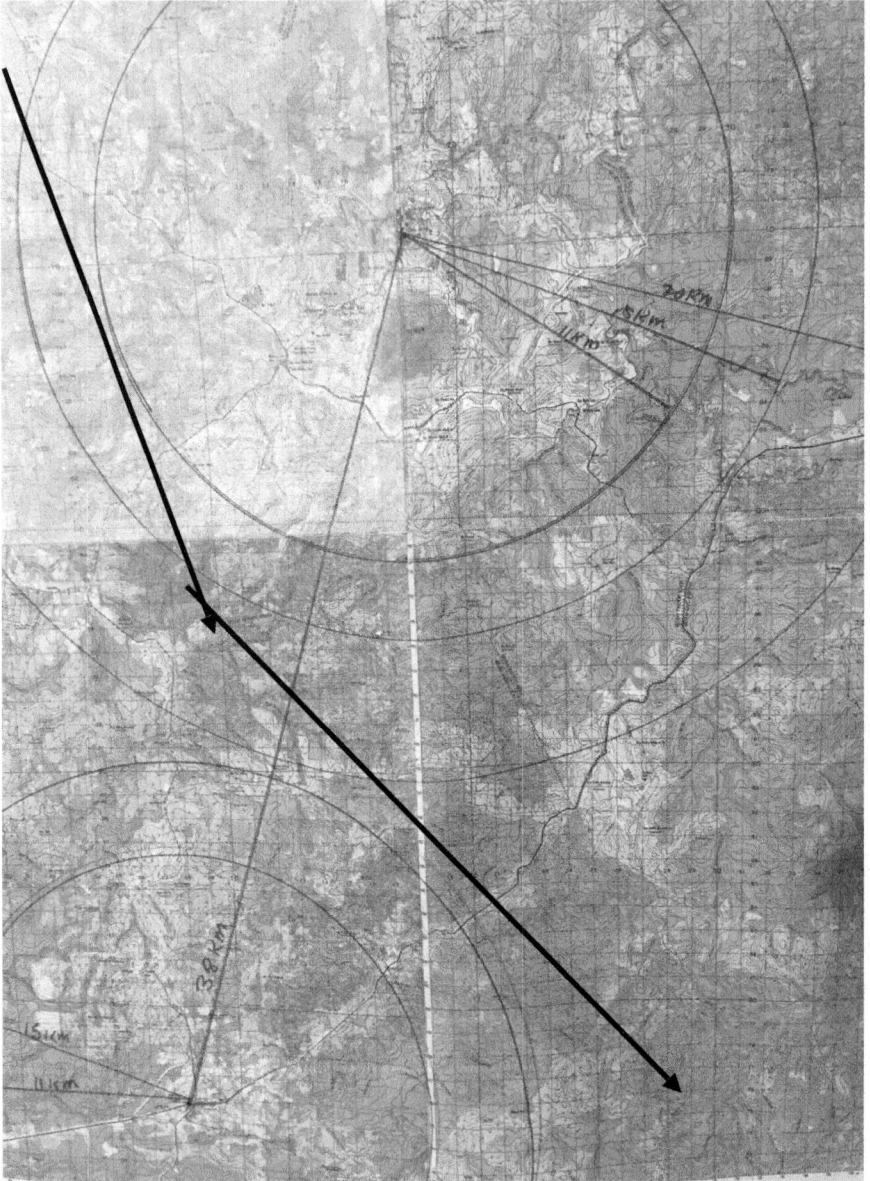

Figure 32.1   Topo Map showing artillery ranges for Song Be and Dong Xoai. The dark line is the infiltration route.

counterparts received information about Viet Cong movement in this area; usually from Montagnards who hated the Viet Cong with a vengeance and were more than willing to provide us with information. Their information was the basis for many of the operations around Dong Xoai.

A series of these Montagnard reports generated a sense of dread in the Regional Force (RF) command and the advisors at Dong Xoai. The reports started coming in over the course of several days from different groups of Montagnards. Their reports from areas north along the Cambodian border mentioned soldiers in twos and threes. A report from further away from the border had them going up to form squad size groups. One from an area close to Dong Xoai indicated the squads were joining up forming companies. A much closer report had them singing as they moved through a fairly open area. By the time these reports were collated into something meaningful, it was estimated that we had group of about 2500 soldiers, possibly North Vietnamese Army regulars moving just beyond our artillery range (the smaller circle in the lower left corner on the map in figure 32.1 — about 11 KM). We requested an

Figure 33.2 33 Quebec in the rear seat of a Bird Dog

aerial observation, and Province arranged for the recon. An 0-1 BirdDog landed at the airstrip outside Dong Xoai, and I climbed into the rear seat for the flight. The jungle was thin but not thin enough to positively identify movement, however there appeared to be signs of areas that were trampled. One way to know what is down there is to fly low and slow to let them shoot at you. Then, if you have artillery that can reach the area (and they don't shoot you down), goodbye Charlie. We did not have artillery, but I did have an M-79 grenade launcher, so we flew low and slow, but no one shot at us; I really did not see anything. If they were there, they were well trained. I was flown back to Dong Xoai in the late afternoon without incident. It might have been possible to spot fires after dark but the Bird Dog had to return to base before nightfall.

We called Province to ask for any assistance from American units that might be available, ranging from some type of high-tech reconnaissance such as SLAR (Side Looking Airborne Radar) along with Air Force tactical air and Army helicopter gunships — anything to bombard the area this mass of troops was thought to be in. There were two problems with the request:

ONE - Several working rubber plantations were in the area we wanted to saturate with ordinance. Bombing and strafing the area would require the Army pay Michelin for damaged rubber trees — apparently, they "bleed to death" if they are hit by bullets or shrapnel. Without firm visual evidence that the enemy was there, the attacks would not be supported by higher up.

TWO - Much of the requested support was not available or no longer in country making the first problem moot.

Province relayed this information and wished us good luck. GOOD LUCK! THAT'S IT! Why didn't they just say, "Call us in the morning if you're still alive?"

This is the night I learned to REALLY drink coffee. Before that I usually just drank it when I was in the field. To this day, 49 years later I still drink coffee — not the good stuff; not Starbucks. Just bad coffee, because the coffee I drank that night was bad — very bad, and I learned to like it.

Apparently, this mass of troops wanted to attract as little attention as possible because they moved around us causing us no problems of any type. I accompanied the RF troops to reconnoiter the area after they had passed, and we found signs of movement of a large number of troops and several overnight positions. This was reported up to Province and Province reported it up to III Corps headquarters in Ben Hoa but, to my knowledge no action was taken.

It is possible that these troops were part of an Easter Offensive launched in February, 1972 that hit numerous places in III Corps and overran Dong Xoai once again. The RF companies, with the aid of the Vietnamese Air Force were able to retake Dong Xoai in October, 1972 demonstrating that the training provided by the special forces and maintained by our MAT team had not been lost.

Story 33 - Medivac for the DSA

The MAT Team Captain was out of camp on compassionate leave. Things had been quiet for a while, and we had no intelligence to indicate this would change. What we did not know was that an American convoy including artillery ammunition was south of Dong Xoai traveling north. Reaching Dong Xoai, the convoy would turn west heading for a US base in the neighboring province where several artillery units were located. Their senior command must have felt that even though the road had not been cleared, the area through which the convoy would pass was secure enough to send it with minimum security elements. This meant that the convoy needed to reach the US base before dark. The convoy had problems from the start and was running behind schedule. Traveling faster than the roads dictated in an attempt to make up time, one truck ran into a ditch spilling its load of artillery ammunition. None of the shells exploded but they scattered widely and had to be collected and moved away from the truck by hand before it could be pulled out of the ditch. Once the truck was out of the ditch and back on the road, the ammunition had to be reloaded on the truck; again, by hand. We pick up the story at this point:

Call #1 - Radio: The convoy commander calls us when he realizes that the convoy is not going to make it to the US base before dark. He was not sure the convoy would get to Dong Xoai before dark, and he requests our help because there were no US units close enough to provide security. Our District Senior Advisor (DSA), the Major takes the radio call. The Major replies that his team will discuss the options and get back to him.

Call #2 - Land Line: Following a discussion among the Major's NCO, the Intelligence Captain and me, the Major calls the Regional Force (RF) commander and asks him for enough soldiers to provide a security perimeter around the convoy. The convoy is well within range of the RF's 105 MM howitzers and the MAT team would be there as liaison between the RF and the Convoy Commander. The RF Commander agrees and says his troops could be loaded and underway in thirty minutes and at the convoy location within the hour. It was a simple plan that would be easy to execute. Besides, there was no intelligence indicating any Viet Cong activity south of Dong Xoai.

Call #3: Radio: The Major calls the Convoy Commander and makes the offer to arrange for an RF security perimeter for the night. The Convoy Commander rejects this outright. He replies that he does not trust the RF troops and wants to be inside the Dong Xoai perimeter tonight. Irritated, the Major signs off and remarks out loud, "Just who does he think will be providing security at Dong Xoai?"

Call #4 Radio: After another brief discussion among the three of us, the Major calls and suggests sending an RF company to escort the convoy to Dong Xoai. The Convoy Commander rejects the idea too. The Major signs off throwing the handset down on the desk in disgust. This was new for him. He had always been the calm member of both teams who had always reacted to negative events in a smooth, even manner. But his disgust did quite accurately reflect our collective reaction to this outright prejudice against the RF by the Convoy Commander.

The Major has not been himself lately. A few days earlier, I was on radio watch and took a call in the evening with a report on something trivial and before I could reply, the Major, who was reading a book in the nearby briefing room called out to me, "Tell them, 'Roger'" ("Roger" means, "I understand"). I didn't need to be told that. This behavior was becoming familiar to the rest of the team. Over the past few weeks, he had gradually begun to try to make every decision; on even the smallest detail. He was becoming an obsessed micromanager. Everyone had been at Dong Xoai long enough to deal with the routine happenings. And we knew when to consult the Major or either Captain. We did not need to hear, "Is it time to switch the generator?", "Better check the gas in the jeeps," "We need to check the ammunition for the machine gun." This wasn't typical behavior for the Major, and we were not sure what to do. Right now, practical and workable options were not being accepted by the Convoy Commander, and the Major, who was usually rather relaxed and laid back was beginning to show an extreme level of agitation.

Call #5 - Land Line: The Major calls the RF commander to tell him to have his troops stand down, and he would get back to him. He thanks the RF commander before terminating the call.

Call #6 - Radio: The Convoy Commander calls and asks us to provide artillery illumination over the road while they move to Dong Xoai. The Major replies, "Wait one, OUT." Illumination rounds[50] were like gold. They were difficult to obtain, and other units did not want to share them. They only provide illumination for about sixty seconds — one minute. We doubted that the Convoy Commander had any experience calling in artillery, and the process would be very clumsy. The Commander would have to encrypt the coordinates of the place he wanted the shell to illuminate. We would have to decrypt them, give them to our interpreter who would call the RF howitzers on a land line to provide the coordinates.

Call #7 - Radio: The Major calls the Convoy Commander and suggests that he send the MAT team to call the artillery. We had pre-plotted targets around Dong Xoai and we could call a shift from those points to the place the illumination was wanted, "From Cadillac, right 2000, drop 500." Cadillac was a previously plotted artillery target. "Right 2000" meant shift the target 2000 meters to the east and "drop 500" meant shift the target 500 meters south. There would be no need for encryption. Our interpreter would call it in directly to the RF howitzers. It would be a much simpler and much quicker procedure. The Convoy Commander rejects this. The Major angrily replies, "Wait one, OUT."

Call #8 - Land Line: The Major calls the RF commander and asks for illumination support. The RF commander replies that they may not have that many illumination rounds. Then the RF commander asks who was going to replace the shells? They were difficult to acquire and his supply chain would not replace shells used in support of an American unit.

---

[50] Illumination rounds explode high above the ground igniting a magnesium flare that burns brightly illuminating the ground as it slowly descends by a small parachute. It burns out before it reaches the ground.

Call #9 - Radio: The Major calls the Convoy Commander and asks if he can replace the illumination rounds for the RF company. The Convoy Commander replies that he can and that the convoy is getting ready to move. He presses for a confirmation his request. The Major again replies, "Wait One, OUT."

Call #9: - Land Line: The Major calls the RF commander, tells him that the rounds will be replaced, and asks for the support. Somewhat reluctantly (my opinion), the RF commander agrees.

Call #10 - Radio: The Major calls the Convoy Commander telling him to call the illumination as needed but that the number of rounds available is limited.

Call #11 - Radio: The Convoy Commander calls to transmit coordinates. The Major writes down the encrypted coordinates. I am standing there with the whiz wheel ready to decrypt the coordinates when the Major takes it out of my hand and does the decryption. He sets the wheel down and walks over to the map on the wall to check the

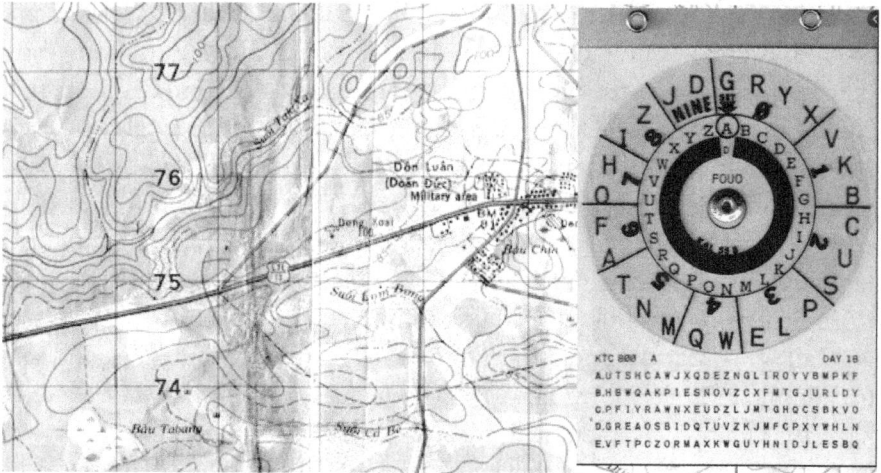

Figure 33.1   A Topo map of Dong Xoai and a Whiz Wheel. Whiz Wheel image courtesy of Ralph Simpson.

location. Five of us are standing there and it is as if none of us exist. He is someplace, somewhere else, alone and has to do everything himself. As the Major turns to walk back to the radio, his NCO says something to him that we cannot hear. The NCO is ignored — the Major does not hear him.

Call # 13 Land Line: The Major hands the coordinates to our interpreter who relays them to the RF howitzers. We hear the round going out less than two minutes later.

Call #14 - Radio: The Convoy Commander calls and says the round is off target. The Major replies, "Are you sure of your location? We put the round over the road where you asked for it." In a **COMMAND VOICE** the Major's NCO says, "Sir, the coordinates you gave the RF artillery are not over the road," apparently repeating what he had quietly said to the Major a moment ago. The sergeant's voice brings the Major back to this reality. He slowly sits down at the radio watch position, and puts his head in his hands and begins to breathe — rapidly — too rapidly — hyperventilating. Somewhere our medic finds a paper bag and moves to the Major's side eventually getting him to breathe into the bag.

Call #15 - Land Line: The Major's NCO picks up the whiz wheel, decrypts the coordinates again and hands them to our interpreter to relay to the RFs. A second round is fired.

Call #16 - Radio: The Convoy Commander calls to say the round is on target.

The medic manages to get the Major who is still breathing into the bag, but less heavily, on his feet and slowly moves him towards his room. The Major's NCO takes the Major's place at the radio, decrypting the incoming coordinates from the Convoy Commander for the following rounds and relaying them through our interpreter to the RF artillery unit. The convoy proceeds towards Dong Xoai.

Eventually, the convoy pulled into our perimeter having encountered no problems. The Intelligence Captain and I left the team house to find the Convoy Commander and tell him where to deploy his trucks and where his troops should set up for the night. When asked about replacing the illumination rounds fired, the Convoy Commander said he would have them unloaded at the artillery position in the morning adding that he would give the RF artillery two rounds for every one they fired.

While we were outside, the medic and the Major's NCO checked on the Major. When we came back in, the news was not good. He was no longer hyperventilating but was lying in his bunk clutching his poncho liner[51] tightly in his hands and almost incommunicable. With the Intelligence Captain's concurrence, the medic called Province and explained the situation to their senior medic. The senior medic replied that a Medivac helicopter would be called in the morning, if the Major's situation was unchanged.

Figure 33.2   A Medical Evacuation Helicopter (medivac).

The next morning the medic called Province and reported that the Major's condition had not improved, so Province was called for a Medivac. When it arrived, the helicopter's medic examined the Major and, with the help of the MAT medic moved him onto a litter. He was still clutching his poncho liner tightly when the two medics carried him out of the team house and placed the litter across the back of one of our jeeps. The two medics held the litter in place while the District NCO slowly drove the jeep the short distance to the helipad where the medics put him on the helicopter. That was the last time any of us ever saw the Major. He never returned to Dong Xoai and he was not replaced —

---

[51] A poncho liner is the Vietnam equivalent of an Army blanket. Camouflage covering, very light, easily compressed into a small bundle to fit into a pack, and capable of conserving body heat when it is wet.

Vietnamization was at work…

The Major's NCO packed up the Major's gear and personal items and took it to Song Be. The MAT Team Captain would learn upon his return to Dong Xoai that he was now the acting District Senior Advisor for Don Luan District for the remainder of his tour.

Story 34 - YB DEROSes

I am not a drinker. I did not drink in high school or college — I just did not like the taste of alcohol. In Vietnam I had the occasional beer when it was dictated by the social situation. I drank the fermented, vile tasting Montagnard brew and managed somehow, to avoid hepatitis that frequently accompanied it. Today I have the occasional glass of wine or can of beer. I can honestly say that I have been drunk one time in my life — the evening before YB left Dong Xoai to DEROS.

YB was the Intelligence Sergeant for the District Team at Dong Xoai. He and I became friends the night we had a close-up view of a Viet Cong mortar shell exploding in his room. His being a member of the District Team and my being on MAT team meant that we did not operate together in the field, but we both manned the same machine gun position during attacks on the camp. We have remained in touch throughout the years, and he has been commenting on these stories as they were being written.

Figure 34.1   YB in the village.

He was the youngest member of the team and was always in a good mood with a positive outlook — even when things were bad. This quality followed him to the village. When YB was in the village, he was usually surrounded by kids.

By June, 1971, Vietnamization was in full swing. American units were being pulled out, and the number of Americans in Vietnam was being reduced as rapidly as the immediate tactical situation allowed. The Army was offering "Early Outs" for soldiers who wanted to attend college. The GI Bill allowed many soldiers to request the College Early Out, and YB was one of them. His early out moved his DEROS of early December to August. Processing out at Province and at MACV annex usually took 7 to 10 days, so YB was leaving tomorrow morning on an Air America flight to Song Be. The Major was gone; medevaced and not replaced. The MAT Team Captain was in the States on compassionate leave. The Intelligence Captain, who had a bit of "flower child" in him, was in

Figure 34.2 The Intel Team Captain at one with a grenade.

charge, so, we had a goodbye party for YB.

That is not quite accurate — We had a PARTY! We managed to drink all of the beer remaining in the cooler (we were running a bit low before the party began) so we sent the interpreters to the village to buy Ba Muoi Ba ("Beer 33")[52], which was almost as bad as the Montagnard brew. By the time we were drinking the local swill, we had turned the volume on an old 8 track tape player up to its max and were dancing inside the team house. Some of the Vietnamese soldiers crept up to the windows to peek in to see what was going on. At one point, the District Team NCO was wearing a plastic chair as a party hat. Every advisor was involved (the interpreters had disappeared after buying the resupply of beer), and it was not a good image for the Army to be presenting to Vietnamese counterparts. Had we been attacked that night; we would have been of no use. In fact, we probably would have been a hazard.

Every night at midnight, Radio Watch had to re-key a radio scrambler called the "Green Machine." To re-key the scrambler, the key had to be set. Setting the key involved opening up the two-part, metal key-box which had 64 small rods that had to be moved to different marked positions. Once these rods were positioned, the key-box was closed and inserted into the green machine. If the rods were set correctly, we could talk to Province "in Green" meaning that the voice transmission was scrambled so the Viet Cong could not listen in. If the rods were not correctly set, the green machine emitted a loud screeching sound. The specific settings for each rod were part of the Signals Operating Instructions (SOI) we received monthly. The settings for each day were on a separate page in the SOI. The rods were spring loaded and snapped back to their "rest" position when they key was removed from the green machine. If one rod was set incorrectly, all of them had to be reset.

On a normal night, Radio Watch usually asked someone to help him set the key; one person would read the settings and the other position the rods. Two sets of eyes usually meant that the key would be set right the first time. Province did not appreciate hearing the loud screech on their end of the radio call.

---

[52] When the North took over, they kept the brewery going but added an additional 3 to the name: Beer 333. Beer 333 is for sale at several beer distributors in the Pittsburgh area and, NO! I have not tried it.

Two sets of eyes may be better when things are normal but not when everyone is drunk. We tried to set the key. We tried several times and all we got was screech. And Province was beginning to ask what exactly was going on. Thank goodness it was night or someone would have flown down on the work chopper only to find us incapacitated. Finally, someone said we were having generator problems and would call back tomorrow morning after we fixed the problem. Province seemed ok with this — maybe they were just tired of the screeching sound.

Several of us decided to sleep outside on the bunker because we did not want to get sick in our bunks. Our maids would clean up almost anything but not that. It had started to rain during our party so we got ponchos, covered ourselves with them, and slept outside in the rain on the cold, wet concrete of the bunker roof.

The next morning was my first and only hangover. I promised myself, "Never again!" and I have kept that promise. Someone did start the generator and we managed to see YB off at the air strip. I am not sure how, but we were all there. The Intelligence Captain had his Vietnamese counterpart contact Province to report that we were still working on the generators and would check in as soon as we got them running. There was a problem with this lie; the Vietnamese used our generated electricity to power their radios. If they could communicate to Song Be, we should be able to do the same. To my knowledge, no one at Province pointed out this inconsistency. Regardless, the lie allowed us to get some sleep in our bunks that morning and recover to some degree from the previous night.

Several of us managed to set the Green Machine key positions and someone else checked it to be sure they were right. Another someone called Province in Green and all was well. I think the reason given to Province was that we had water in the gasoline used to run the generators. Whether or not Province actually bought the story was unclear, however nothing was ever said, and that night was never spoken of by anyone who was there. YB remembers very little about this party. He does remember everyone seeing him off at the air strip that next morning. It was a night to remember but the fog of 49 years, aided by alcohol and hangover, makes it difficult to do so with any accuracy.

Story 35 - YB's Return to the World

told by Gary Weinreich — YB

About half way through my one-year tour of duty in Vietnam, word came down from the powers-to-be that they would be granting early outs for certain reasons. They would grant up to 90 days off your enlistment if you had signed up for college and needed to start before your enlistment ended. I applied for acceptance to Cal-State Long Beach and was accepted for the fall term beginning in early September of 1971. I then applied for a College Early Out and that was approved. Instead of going home on 4 December, 1971, I would be going home on approximately 4 September, 1971.

As that early September date approached, I grew anxious to get home. When the Major found out that I was not going to be replaced, he told me in front of everyone that he would not have approved my early out had he known that there was not going to be a replacement for me. As it turned out, the Major soon had some medical problems and he was put on a medivac helicopter, and we never saw him again — he was not replaced either. Many men were going home early to get troop numbers down because of the Vietnamization program.

I am told that they threw a going-away party for me that included a lot of music and drinking. I don't remember much of that party. I said my good-byes to my Vietnamese counterparts and packed my bags. An Air America (CIA run airlines that we often used) Porter landed at Dong Xoai airstrip for the first leg of my travel to Song Be and then to Saigon and out-processing. I remember almost all the guys from both Advisory Team 67 and MAT-111 came out to the airstrip to say, "Good-bye" to me. It was a sad/happy day as I would miss all these guys greatly, but was excited about going home. And they were left behind in harm's way.

On the way to Saigon, the Air America pilot became lost in a thunderstorm and had to turn around. I thought that some force was trying to keep me in Vietnam. Finally, he was able to return to a course for Ben Hoa and we made it there safely.

Out-processing at MACV headquarters was accomplished over a couple of days. I turned in my Army equipment and finally got a seat on a "freedom bird" bound for the "world." All of us home-bound GIs were subject to several drug searches. When the plane (a Boeing 707) finally took off, there was cheering from the many passengers. The flight home took somewhere around 23+ hours with a refueling stop in Guam. Guam was a large rock with a long runway down the middle of it as I recall. Lined on each side of the long runway were fully loaded B-52 bombers with drooping wings. It was from Guam that a lot of the bombing of North Vietnam took place. Another reminder of the war that was still going on.

Our destination in the states was Travis Air Force Base near San Francisco. I remember we all had a grilled steak dinner upon arrival there. I can't remember the time sequence, but since I was about to muster out of the US Army, I was put on a bus to Oakland, California where the US Army out-processing center was located. For some reason, the bus dropped a number of us short-timers a block or two from the out-processing center. I was wearing my Army kaki summer uniform, as were the other guys. During the short walk, which was in the day time, I was accosted by two different cars of drive-by anti-war protesters, both of which pulled up to the curb right next to me and the first car's occupants called me a "baby killer" several times. Soon a second car pulled up to the curb and the occupant's spit at me, yelling anti-war slogans. I continued to walk on and did not respond to them, but their comments really hurt. I felt like I was dropped off in the wrong country — this couldn't be the America I had left 9 months earlier. But it was. The anti-war protest movement had really grown. I immediately thought of all my fellow teammates that I had left behind in DX. I knew that neither I nor any of my teammates had done anything worthy of being called a "baby killer" or being spat upon. And my friends were still in harm's way.

At the out-processing center, several hours were consumed with paperwork, pay, etc. I remember they took my class-A uniform jacket, which I had hardly worn, and cut a large "X" with a razor blade in the back of the jacket so it could not be used again. Then they issued me a new uniform to wear home. I flew from San Francisco airport to Orange County Airport for a reunion with my wife. Cindy had brought along her sister-in-law, Karen, whose Air Force FAC[53] husband was killed earlier in the war in Vietnam. That was a little uncomfortable: I came home alive, and her husband did not.

It was tough to adjust to life in the states. Remember, I went from Team 67 in the jungle boondocks of Vietnam to the busy life in southern California in less than a week. No gunfire at night. No artillery fire. Just lots of vehicle traffic and busy freeways. Nobody trying to ambush you.

A few days after my return to southern California, I attended my first classes at Cal-State Long Beach after a two-hour freeway ride to the campus. I wandered across the university commons (a large grassy area) in search of one of my next classes. Inadvertently, I stumbled right into the middle of a very large anti-war rally going on in the middle of the commons area. Many long-haired anti-war protestors were there with pot smoke, lots of anti-war music, and anti-war chants filling the air. Of course, I was the only one there with a military haircut, and I was the brunt of many angry stares. Again, I felt like I was in the wrong country, and my mind was immediately turned to my fellow soldiers still at DX, who were not baby killers or worthy of spitting. That really hurt me. All I could think of were my fellow soldiers still serving at DX.

I eventually did survive and made the transition to peace time in the USA. About 15 years after my return, I did come down with a good case of PTSD associated with a lot of depression. I looked up LT who was living in western Pennsylvania, and we visited the Vietnam War Memorial the spring of 1983, the year after it was dedicated. I eventually had 10-12 counseling sessions with a VA psychologist, and I did put that PTSD behind me. I have talked with numerous other Vietnam vets who received much of the same treatment as I did upon their return to the

---

53 FAC: Forward Air Controller - a pilot who flies a small unarmed airplane and directs attacking Air Force jet aircraft in support of American ground troops.

states. I have talked with Vietnam vets who were spit on and called "baby killers" as I was, some were physically assaulted, many were verbally assaulted, some had fresh dog feces thrown at them, and many encountered "social distancing" where people in airplanes or airport terminals did not want to be seen sitting next to a Vietnam vet. It was tough to try to understand why people in your country hated you so much for doing your job. Even some of the WWII veterans' organizations like the VFW and American Legion at first were not very friendly towards Vietnam vets. That's why many Vietnam vets will welcome one another with the, "Welcome home" that we did not get from the general public.

Figure 35.1 Gary at the Vietnam War Memorial.

Story 36 - Being Useless

Have you ever felt terrified and completely useless — so scared and useless that all you could do was sit and shake uncontrollably, hoping you could just control your bladder? I have! One time, for about 10 seconds before I stopped feeling sorry for myself and did something useful.

Day 1: By early November, MAT 111 consisted of me. Everyone else was gone. Only two members remained on the District Advisory Team. Having no MAT 111 NCO with whom to operate, Province was sending me on operations in the other districts with other NCOs. For the most part the operations went "OK," where "OK" meant that the NCO and I got back in one piece. By this time there were very few American units (artillery, gunship, medivac) available for support. For the most part we were really on our own. Rapport with a Vietnamese counterpart, such as a Company Commander, takes time to develop. Working with a different Regional Force (RF) company on each mission did not provide time to develop that rapport. What was always a lonely war had become even lonelier.

The radio call came in right after breakfast. I was going to another district to run their radio watch while the two remaining advisors; the Intelligence Captain and his NCO, were going out on an operation. I would be there between three and five days. So, I packed accordingly. I grabbed my laundry bag put things in I would need in their camp. I got my web gear ready. I did not carry my .45 pistol in the field, but for this I attached it to my pistol belt, which already had the usual gear attached. I put my compass in one chest pocket and my SOI (Signal Operating Instructions), whiz wheel, and a small notebook and pencil in the other. I did not have a map so I would have to get one at the District.

A few minutes later the helicopter called, saying it was ten minutes out, so I put on my web gear, picked up my M-16 and the laundry bag, and walked out to the helipad. When the bird settled onto the "H" in the center of the pad, I started to walk out to board the chopper and was surprised to see the Province Senior Advisor, a Colonel jump out of the cabin and head towards me. He looked at me as he approached and said, "Lieutenant, where is your gear?" I pointed to my laundry bag and said, "Here, sir." His reply was terse, "I meant your rucksack." I feebly replied "Sir, I am not going to the field and…" He cut me off, "You are leaving this camp, this district, aren't you? You are going to the field, **Lieutenant**. Get your ruck now!" I replied, "Sir, Yes Sir!" returning to my OCS formalities.

Fortunately, 33 Tango taught me to pack my rucksack immediately after returning from an operation, "You never know when you are going need it." He was right. I dropped my laundry bag where I was standing, ran back to the team house, and picked up my rucksack. I jogged back and was standing in front of the Colonel within a few minutes, but I don't think he was impressed.

The Colonel and I had no interaction during the flight to the other district. The chopper landed, and we got out. I followed him to the waiting jeep and got into the back. The ride to the District Team house was just as quiet.

Once we got to the team house, I learned that I would not be standing radio watch but going to the field — not as the senior advisor with a supporting NCO but as the supporting officer for the Intelligence Captain — he would be the senior advisor.

Let's consider this a moment… The Intelligence Captain was not a field officer. He would have had some field training somewhere in his career but it would have been at a very basic level and at least two years ago. Had he ever operated in Vietnam? Can he read a topo map? Had he carried a pack weighing 60 to 80 pounds? These were just a few of my thoughts.

The Colonel and the Captain discussed the operation while looking at a map on the wall in the team house. I was just an observer, so I took some notes. When they appeared to finish discussing the details, I asked if I could ask a question. They looked at me, and the Colonel coolly replied, "Yes?" I asked what the radio frequency and the call sign of the Vietnamese commander would be. I received two glares as if to say,

"Why in the world would you want to know that?" I put the small pad of paper and pencil back in my shirt pocket and said nothing further.

The Colonel took his leave and was driven back to the helipad. I introduced myself to the Intelligence Captain and asked him some questions about the RF companies we would be accompanying. Then I asked him where I could get a topo map of the area in which the operation was based and he replied, "I have one; that will be enough." I said, "Sir, my Sergeant and I always carried our own maps in case we got separated. I would prefer to have my own map." The Captain huffed, "Lieutenant, one will be sufficient." So, I spent much of the remaining time until the mission mounted up studying the map on the wall, trying to memorize as many of the terrain details about the mission AO (Area of Operation) as possible.

The mission was "simple" on paper. The district's two 105 mm howitzers would be towed by trucks in a convoy and set up for fire support of the operation. This was going to be a big operation — bigger than any I had been on, involving elements of three companies. Platoons would patrol the area around the mission base on day two, three, and four, with the artillery supporting them. Day 1 would be spent traveling to the operation base, setting up the defensive perimeter, and positioning the howitzers.

When it was time, we got into the jeep (the Captain was driving) and joined the RF company. I started to get out when the Captain asked, "Where are you going?" I replied that I was going to travel with the Mission Commander's Executive Officer (XO) and asked if he was going to ride with the Mission Commander. His reply surprised me, "Of course not. Get back in." So much for advising protocol. I decided then and there to keep my mouth shut — unfortunately, a decision that was quickly forgotten.

Instead of driving at the lead of the convoy, we were near the rear. Even though the road had not been cleared of mines and booby traps, travel to the area that would serve as a base for the operation was uneventful save for the numerous deep holes and ruts in the road. Fortunately, the convoy traveled at a fairly slow speed.

The RF companies seemed well trained, and the Mission Commander and his XO, neither of whom I had met, directed the preparations of the perimeter at the operation base very professionally, and the defenses were in place in short order. The Captain called in to the District where his NCO was standing radio watch to report that all was quiet. We set up apart from the command group near the two howitzers; away from the center of the perimeter — not a place I would have chosen.

I asked the Captain if he wanted to walk the perimeter with me, and his reply was a curt, "Why?" OK — So I got out my entrenching tool and started to dig a hole. This was the first hole I had dug in my tour, but with nothing to do, it seemed like a good use of my time. The ground was dry and higher than the water table, so it would not fill with ground water, and the digging was easy. The hole was deep and round enough for me to sit in. Kneeling, I could see over the edge and fire my weapon if that ever came to pass. When I climbed out, the Captain called over asking, "When are you going to dig my hole?". My reply was somewhat terse, "When you make Colonel, Captain." With that he asked if he could borrow my entrenching tool. As much as I wanted to say that I don't loan vital gear on an operation, I tossed the shovel to him.

I walked over to the Mission Commander's location and introduced myself with my best-spoken Vietnamese; he seemed surprised and pleased. He asked me to walk the perimeter with him. His troops were well trained. Their positions were well situated, and the machine gun emplacements had good fields of fire. Somehow, they had acquired anti-personnel Claymore mines which were usually not available to the RF companies and positioned them in front of their well dug in defenses. I commented on this to the best of my ability as we walked, and he seemed to appreciate what I was trying to say. I felt better about this operation for the first time.

I walked back to our position to find that two more holes had been dug. The interpreter was just finishing his. He remarked that he had also dug the Captain's hole and did not seem too happy about that. Our radio was on the ground between the Captain's and the interpreter's holes, well out of my reach. I guess that is why I did not need any call signs or radio frequencies. It was very clear that I was here just to be the required second American, which was standard operating procedure in the province; no American went to the field alone. I began to realize that the toughest thing on this op was going to be doing absolutely nothing.

After eating my C-Ration supper, I asked the Captain if he wanted me to take the first watch tonight. He replied, "What do you mean?" So, I explained that in the field the two Americans usually took watch through the night in two hour shifts so one of us would always be awake. The Captain replied that we were not going to do that. "You can stay up all night if you want to." We slept on the ground next to our holes. It was a quiet night until the 105 howitzers began H&I (harassment and interdiction) firing shortly after midnight. The place the Captain had chosen for our position was very close to the guns, so we received a lot of noise and good bit of the concussion when each round was fired. That is why I would have set up elsewhere. Once the firing was over, the night returned to quietness.

Day 2: The next morning after breakfast I noticed the Mission Commander gathering the company commanders and platoon leaders for operations orders. The Mission Commander was wearing his gear so it looked like he was going to accompany one of his platoons. I went over to the Captain and asked him if we were going to accompany the Mission Commander. I received the familiar curt, "Why?" In return I thought about asking the Captain, "WHY are we here?" but Lieutenants are never supposed to ask "Why?" "Why" is above our pay grade. We are trained to ask only, "What do you want done? Where do you want it done? When do you want it done?" How it's done is my problem — that is why I am wearing a silver (actually black) bar on my collar. But, "Why?" as I said, is above my pay grade.

So, we sat on our butts doing nothing. There was no shade to speak of in the perimeter and it was hot and humid. The perfect day had the perfect setting to do nothing.

In the late afternoon, the platoons returned from their sweeps and moved to their positions to eat their dinners. I decided to do the same thing. I always carried two clay like blocks of C-4 explosive in case something needed blowing up. Because C4 burned much hotter than the heat tabs the Army provided, I broke off two small pieces from one block and started heating a can of C-Rations and a canteen cup of water. The Captain looked over and asked me what I had there. I threw him a packet of heat tablets; I was in no mood to share the good stuff.

Early that night small arms fire began; then the explosions. When I rolled into my hole, the shaking started. It took me about ten seconds to get control of myself. Looking back, the fear was there because I had absolutely nothing to do. NOTHING! The radio was not the answer; it was out of reach. The hole was not a fighting position for me, unless we were being overrun. Firing my weapon from the hole would only shoot into the backs of the RF soldiers around me. Besides that, I had nothing to shoot at! Doing nothing was truly terrifying. Finally, I managed to pull myself together and crawled out of my hole moving slowly to the Captain's hole. He was sitting in his hole doing the same thing I had been doing just a few seconds ago. I turned and started moving towards the Mission Commander's location. Listening to the sounds as I was crawling, I realized that there was only M-16 and M-60 machine gun firing. There was nothing that sounded like AK-47 fire. There were no "POPs" that a mortar tube makes when it fires, and the explosions sounded more like grenades than mortar shells. As I was crawling as close as possible along the ground, I realized that all of the fire was outgoing. There was no incoming fire. I stood up and brushing off the dirt on my fatigues, walked the rest of the way to the Commander's position. He was on the radio and sounding very angry. He saw me in the moonlight as I approached his position and waived me in saying, "Toi xin loi" — "I'm sorry." He explained that apparently one of the squads on the perimeter opened fire on an animal moving in front of their position. "Cam on" — "Thank you" was my reply and I returned to our position. The Captain was on the radio talking to his NCO back at their team house reporting, "... incoming mortar fire and small arms fire but the probe was pushed back. No causalities..." Ok, fine. I dropped down next to my hole onto my poncho, pulled my poncho liner over me and slept the rest of the night.

Day 3: It appeared that this would be a repeat of Day 2, but by mid-morning I was proven wrong. An RF soldier approached and talked to our interpreter who turned to me and said the Mission Commander wanted to see me. I picked up my M-16 and followed the RF soldier and our interpreter to the Commander's position. He explained through our interpreter that the he wanted me to accompany his XO back to the village to pick up some important documents. I replied through the interpreter that this was ok with me and told the interpreter to tell the Captain where I was going. The interpreter returned to our position and the XO signaled me to follow him over to a jeep. Laying in the front passenger seat was an M-60 machine gun and two cans of ammunition were sitting on the floor. He got into the driver's seat and pointed to the passenger seat motioning me to get in. I put my M-16 in the back, picked up the M-60 as I got in. I opened one of the ammo cans and pulled out a belt of machine gun ammunition. I loaded one end of the belt into the machine gun and chambered a round. Seeing the gun loaded, the XO exited the perimeter and took off at high-speed heading back the way we came on Day 1. Just the two of us, an M-60 machine gun, 400 rounds of ammunition, no radio and lots of holes and ruts in the road. I hung on to the gun and to the jeep. It was difficult but I managed.

We got back to camp with no problems other than a sore butt and a few other bumps. The XO went into the RF Headquarters office for a few minutes and returned with a dispatch case. He got in, and we pulled out of the compound but did not start back to the operation. The XO stopped at a bar and got out of the jeep. He motioned me to follow. I held up the M-60, and he pointed to the back of the jeep. I put the machine gun in the back and grabbed my M-16. Inside, the XO ordered a beer, and I ordered a coke — without ice. Ice in the village, when it was available often came with embedded insects included at no extra charge. A warm Coke would be just fine. After we finished our drinks, we returned to the jeep and headed back on the rutted road to the operation base; more bruises, more bumps and an even sorer butt. Like the trip to the village, the trip back to the camp was essentially uneventful. I am not sure why the Commander wanted me to make the trip. Other than carrying a machine gun, something any grunt can do, I did nothing other than bounce around in the jeep. Maybe the Commander was giving me a break from the Captain. I did not know then and still don't.

I limped over to our position to find that our interpreter had some RF soldiers weave thatched sun screens for his hole and the Captain's. Mine was in full sunlight. At least the Coke was refreshing and the rest of the day was quiet, save for the H&I fires that night.

Figure 36.1   A typical village bar.

Day 4: Much of the day was the same as Day 2, minus the evening fireworks because, we broke camp mid-afternoon and returned to the village. It was too late for me to catch the work chopper, so I spent the night and returned to Dong Xoai the next morning.

Back at Dong Xoai I received a radio call from the S-3 (Operations) Major at Province asking me to, "Meet him green". The S-3 asked me about the contact. I told him that there was no contact and explained what happened. The S-3 asked if I was sure, and I told him that I was at the Mission Commander's position when this was sorted out. There was no enemy activity of any kind. Then I broke the cardinal rule — I asked, "Why do you want to know?" The S-3 replied that the Intelligence Captain wanted a CIB because he was acting in an infantry position and was in contact.

"Sir, I don't think so…"

The CIB is my most valued award. I wear it today with pride. To earn the CIB, you had to be in an Infantry position at least 30 days and be involved in close contact with the enemy. A mortar attack did not even qualify you for a CIB. Someone had to be shooting at you.

Figure 36.2   The Combat Infantry Badge - CIB

Story 37 - The Thanksgiving Turkey

By early November, 1971, the count of Americans at Dong Xoai had fallen from the nine when I arrived to three. Two members of the District Advisory Team were all that remained: the Intelligence Captain and the District Team NCO. I was MAT 111. The other four members of the MAT team were gone; three had DEROSed, and the medic had been pulled back to Province because Dong Xoai was considered to be too exposed. Support from American combat units, namely helicopter support (medivacs, airlift, and gunship) was essentially non-existent. Militarily, things had changed during my tour from being a very lonely war to an extremely lonely war.

One day in mid-November, the District NCO found me and told me to call Province; the S-4 NCO (supply) wanted to talk to me. When I called in, the S-4 NCO got on the other end and told me that he would be sending a frozen 25 pound Thanksgiving turkey out to Dong Xoai; enough turkey to easily feed 25 people. Now, this might sound like a great treat for three soldiers far from home, but it presented some logistical concerns for us:

- Butane gas for cooking was becoming a problem. We had two tanks at Dong Xoai. One was empty and one was being used. When Province delivered a full tank, we would exchange it for the empty tank. This was almost a monthly event. With Vietnamization in full swing, Province was having trouble getting resupplies of butane. Running the gas oven for the four or five hours to roast the bird would not be a good use of what was becoming a scarce resource.

- The three of us could not really eat that much turkey. We discussed this among ourselves and decided to decline the offer. I called Province and asked to speak to the S-4 NCO. I told him that he could keep the turkey and serve it to the troops at Province. The Supply Sergeant replied that he could not do that. Apparently, someone much higher up in the

Figure 37.1   Tei Lai, our cook making supper.

chain of command — far above Province — had acquired the turkeys and ORDERED that they be delivered directly to the District Teams in the field. Province was also getting a small turkey but it would not come close to feeding everyone based at Song Be. I explained our concerns at Dong Xoai, but the S-4 Sergeant was not willing to disobey a direct order, and I don't blame him. There was no S-4 officer at Province, so I asked to talk to the S-2 (intelligence) or S-3 (operations) Majors, if either were available and signed off.

A bit later the S-3 Major radioed back, and I explained the situation. He replied that he would see what he could do. Apparently, he was able to convince someone up the chain of command that we would not be able to cook the bird and got permission to cook it for us at Province. We agreed that they would cook it, carve it, and send us three meals worth of turkey. The rest would be served to the soldiers at Province. This would be a win for everyone and, it would soon become an even bigger win for me with the S-4 NCO.

As it turned out, I was in Saigon on Thanksgiving Day and had a nice turkey dinner at the MACV (Military Assistance Command Vietnam)

Annex cafeteria. When I returned, the two advisors reported that three very hot meals with turkey and all the trimmings had been flown down by the work helicopter and that two of them enjoyed their meals, along with mine. Those three meals were probably some of the most expensive takeout meals ever delivered; three hot meals delivered by helicopter.

Story 38 - Why Are You Here?

It was the week of Thanksgiving, 1971. Things for me had moved beyond useless when it came to my being an advisor. I was the last member of MAT 111 remaining at Dong Xoai and possibly the last MAT Team member in Phuoc Long Province.

Recently I read (https://en.wikipedia.org/wiki/Mobile_Advisory_Teams) *that at this time in 1971 the number of MAT teams had been reduced from a high in 1968 of 487 to 66.*

On the recent operations with units new and unknown to me accompanied by NCOs with varying skills and experience, the only American I had talked to over the radio was the Province S-3 (Operations) Major when he happened to be overhead in the work chopper. There was no American support of any kind available: artillery, resupply, medivac, gunship, or airlift. There was no rapport between me and the Vietnamese unit commander, so my advice was not welcomed much less considered when it was offered. The interpreters for these missions were new to me and for the most part unreliable, due to their poor language skills, their unwillingness to tell my counterpart the truth, or their cowardice. As an RF soldier, Sgt. Yung, my usual interpreter, could not work with me outside his home district where Dong Xoai was located. I understood the risks when I enlisted and volunteered for Infantry OCS, but this had reached a point beyond ridiculous.

The Province S-4 (Supply) NCO and I had just worked out a situation with frozen turkeys and things were quiet. The Montagnards had reported no activity of any kind around Dong Xoai in the recent days, and Intelligence was not anticipating anything happening in the coming week. With this lull, I caught the Air America flight to Ben Hoa and a helicopter to Saigon on the Wednesday afternoon before Thanksgiving to try to call Linda (my wife), and to check on some paperwork.

The Army was trying to comply with the reduction of force mandated by the policy of Vietnamization. With the entire war effort being shifted to the Vietnamese Army, the combat operations of the American units were being reduced, and soldiers were being sent home. One mechanism being used to reduce the number of soldiers in Vietnam was the "Early Out" program that had various categories for the requests. YB DEROSed at the beginning of September instead of his original date in December by getting an Early Out for College. There was also an Early Out category for teaching jobs, and I was a science teacher before enlisting. Linda found a job for me at Girard College, a private school in Philadelphia where she was in her fourth year of medical school. All I had to do was be interviewed to get the job. She had sent me a letter with the qualified offer signed by the Headmaster of the school. Using this letter, I applied for the Early Out but had heard nothing back. At the same time, I applied for an Early Out in another category — Christmas, which was actually a category — the Army had to reduce the overall numbers of troops in Vietnam. I had heard nothing about that request either.

After checking in at MACV Annex and getting a bunk, I ran some errands. It was the wrong time to call Linda — her time was 11 hours behind so 5:00 pm here on Wednesday would be 6:00 am Wednesday at her home in Western Pennsylvania where she was for Thanksgiving. Calling her that early could be upsetting and besides, I had no information about an Early Out.

The next day was Thanksgiving, and I took it easy but did not leave the annex to tour Saigon. I did that when I originally arrived in Saigon in April and found that city's wartime scenes catering to American GIs in various ways designed to separate them from their money too depressing. The quiet of the annex suited me. Besides, the buildings were air conditioned. I slept in, had a late breakfast at the MACV Annex cafeteria which served good food. Then I had a mid-afternoon Thanksgiving meal of turkey carved in front of me, mashed potatoes, cranberry sauce, and other trimmings. And I had a glass of real milk. I had pumpkin pie and ice cream for dessert. Almost like being back home — nah... no way! But the food was good.

Very early Friday morning I went to Personnel to check my Early Out status. A very pleasant and young Specialist Fifth Class (Spec-5) called me up and told me to take a seat. I told him why I was there, and he asked me to wait a few minutes. With that he disappeared. A few minutes later he returned with my 201 file[54] — that was AMAZING to me; he actually found my personnel file and in less than ten minutes — it might be my lucky day.

The Spec-5 looked through my folder and frowned; maybe not so lucky of a day. He explained (you may need to read the following bit several times — it sounds like it came from a Monty Python skit): "Your original enlistment was for three years, which is to end on 29 June, 1972. Your commissioning as an officer committed you to two years of service after commissioning. That was on 15 May, 1970. This meant that you would leave active duty on 14 May, 1972, reducing your original commitment by 45 days. You will be separated from service on your DEROS, which is 1 April, 1972, which further reduces your original commitment by another 43 days for a total of an 88-day reduction. The Army would have to grant you another 89-day reduction of your original commitment to give you an Early Out for Christmas. That totals 177 days and that is too many days to qualify for the Christmas Early Out."

He went on: "As for your Early Out for Teaching, you have to have the job to qualify, but you only have an offer." I replied, "But I have the job, if I get out early and have the interview." He sighed saying, "But you can't get out early for the interview if you don't have the job — Catch 22.[55]" I repeated, "Yeah, right, Catch 22."

He offered me his hand and said he wished he could have given me better news. I thanked him for his time with all of this and asked if I

---

[54] Every soldier has a 201 File. It is their personnel file with all of the pertinent information about the soldier.

[55] *Catch 22* was a book by Joseph Heller turned into a movie starring Alan Arkin in late 1970. Set in the dessert in Northern Africa, the main premise is B-25 bombardier John Yossarin's attempts to get out of the Air Force. Medical regulation #22 said that to get out early, you had to be insane but if you asked to get out early, you just proved that you were sane — Catch 22.

would see him in late March when I DEROS. Frowning, he replied that he would probably still be here.

I took a slow walk to the Army hospital outside the gate of the Annex, where there was a little-known lounge with a telephone that I had found earlier in my tour. The phone was set up to call the states and there was no charge. I had used it several times to call Linda. I was hoping that at this early hour the lounge would be empty and it was. It was 8:00 AM Friday here so it would be 9:00 PM Thursday at Linda's home. I had said I would try to call about this time on this day in a letter sent last month.

I lifted the receiver, dialed 32 and the voice asked me for the number. A phone rang and Linda's voice was the nicest sound I had heard in a long time. After assuring her that I was fine, I relayed the news I had just received. Her reaction was not suitable for printing here — let's leave it at, "She was extremely displeased." We talked a good while longer, I promised I would try to call her at Christmas, and we said goodbye. I am not a drinker and besides, it was too early in the day to start. So, I returned to the bunk room and took nap. I was suddenly very tired.

Later I went to the Annex Cafeteria for lunch and returned to my bunk to get my stuff, so I could try to catch the afternoon flight back to Dong Xoai. There was nothing more to do here. The room had a bulletin board where notices could be pinned if the person was not there when the message arrived. As I moved to my bunk, a Lieutenant in similarly faded fatigues asked if I was Roberts. I nodded, and he said there was a message on the board for me. Nice of him — I would have never looked. The message was from the Spec-5 I had talked to this morning. It asked me to see him "ASAP." Now what?

I walked over to the Personnel shop, and he was at his desk. I walked up to him and before I could say anything, he looked up at me and asked, "Why are you still here?"

Totally confused, I replied, "Uh, didn't you send for me?"

"NO! I mean, why are you still in Vietnam?"

I wish I had a picture of the look on my face because I have no idea what it looked like — I just stood there staring at him. He went on, "After you left, I got curious and did some digging. Your team was deactivated six weeks ago. At that time, you had less than six months to go on your tour. Current policy is that any member of a deactivated unit with less than six months remaining on their tour is to return to the States. Simply put, you are not supposed to be here."

Me: "I never received any orders, and I don't know anything about this. All I know is that as my team members left, they were not replaced. Now I am the only one on the team."

Spec-5: "Now you know why. Your team has not existed for some time. Your Commanding Officer must have held your orders."

Me: "Can he do that?"

Spec-5: "Apparently. When do you want to leave?"

Me: "Are you serious?"

Spec-5: "This is not something to joke about."

Me: "How about tomorrow?"

Spec-5: "You have to clear your Province and Saigon. That usually take 8 to 10 days. Let's walk down to the booking office and see what's available."

Still dumbfounded, I followed him to the booking office which was just down the hall. The booking clerk said that he could put me on a flight this coming Thursday, if I could clear everything. The Spec-5 asked me if I could do that because if I did not, they would not let me on the flight. I replied that I would do it. So, they signed me up for a seat on flight United 284 to Travis Air Force Base leaving in the afternoon of Thursday, December 2. I was going home!

We returned to the Spec-5's desk, where I signed some papers and he gave me a list of things I had to do and forms that I had to have signed by appropriate people at Province and then here in the MACV Annex to make the flight. He said to return tomorrow morning after 5:00 AM when he would have signed copies of my orders, so I could begin to process out of Vietnam. I was going home!

I don't remember much immediately after that. There was no one in Saigon with whom I could celebrate. I decided not to call Linda today. I wanted those orders firmly in my hands before I made the call. I just remember that it was a very long day. I did check with the Air America office in Ben Hoa and reserve a seat on tomorrow morning's flight to Song Be. It would be tight but I should be able to make the call to Linda and get a chopper ride to Ben Hoa in time to make the flight. Besides, Air America would probably wait for me.

Saturday morning, I was up early — actually I did not sleep much that night. I was at the Spec-5's desk a bit after 5:30 AM, and he had my orders sitting on his desk. Apparently, they were printed overnight. He handed them to me and asked if I wanted him to send them through channels to Province. I told him to take his time. I did not want the Colonel to have a chance to sit on these. He smiled and said he would do that.

I went back to the hospital, to the lounge with the phone to call Linda. 6:00 AM in Saigon is 7:00 PM the previous day in the states. When I called her home, there was no answer, so I figured she was still at a family gathering. I made a second call to my parents who were home. After reassuring them I was ok, I asked them to call Linda's relatives and have them tell her that I would call her at her home about 9:00 PM. That nothing was wrong — I just needed some information.

They said they would, and we hung up. I would make the third call at 8:00 AM my time. That gave me enough time to run an errand. Then I went back to the annex, picked up the few things I had brought with me, checked out of the annex, and returned to the lounge to wait until 8:00 AM.

I called Linda at 8:00 AM my time, and she answered in a worried voice. When she said, "Hello" I replied, "I'm coming home, I leave this coming Thursday." That was essentially the end of the call. All I can remember is that she was no longer displeased. I said that I would call with details, and we hung up.

I got a ride to the airfield, hopped a chopper to Ben Hoa, and made the Air America flight with time to spare. As I was getting off of the plane in Song Be, the S-3 (Operations) Major who was apparently meeting another passenger walked up to me and said, "Glad to see you, Lieutenant. I have another mission for you. Be here tomorrow for a briefing." I replied, "Sorry, Sir, I have orders. I'm going home!" I did not wait for a reply. I had to find the Supply Sergeant to start clearing Province.

Story 39 - Clearing Province

My run of good luck continued. When I got off of the Air America plane at Song Be, there were several jeeps waiting at the airstrip, so I got a ride back to the compound. I had a packet of freshly printed orders in my hand that said, **"I'm going home!"** It was Saturday, and my flight was this coming Thursday. Processing out, better known as, "clearing" usually takes ten days, so I had a lot of work to do in less than half that time. Where to start?

I had to turn in everything that I had been issued at Province and get a form signed by the S-4 (Supply) shop indicating that I had done so. Anything not turned in would be charged against my pay. That might be a problem. Other than personal equipment issued to me when I arrived at Song Be, I had not signed for anything when I arrived in May. As the assistant team leader, I was responsible for all of the MAT team's equipment: jeeps (we were supposed to have two but only had one), trailers (ditto), field radios, M-60 machine gun, the team's conex (a secure lockable steel storage container that can be airlifted by helicopter), and its contents. We had the conex, and I knew what was supposed to be in it, but I had no idea what was actually in there and what was missing. We took out the tools when we needed to use them and returned them when we were done, but the contents were never inventoried. That was the catch — hopefully not a Catch 22.

When I joined MAT 111, the former assistant team leader was still here. He signed out at Song Be and apparently signed over the MAT team equipment to the S-4 shop. After the other Lieutenant left Dong Xoai, I got a call from the S-4 NCO asking me to come to Song Be and sign for the equipment. I told him that I would sign when the equipment was inventoried, so I knew what I was signing for. This meant that he would have had to fly down to Dong Xoai and go over everything in the conex with me. He never made the trip and never mentioned it again.

Maybe he did not want to venture out into the dangerous "boonies".

That S-4 NCO had DEROSed, and his replacement never mentioned it to me either. I got along well with the replacement S-4 NCO and had just helped him with his turkey problem for Song Be's Thanksgiving dinner, so hopefully, that would go in my favor. He was still at his desk when I knocked on the door of the S-4 shop. He looked up and asked what I needed. I explained the situation, and he checked his file cabinet. The only items on an inventory form with my name and signature were the field gear that was issued to me when I arrived: a rucksack, a hammock, a poncho liner, and a poncho, canteens, magazine pouches, gas mask, flak jacket, steel helmet. There was no mention of jeeps, trailers, a conex, or equipment. As far as the Army was concerned, all I needed to do was turn in the gear on the form, and he would sign it, clearing me at Province.

I said I needed to fly up to Song Be on the work helicopter tomorrow (Sunday) morning to get the Air America flight to Ben Hoa. He said that he would have the chopper stop for me at Dong Xoai on its way north and reserve a seat for me on the Air America Flight. He even went one further. He offered to meet me at the air strip to pick up my field gear and sign off on the clearance form. That Thanksgiving turkey was really paying dividends.

As I stood up to leave, he offered his hand and smiling said, "L T, you might want to hold on to your orders. The S-1 (Personnel) will find out you are leaving soon enough, when your orders come up through regular channels." I shook his hand, returned his smile and said, "Thank you." The Thanksgiving turkey had returned dividends far beyond what I could have ever imagined.

The work chopper flew me back to Dong Xoai in the early afternoon when it delivered the mail. I told the remaining two Americans that I was leaving, and we all had a beer to celebrate. Not anywhere near the party YB had when he left, but one of those per tour of duty was enough for me. When I arrived in May, advisors on the two teams consisted of 9 Americans and 3 interpreters. The two team houses had only a couple of unoccupied rooms. Now most of them were empty. For the Intelligence Captain and the District NCO, the war had become even lonelier.

They were happy for me but less than thrilled to have their numbers reduced by a third. I spent part of the afternoon cleaning my rifle and my gear and packing up what I had brought with me. I pulled my khakis out of my duffle bag; the uniform I had worn when I traveled to Vietnam from Pittsburgh in April. Also, in the bottom of the bag were my black oxford shoes and my field jacket. It was still cold when I left the States, and it will be cold when I return; I was glad I had the jacket with me. They had been in my duffle bag ever since I was issued my jungle fatigues in Saigon. The khakis had not been cleaned and did not look too good. I had removed my brass and other insignia from my shirt and put them in a black sock that was stuffed into the oxfords. Fortunately, the shoes had not mildewed. I am not sure why but they still looked pretty good; no longer spit shined, but they were wearable. I would get the kakis and the field jacket laundered, a CIB and MACV patch sewn on the jacket, and the shoes polished in Saigon.

I went over to the Regional Force (RF) company headquarters to tell Captain Ky, the RF Company Commander with whom I worked that I was leaving, and he insisted I have a drink with him to say goodbye. I had been having tea with him once or twice a week when we were in camp, and we helped each other with our language skills. His English was fairly good when I arrived, and it seemed to be somewhat better now. He poured two glasses of something from a bottle that looked expensive. I have no idea what it was but it looked good, smelled strong, and tasted even stronger. Then he handed me a new blue beret with a silver bar on it. The blue beret was the ceremonial head gear for the RF companies. The silver bar on it meant that he had been planning for this moment. With that, he shook my hand, and we both spontaneously saluted each other — the first salute I had thrown in a long time. That left one more dinner, one more night, and one more breakfast in Dong Xoai — all three were good.

The next morning, the District NCO offered to drive me the short distance to the helipad. I piled my duffle bag and rucksack on the hood of the jeep — the same place YB had put it when I arrived and climbed in for the thirty-second drive. The radio on the jeep came alive as the pilot called to say he was inbound. The NCO took a smoke grenade and

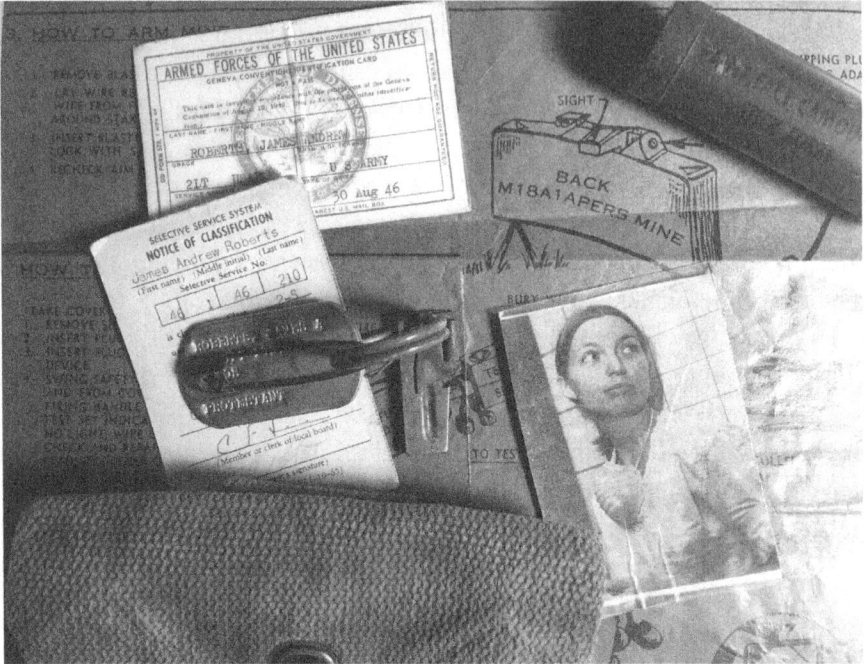

Figure 39.1 The grenade ring and pin still holds my dog tags, a black bandolier safety pin, and my P-38. Part of an old draft card is under the dog tags. My Geneva Convention ID card is above that. The picture of my wife was carried in my shirt pocket every day I was in Vietnam. The background is a Claymore mine bag with illustrated instructions for using it.

handed it to me — the last grenade I would throw in Vietnam. I pulled the pin, tossed the canister off to side of the helipad and put the pin in my pocket. I still have that pin; it holds my dog tags and my P38.

I had acquired a flight helmet because I had spent a good bit of time on reconnaissance flights during my tour, so I put it on as the helicopter was touching down. The NCO grabbed my duffle bag, I picked up the rucksack, and we walked out to the chopper. As I hopped up on the floor of the chopper, the NCO tossed the duffle bag in beside me, held out his hand and mouthed the words, "Good luck, L T"; the noise of the chopper drowning out his voice. I replied, "Thank you."

As the bird lifted off, I held up the end of the cord from my helmet and the door gunner handed me a cord for the plug. It was on the intercom circuit of the helicopter, so I pushed the button and asked what the flight was like. The pilot replied that it was good, but they were getting concerned. There was a morning fog developing north of Dong Xoai over Song Be... I was sitting on the floor of the helicopter with my legs hanging out. Looking forward I could see the top of Nui Ba Ra, the ancient volcanic cone next to Song Be. The airstrip was at the bottom of the cone. There were some light clouds around the cone. Flight time to Song Be for the helicopter at cruising speed is about 10 to 15 minutes. About half way into the flight the pilot asked me if the road was clear of wires. I told him that it would be ok until we got closer to Song Be. He said that the fog had gotten thicker, so he was going to try to follow the road. He did not want to have to descend through the fog at Song Be not knowing exactly where he was. His voice did not sound like it was a flight path he wanted to fly.

I noticed that the door gunner near me moved to lay on his stomach with his feet in the center of the cabin and his head and chest out of the door looking forward. I assumed the same position thinking that I might help looking for wires and other problems. We were ok for a while, when one of the gunners called, "WIRES" and the ship rose abruptly through the fog and into clear air. The top of Nui Ba Ra and the top of the fog were all that we could see. The fog had become thicker and there were no holes through which we could see the ground. A voice called me on the intercom saying, "Tell us about the mountain."

Me: "What do you want to know?"

Voice: "Are there any high antennas or poles or wires on that mountain?"

Me: "There have been communication antennas on top but nothing that I know of on the slopes below the top. Why?"

Voice: "Fuel is going to be a problem. We are ok but we do not have enough to go back south for more. If we fly back to Dong Xoai to wait, we will not have enough to return to Song Be for refueling. We need to find a way to set down until the fog lifts; preferably at the airstrip at Song

Be."

Great — my last day in province and another adventure — one I would prefer to avoid. I pulled out my topo map, which out of sheer habit I had put into the cargo pocket on my pants this morning and looked at the area around Nui Ba Ra. I went back on the intercom, "On my map it looks like you could fly a straight line down the slope of the cone right to the foot of the airstrip. There is nothing built up around the air strip, so it should be a clear path all the way down."

Voice: "I agree. This is going to be an interesting descent. Let's hope the fog does not reach the ground."

With that the pilot moved the helicopter to the side of the cone opposite the air strip, reduced the chopper's airspeed as much as practical and flew low and slow over the top of Nui Ba Ra to begin the descent through the fog, following the tops of the trees down the slope of the ancient volcano. Though the fog was thick, we could see the treetops when we were a just a few feet above them. Flying as slow as possible, the ship crept down the slope with three heads (two door gunners and

Figure 39.2   Nui Ba Ra at the end of the airstrip. The white arrow marks the path the helicopter followed down the mountain side in the fog to the airstrip.

mine) peering out from the cabin floor, looking for anything that would cause problems…

Finally, the helicopter emerged from the fog about twenty feet above the ground and there was the airstrip —right where the map said it would be. The pilot flew the ship down the center of the airstrip to the far end pad and settled down on the "H." I gave a hearty thanks to the crew and shook four sets of hands. They all wished me a much quieter trip the rest of the way back to the World.

The S-4 Sergeant arrived a few minutes later in his jeep. I sat my duffle bag down by the jeep and put the rucksack in the back of the jeep. He had some forms on a clipboard and handed it and a pen to me and asked me to sign them. It was an inventory form with a list of the gear I was turning in. I asked him if he wanted to check the list against what was in the rucksack and he shook his head, "No" saying, "That won't be necessary." I signed the forms. He signed the forms. I took one copy and put a copy of my orders under the clip on the board, and handed it back to him. Then I handed him the Province Clearance form which he signed and handed back to me. That was it. I had just cleared Province. We shook hands, and he wished me good luck. He got into his jeep and drove away. I sat on my duffle bag and waited for Air America to show up for my final flight to Ben Hoa, while the helicopter crew waited for the fog to lift, which it eventually did. Soon after the chopper lifted off to get fuel, Air America approached and landed.

The flight to Ben Hoa was in clear, smooth air, and the pilot was awake the entire trip. The helicopter ride from Ben Hoa to Saigon was the same. The air did not seem so fetid this time when I got out of the helicopter in Saigon. Now, all I had to do was clear Saigon. Standard protocol dictated that I should have tried to see the Colonel, the S-1 (personnel), the S-2, and the S-3 before leaving but I decided to skip that. Apparently, the Colonel had put the original orders sending me home in his desk drawer, which to my thinking was his own personal protocol, so I decided to follow my personal protocol for leaving Province.

Story 40 - Clearing Saigon

The Air America flight from Dong Xoai to Ben Hoa was smooth and quiet. From the Air America terminal, I hopped a chopper to Saigon and the MACV annex. We were not allowed to carry weapons in Saigon, so the first order of business was turning in my M-16. The pistol I carried was not on the books. It was given to me by the assistant team leader I had replaced, and I passed it on to the District Team NCO at Dong Xoai. The armory was a short walk from where the helicopters landed — intentional in its location, so soldiers could check their weapons overnight and pick them up when they were heading back to the field.

There were two doors on the building; one was marked, "Temporary Storage" and the other was marked "DEROS: Turn Weapons in Here." The "DEROS" room had a counter with two armorers behind it. On the other side of the room were several work benches with weapon cleaning supplies. I put my duffle bag along a wall and joined a line of about eight soldiers, NCOs and Lieutenants who were wearing faded fatigues like mine. All had MACV patches on their shoulders and several had CIBs above the chest pocket on their shirts.

We struck up some small talk that got around to, "Where were you stationed?" I replied, "Dong Xoai in Phuoc Long Province" getting some questioning looks. One asked, "Was that with the First Cav?" and I remarked, "No, I was on a MAT team. Dong Xoai was the village I was based in." That generated some "interesting" looks — I still did not fully realize how other advisors regarded a MAT Team assignment.

The line moved along slowly, but we were not in any hurry. One of the armorers would take the weapon from the next person, check to insure it was not loaded and inspect the weapon. He checked the bolt, the chamber and looked down the barrel. While he was doing that, the soldier emptied the cartridges from his magazines into a tub and put the empty magazines in a box next to the tub. The armorer filled out a form and asked the soldier to sign it. The soldier produced his clearance form for the armorer to sign along with a copy of his orders. The armorer returned the signed form, put the copy of the orders with his form, and it was done.

I was about fourth in line when two Majors entered. They too had MACV patches on their shoulders, no CIBs, and their fatigues were not faded like ours. They had no visible stains or tears and were ironed and possibly starched. They walked to the front of the line with one of the Majors smugly remarking as they moved past us, "Rank has its privileges." We stood quietly, but I am sure we were all mentally screaming the same obscene thoughts.

The armorer looked at the first Major, inspecting his neat uniform as he took the Major's weapon. He performed the same checks that he had done on the previous weapons and then he did something additional. He pulled off the hand guards that surround the barrel. These are difficult to remove, and it is not normally done. Even during weapons inspections in OCS, the hand guards were never pulled. There was dust and some dirt under the guards. The armorer, a Specialist 4th Class (Spec-4) handed the rifle back to the Major saying, "Sir, you will have to clean this weapon before I can accept it." Pointing to the cleaning benches on the other side of the room. The Major, somewhat stunned, was not going to be ordered about by a mere Spec-4. He replied, "You can clean it yourself." Pointing to a sign in large letters on the wall behind him, the Spec-4 said, "Sir, I cannot do that." The sign read, "All personnel regardless of rank will clean their own weapons prior to turning them in." followed by a name with the rank of Colonel. The other Spec-4 did the same thing with the same results to the second Major when it was his turn. Those of us with the faded, wrinkled, torn fatigues smiled to ourselves and proceeded to turned our weapons in one at a time with no problems. Rank does indeed have its privileges. The two Majors were still standing at the benches cleaning their weapons when I left the facility. One important item was checked off my list, but I had more to do. I checked in at MACV Annex and got a bunk for the rest of my stay and proceeded to work on the clearing check list.

I had a physical and a blood test and both pronounced me fit to return to the States — translation: I had no obvious communicable diseases. I visited other offices and cleared my checking account at Bank of America, getting more items checked off the list.

The only real problem was the urine test for drugs. NO! — I was not on drugs. I just have a problem urinating into a small container; I still do today. The only thing I hate more when I have my annual physical, is the prostate exam. It is probably due to some deeply buried early childhood psychological embarrassment. This "problem" was exacerbated by having to produce the specimen standing in a line, shoulder to shoulder with four other soldiers, pants down around our ankles, who were doing the same thing while being closely watched by the medic who was standing in front of us. It was as if my bladder went on vacation, moved without leaving a forwarding address, or had an unlisted phone number. It just refused to answer the door or take my call. My first try yielded too small of a specimen to test. At the suggestion of one of the other "five in a line" crew who was having similar problems, we went to the Officer's Club in the Annex and drank a few beers. I returned and produced a copious sample (I am sure the beer helped me in more than one way), but it was too dilute to be assayable. The next morning, I got up, dressed and rushed over to the testing office — really having to go so badly on the walk — and managed to produced enough of a specimen with sufficient density for testing followed by a quick trip to the latrine. Aaahhhh… the indignities endured in military service never seem to end.

I attended a class on how to return to the states and what to expect upon arriving. Since I was not only DEROSing but also separating from the Army, there were other forms to fill out and other places to get checks and signatures on my forms.

I took my khakis, field jacket and shoes to a shop run by Vietnamese in the Annex for cleaning and polishing so I would look decent for the trip back to the states. I had the shop sew a subdued MACV patch on the right shoulder of the field jacket, which is reserved for the patch of the unit with which you fought in combat. I had a CIB sewn on above the pocket.

I managed to visit the appropriate places, see the right people, and do the right things to get all of the blanks checked off my list and the appropriate forms signed by early Wednesday morning. I took them to the booking office that I had visited the previous Saturday and turned them in. In exchange they gave me a transit ticket for the flight home and a list of instructions on what I could and could not take back to the States. Unfortunately, I would not be able to bring back everything that I had with me. I had to turn in my jungle fatigues and one of my two pairs of jungle boots. I also had to turn in my flight helmet. The green underwear, socks and green towels could travel back with me. We would go through customs before boarding, so anything we were not allowed to take back would be confiscated there or we could turn it in before the flight.

After I received my transit ticket, I stopped by the Spec-5's desk, who started my DEROS journey and thanked him profusely. From there I went to the lounge at the hospital where the phone was and called Linda

Figure 40.1   The subdued MACV unit shoulder patch and the subdued. Combat Infantry Badge.

to give her my arrival date and time. We agreed that I would call her before I left California to tell her the flight number and arrival time in Philadelphia. It was a very good and very long call. I was so glad to have stumbled onto that phone earlier in my tour.

With everything done, I was able to relax the rest of Wednesday. I picked up my khakis, field jacket, and shoes. I polished the brass belt buckle, my collar brass and pinned it and my CIB on my shirt. I had one "suspect" item I was taking back that was not listed as illegal to take home. It was the tail fin section of the Viet Cong mortar shell that wounded YB in May. I was bringing it back for him, and I was concerned it would be confiscated before I boarded the plane. I wrapped it in a sock and stuffed it deep in the toe of the one pair of jungle boots I would be taking home followed by more socks. I packed my duffle bag, putting the jungle boots on top hoping the inspecting MP (Military Police) would be more interested in what was buried at the bottom of the bag. Maybe it would work.

I had a good dinner Wednesday evening and tried to get to sleep early but that did not work. My flight was for mid-afternoon on Thursday with a reporting time of noon. I got up and put my jungle fatigues and boots on for the last time and walked over to the cafeteria for breakfast. Somehow the sounds and smells were different today. I couldn't describe it then and cannot today. But they were different. After breakfast, I returned to the bunk room and laid down for a while.

I wanted to have some lunch before reporting for the flight so I changed into my freshly washed and ironed khakis and polished shoes — they felt very strange, very constricting; I had been wearing nothing but loose-fitting jungle fatigues and jungle boots ever since I arrived in country. Checking myself in the mirror, I put on my overseas cap. Then for some reason I returned to my duffle bag and put the overseas cap in and took out the blue beret with one silver bar Captain Ky had given me a couple of days ago as a parting gift. Unauthorized or not, I was wearing this blue beret. After eating lunch, I returned to the bunk room to get my duffle bag. My last chore was cutting my name tags off of my jungle fatigue shirts because I had to turn them in before boarding the flight.

Carrying my duffle bag, I headed to the bus stop to get a ride to Tan Son Nhut airport for my flight home. The bus back to the airport was just like the one I rode in from the airport in April — it had wire over the windows so no one could throw a grenade into the bus. The wire that was so shocking and disturbing in April seemed perfectly normal today.

At the airport I dropped my jungle fatigues, one pair of jungle boots and my flight helmet in a bin. My papers were checked, my transit ticket taken, and I was given a boarding pass. Next was a window where I converted my MPC (Military Pay Certificates) to US bills and coins — the first real money I had seen since I arrived in Vietnam. Then I moved to the customs line to have my baggage checked. An MP emptied my duffle bag on a table and went through everything. Finding nothing (the fin section of the mortar shell was not detected), he told me to pack my things up. When I finished, a Spec-4 put a baggage tag on the duffle bag, handed me the claim stub and put it on a cart for loading onto the plane. When he was done, he pointed to the next station in the customs line. There another MP frisked me thoroughly from head to toe and removed my beret to check it carefully before handing it back. When he was done, he pointed to a doorway and told me to wait in the departure lounge.

Figure 40.2 The departure point on the trip home.

Everyone, in the lounge was subdued. There were no signs of excitement. Bits of nervous talk could be heard among some of the 150 or so soldiers waiting to leave, but there was little kidding around. It was as if we all felt we were in a dream and afraid we would wake up to find ourselves back in the jungle. The time dragged to a point of almost stopping.

Finally, we were called to board the plane as a group with no particular order. I would have thought that they would have boarded us by rank, but I guess they thought better of it. Soon now, I would be able to say, "Goodbye, Vietnam!"

Story 41 - Flight to the World

It was Thursday, December 2, 1971. I had arrived in Vietnam on Friday, April 2, 1971. Thanks to Vietnamization, I was leaving Vietnam four months ahead of my initial DEROS. I had no mixed feelings about leaving early. It was time for me to go. The processing and waiting were done. The plane was fueled and waiting on the tarmac at Tan Son Nhut for us to board. With about 150 soldiers heading home and many of us also separating from the Army, rank was apparently not considered for

Figure 41.1 The departure board for the flight home.

the order in which we boarded the aircraft when our flight was called.

We walked out of the departure lounge across the tarmac and up the stairs into the plane. There was no first-class cabin in the aircraft. Just rows of seats and an aisle down the center. This was 1971, so airlines had not begun the process of shrinking seat sizes, leg room and applying other "sardining" features found in aircraft today. Regardless of where you sat, you had leg room, and the person in front of you could actually lean their seat back without crowding you; getting out of a row from the window seat did not require a gymnast's ability. It would not have mattered. After finishing your tour, any seat, even in the bathroom, would have been welcome to this group. I found a window seat somewhere in the middle of the cabin. I put my field jacket in the overhead bin and sat down. After fastening my seatbelt, I started to look out the window, which was facing away from the terminal building. There were lots of aircraft moving around on the ground, taking off, and landing. Soon we would be joining them.

The cabin was extremely quiet. The cabin crew, all women, moved up and down the aisle checking our seat belts, seat back, and tray tables. Many of the soldiers just gazed at them as they moved through the cabin. Probably veterans of many such flights, these women seemed comfortable with the looks. I hope they remember today how much their presence, their voice, their occasional touch on the shoulder meant to us at that time. They gave the usual pre-flight passenger instructions about seat belts, life preservers under our seats, emergency exits, life rafts, and oxygen masks. The plane began taxiing to the runway. After a few minutes it moved onto the end of the runway, turned to face the long strip of concrete and began its acceleration, pushing us back into our seats. Once the wheels left the pavement, there was (what was probably typical of "Freedom Bird Flights") a loud cheer from everyone on the plane. Unlike most flights, the pressure did not ease. Rather it pushed us back into our seats even harder as the pilot increased the upward angle of the plane to the max allowed before an aerodynamic stall. He wanted to get as much altitude as soon as possible to avoid enemy gun fire and a possible ground-to-air missile hit. Once the plane reached a safe altitude, the angle eased a bit, and the pressure disappeared; there was another cheer. We were on our way home; total flight time about 24 hours plus 2 stops.

The first leg was about 11 hours to Guam for a crew change and refueling. There was not much activity. A few card games, some book reading, and a lot of sleeping. Conversations were muted. The cabin crew circulated offering drinks (no alcohol), snacks, and meals at appropriate intervals. Even with the muted excitement before liftoff and the cheers during takeoff, the flight was somewhat boring and very slow. There is no easy way to pass time, when all you want to do is get back home.

With the flight distance and time zones, it was about 4:00 am when we landed in Guam. We were allowed off of the plane into a lounge to stretch our legs. Given the time, there were no services, so we took advantage of the vending machines until they were empty.

Then an announcement came over the PA system telling us that an engine component on the aircraft had failed during the flight. The plane had landed safely because there was a backup, but the plane could not take off until the failed component was replaced. The announcement went on to say that the pilot had called ahead, and the replacement part was coming on the next flight from Hawaii. The delay time would be between 3 and 4 hours. We could remain in the lounge, on the tarmac around the plane or return to the cabin, but we could not leave the immediate area.

A few of us had walked back outside to get some exercise and some fresh air, when it began to rain. So, we moved under the wings of the plane and stood there watching the rain puddle on the tarmac. At least it wasn't a Vietnamese rain.

Eventually a vehicle rolled up to the plane and two men got out and removed an access panel and went to work. A while later another vehicle drove up and two more men got out. They did something and they closed the access panel. Shortly after that, the soldiers on the plane exited and joined those of us outside. Then the PA announced the boarding of the plane for the next leg. We went up the stairs and called out our names as we entered the cabin to be checked off the manifest. With everyone accounted for, the door was closed, and the new cabin crew repeated the instructions, checked things in the cabin, and we were off again — with another cheer. The delay had cost us four hours. Would we ever get home?

The next stop was Hawaii — only 5 hours away — less than half the time to Guam. But it seemed longer.

The stop in Hawaii was like the stop in Guam, without the delay. We exited the plane to a transit lounge, again with only vending machines. We milled around for a while until we were called to board the plane.

A new cabin crew greeted us as we entered calling out our names. They repeated the same ritual and we were back in the air for another 5 hours to Travis Air Force Base where a steak dinner would be awaiting us as part of the Army's standard, "Welcome home, GI."

This 5-hour leg was mentally the longest of the three. Everyone was restless having read their books and grown tired of playing cards. There was nothing else to talk about, and we had slept more in the past 23 hours than we did in the week prior to DEROSing. But we hung on and got there — in the middle of the night.

We landed and taxied up to a jetway — no stairs. Walking down the darkened tunnel of the jetway, a lighted sign at the end greeted us saying, "Welcome Home Soldier. Your Country Is Proud of You." Some of us would soon learn about the truth of that poster.

We exited the tunnel to another Customs check — this one manned by Custom Agents instead of Military Police. Why another check? We had a thorough one in Saigon and had no chance to pick up anything illegal during the flight. Nevertheless, they were waiting for us. Our agent was in a sour mood. He greeted the first person in our line with the comment, "Why did you have to land in the middle of the night? Couldn't you have just slept on the plane until morning?" That, "Proud of You" thought gradually began to disappear.

There was another disappointment — even though it had been hours since we had eaten and we were hungry, there would be no steak dinner or dinner of any kind because it was so late. There wasn't even a snack.

They separated us into two groups. One group that was remaining in the Army and the other that was being separated from service. Our group was loaded onto busses and taken to a barracks, where we were told that out processing would begin tomorrow at 0700 hours and breakfast would be available at 0530 hours in the mess hall. Most of the soldiers did not bother to remove their khakis — they just crashed for a couple of hours of sleep. After all, we had lived in our uniforms for 28 hours — so much for looking sharp. I did opt for a shower — a hot, stateside shower and I shaved when I was done to avoid the rush in a few hours.

Someone flipped the lights on at 0500 hours, followed by a number of obscene shouts. Things settled down and people began to move. We walked down to the mess hall, where breakfast was eagerly anticipated having missed our steak dinner the night before. At 0630 hours we filed back on busses with our baggage for the short trip to the Out-processing Center.

The first order of business was a briefing by a Major who began, not by welcoming us home, but by chastising us for traveling in khakis at this time of the year. Khakis were the warm weather uniform, and the regulation dress at this time of the year was Class A Greens. Who wore greens to tropical Vietnam? Looking at the decorations on his uniform jacket, there were no Vietnam Service or Vietnam Campaign ribbons — as a Major with a number years in the Army, he had avoided a tour in Vietnam. That was not exactly a position of strength from which to lecture just returned veterans leaving the service about their travel uniform. His comments were greeted by a good bit of mumbling and grumbling, but the Major continued, ignoring the sounds. He outlined the process and turned the room over to a Specialist 5th class (Spec-5), who had Vietnam Ribbons on his chest. The Specialist sighed as he stepped up, welcomed us home, and we began the process of separating from the Army. It was fairly simple. The reason it would take so long was that there were so many of us. We had our orders checked and were given additional orders and instructions concerning our separation. We reviewed our Form DD-214 and had any additions or corrections made to the form. Form DD-214 is the most important form a veteran receives. It lists your dates of service, rank at time of separation, type of discharge (honorable in my case), awards you are authorized to wear and other administrative information. This form is required for all future benefits including the GI bill, VA mortgages, and VA medical care. They went over our pay status and either gave us a voucher for cash due us or instructions on how to pay back what was owed the Army. Finally, they gave us two travel vouchers: one for a cab ride to the terminal and another for a plane/bus/train ticket home.

The last stop in the Out-processing Center was to receive any money owed us. I gave the cashier the voucher and my Army ID Card and received the money I was due. Without the ID card, I was actually out of the army — a civilian in an Army uniform. That was it. I walked out of the building to find a line of cabs waiting to take me to wherever. It was a cold rainy day. Not unlike the April day when I left for Vietnam. The cold was a shock but my field jacket kept me warm.

Looking back, there was no formal separation ceremony, no certificate, no "Thank you," no hand shake or even a salute for our service. For the soldiers and civilians working at Travis, it was just another day. It did not matter; for us, it was a dream finally becoming a reality.

Story 42 - Flight to Philadelphia

I was no longer in the Army. I was a civilian dressed in an Army uniform: khakis, field jacket, blue beret standing on the sidewalk on a military post. It was a strange feeling walking out of the door of the Out-processing Center without a military identification card. All I had was a lot of cash — real US currency, two vouchers for transportation and a Geneva Convention Identification Card, which did not have a photo or address on it. I did not have a driver's license or a passport. Even with the passing traffic, the air smelled clean and fresh. Soldiers were not wearing web gear. There was no barbed wire and buses did not have mesh wire over the windows. And it was cold and wet. It was a disconnected feeling.

It was mid-afternoon, dark and raining. In front of me was a line of taxis waiting to take me and the other men separating from the Army to the airport, train station, or bus depot for the last leg of the trip back home.

I walked up to the first cab in line and asked for a ride to the airport. The driver motioned me to the back of the car and put my duffle bag in the trunk. I got in the car and closed the door but the driver did not. He found four other veterans heading to the airport and loaded them in. In 1971, the cabs were full size cars with large trunks and seating room for five passengers; three in the back seat and two in the front. It was close but we fit. Thinking about this now, 49 years later, it made sense. He collected five transit vouchers for one trip. Financially he made a nice profit and probably made the same profit every day. My father, a 20-year Air Force veteran, used to call such people "Feather Merchants."

I do not remember much about the ride to the airport, but I do remember arriving at the terminal area. The protesters were there. Arrival at the terminal was a negative memory for many returning veterans in some extremely sad ways: being called "baby killer," being spit on, hearing antiwar and anti-veteran chants. Maybe it was the rain and cold or maybe the sight of five American Army soldiers getting out of one cab as a unit, with one wearing a beret, that was too intimidating for the crowd, but nothing untoward happened when we arrived. If there was chanting, I did not hear it. My memory is that it was oddly silent. I remember that no one got in our way as we walked into the building — it was as if the seas had parted.

Like the roominess of the airplane seats and the size of the cars, flights in 1971 were also different. They were not booked full days in advance. You could walk up to an airline counter, tell the attendant that you needed the next flight to Philadelphia, pay her or him, and get a ticket on a plane leaving within a few hours. That is exactly what I did. When it came time to pay, I handed over my travel voucher and set my duffle bag on the scale to be checked. The person behind the counter gave me a ticket and a baggage claim check. From the counter I took my ticket, walked over to a pay phone (remember, there were no cell phones in 1971), and called Linda to tell her what flight I was on and when it would arrive; 11:00 pm tonight. It was a very emotional and a very short call.

I stopped at a snack bar and got something to eat. If there were stares, I did not notice them. From the snack bar I went to the gate. There were other veterans in uniform heading home, having processed out with me earlier in the day, but none of us stopped to talk to each other. And none of us stopped to talk to any of the civilians surrounding us. It was strange being here. Conversations were easily understood — no translations needed. Again, if there were stares, I did not see them.

The wait at the gate seemed unending. I was tired but not sleepy, so I just sat in my chair and watched this new world walk by.

When it was time, the gate attendant called us to board. Again, in 1971 the airlines did not reserve seats. Boarding was first come, first serve and your seat choice was the same. The cabin crew might ask a few folks to move to balance the passenger load in the plane but where you sat and with whom you sat was up to you. You were, "Free to move about the cabin."

For some reason I did not rush to board. I waited until almost all of the others had entered the jetway before handing my ticket to the gate agent. I had no carry-on luggage; just my field jacket. I walked up the tunnel of the jetway and into the aircraft. A member of the cabin crew welcomed me as she had all of the preceding passengers and told me to choose any empty seat. The passengers had scattered themselves throughout the plane. The flight was not packed, so there were many empty seats and a few empty rows. The area in the middle of the cabin had an open row of three seats on one side of the aisle — I chose that one. I climbed over to the window seat and sat down. Buckling my seatbelt, I sat back for the five-hour flight to the east coast — almost home.

I am not sure where I was mentally for a few moments, but it was not in the airplane, when some stirring brought me back to reality. The people around me, those in the row in front of me, the row behind me, and the seats across the aisle from me started getting up to move. They all began to shift to other seats. No words were spoken, no hushed whispers, just some head nodding and pointing to empty seats as they moved to find different seats in the front or the back of the cabin. Suddenly I was an island to myself. I guess they did not want to sit near a baby killer — one with a deep suntan in December, a handle-bar mustache, and wearing a beret. I was in no mood for idle conversation with strangers, so their moving to more comfortable seats was ok with me.

I had not thought about much about this part of the flight to Philadelphia. Several years ago at a gathering of veterans of all wars sponsored by the Veterans Breakfast Club[56] in Pittsburgh, I was asked to describe my trip home. That was the first time I had really thought about the flight since I came back. That memory was the genesis for this series of stories that I have shared in these writings.

---

[56] The Veterans Breakfast Club or VBC is not a club in terms of membership or dues. There are no requirements for "membership." You don't have to be a veteran. The VBC is the result of the work of Todd DePastino, a historian, teacher, professor, and author who began such gathering of veterans from all wars to share their stories in 2008.

For the entire flight I had three rows of seats to myself. The cabin crew offered drinks, snacks, and dinner (yes, they fed you real food on flights in 1971). If serving a Vietnam veteran bothered them, they did not show it.

At one point an Air Force chaplain, traveling in uniform with his wife and son, came forward to my seat and asked if he could sit down for a moment. I replied, "Sure. Have a seat". It was an uneasy conversation for him. He did not know what to say or ask and I was not effusive in my effort to make him comfortable. He did not ask me what Vietnam was like or what I did. Being in the Air Force, I doubt that he understood what the CIB and the other insignia on my shirt meant or why I was wearing a blue beret and he did not ask. He asked about where I was going and what I was going to do. Through all of this, he tried but was unable to hide his discomfort. Recently I have wondered if he was uncomfortable talking to me or uncomfortable in how the passengers around me had reacted to my presence. I am sure that his being in uniform was a cause for some discomfort for him and his family, given the mood of the country toward the military at that time. It was good of him to try to welcome me back to the States, but all I really wanted was for the time to pass quickly so I could get home.

Flying east crossing three time zones and losing three hours, it gets dark quicker. I looked out the window as the afternoon shifted through evening into darkness and watched the time pass so very slowly.

When the plane landed at Philadelphia, I waited until the others were out of the plane. The chaplain and his family also waited and were in front of me. Why bother the passengers needlessly by walking among them? They did not ask for that.

I walked down the jetway into the gate area, where people were greeting the arrivals. As I came into the room, I could see Linda across the sea of people on the far edge of the crowd with a smile that I will never forget.

I was home!

Epilog

The Covid19 pandemic provided the time to write these stories about my tour in Vietnam. It has been an interesting process. I had not thought about most of these events for forty-nine years; they were buried deep in my past. One day after a Veterans Breakfast Club meeting, I began to think about my flight from California to Philadelphia and decided to write a short story, possibly for the Veterans Breakfast Club quarterly newsletter. Writing that story brought back memories of the flight to California from Vietnam and other events, and I continued to write. With the pandemic raging, what else was there to do?

If this pandemic continues deep into 2021, as it appears it may, I might write another series of stories about events in my service before leaving for Vietnam. If I do write that memoir, the following two stories will be part of it.

Before Basic Training

I was a science teacher; I had a deferment from the draft. Prior to that I had four deferments for being a college student. I was set but then, no I wasn't... My father's father was a Spanish American War veteran who was in Cuba but according to my grandfather, he was still on the boat when the war ended — it was a very short war. My father retired from the Air Force as a Master Sergeant with twenty years of service. I was an Air Force brat. I had changed schools nine times in twelve years and had twelve different addresses by the time I finished high school. Regardless of how much of the country felt about the Vietnam war, I felt it was my duty to serve. So, I chose to walk away from my sixth deferment and enlist in the Army. That was the beginning of almost three years of my life that has led to this series of stories about my tour of duty in

Vietnam. But those stories really began at the AFEES[57] office in Fairmont, West Virginia. When I arrived at the office, a number of men who had received their draft notices were there, and their mood was very negative (to put it politely). I signed in and waited my turn, listening to the muted conversations. Most were centered on the arguments they were going to make to avoid being drafted. And at age 23, I was older than most of them.

When they called my name, I was directed to a Sergeant sitting at a desk. His shirt displayed what I later came to know were the ribbons for the awards of service in Vietnam. He asked for my draft papers, and I replied that I did not have any; that I wanted to enlist. That took him by surprise. He asked a series of questions: education status — college graduate, job — teacher, deferment — yes, 5 with 6th coming for the school year starting in the fall. Then he asked which service and I replied, "Army". Then he asked me to choose three branches and that one had to be a combat branch. He offered the advice that the combat branch should be the third choice. I replied, "Infantry, Armor, Artillery". To this he said, "Son, only one has to be a combat branch; not all three." And I replied, "Those are my three choices, and I want to volunteer for OCS."

With this he pushed back from his desk, stood up, and walked to the back of the office to talk to someone. A few minutes later a Captain returned with him and asked me if I could return on Thursday morning; I replied that I could. They shook my hand and pointed me to the exit.

OK — that was strange but it was a strange time.

I had listed the three combat branches because I felt that if I was going to do this, I was going to be "in there". Given what other men my age and younger were being asked to do, it seemed to be the right thing for me to do. For me — not necessarily everyone else — just for me.

So, Thursday morning I went back at the AFEES station and signed in. In short order they called me in, and I was escorted to a small private

----

[57] AFEES: Armed Forces Entrance Examination Station

room. An officer entered and introduced himself as Doctor Someone. As he continued to speak, I realized why I had to return. Doctor Someone was a psychiatrist, and he needed to talk with me about my enlistment. A PSYCHIATRIST? It seems that when a man with a college degree and a deferment from the draft walks in cold off the street and asks to enlist in the Infantry and volunteers for OCS, all kinds of alarm bells go off — to the Army, sane men do not do this! So, I had to convince them that I was not insane. Apparently, I was successful because they returned me to the Sergeant with whom I first spoke, and we processed the paperwork. I took the required aptitude tests, physical exam, had more interviews, signed papers, and took the oath that every man and woman who has served in the military takes. I would report for my actual induction on June 30. My orders would be coming in the mail. Once again, I shook the Sergeant's hand and left — now a member of the Army Inactive Reserve component until I reported for active duty at the end of June.

So, two major tasks lay before me: finish the school year and figure out how to tell my parents that I had enlisted. Finishing the school year was relatively easy. It was a good school with good teachers, great students, and total community support — Farmington High School in Farmington West Virginia. The previous fall, the Consol Number 9 coal mine exploded killing 78 miners. Almost every student in the high school lost someone in that explosion. It was a tough time for the students and the community. As part of the faculty, I would like to think I helped contribute some degree of comfort to them as they dealt with their loss.

Telling my parents was a different story. Let's leave it to the fact that they were not happy, were disappointed, and very displeased with my decision. I told them it was my decision alone to make, and that they would have to learn to accept it.

I reported early on the morning of June 30 with a gaggle of other younger men (actually boys). We took the oath (again for me), were given a packet of orders and ushered onto a bus for a ride to Ft. Dix, New

Jersey; we were in the Army.

It was a long ride, and we arrived around dark. Several Drill Sergeants entered the bus and started shouting at us to take everything with us and get off the bus. We scrambled and moved off as quickly as possible but that did not end the shouting. Eventually we were herded (as newbies, we could not march) into a mess hall for dinner. Then more shouting and we were herded out of the mess hall and moved to a building where we would sleep that night. More shouting. Linens were on the bunks so we made the beds (we thought we were making them but we would find out tomorrow that we did not know how to make a bunk) and turned in early. What had I gotten myself into? What would the morning bring?

More shouting but it was still dark outside. Get up, get dressed, bring everything with you; we were herded to the same mess hall for breakfast. Then with more shouting we were herded to a supply point, where we were issued our Army clothing: fatigues, khakis, underwear, socks, boots, oxfords, and anything else that was needed to dress as a soldier in the U. S. Army. Somewhere in all of this, we had name tags printed and sewn onto our fatigue shirts. We were also issued a duffle bag into which we shoved this stuff. Before we left the supply point, we were herded into another room and told to put on the Army issue underwear, socks, fatigues, and boots.

They gave each of us a cardboard box. We were instructed to put all of our civilian clothing and items, other than our toilet kits, along with the bag we had brought with us into the box and address it so it could be sent home. These items were the last threads connecting us to our former civilian life and they were being stuffed into a cardboard box and leaving. Gone was almost every immediate relationship to our former lives; the last one would be leaving us in short order. We were now a gaggle of soldiers in new uniforms with boots that were uncomfortably pinching our feet. The only constant throughout all of this was the continuous shouting by the Drill Sergeants.

The Drill Sergeants moved us to another building — the barber shop. This stop was a very well-known rite of Basic Training that every private has experienced. It was simple and very quick. There were probably 10 barbers in the room - 5 on one side facing the other 5. They sheared us like sheep. No finesse — just cut the hair — 5 or 6 passes and we were as close to bald as possible. Then we had to pay for the haircut — yes, we paid to be sheared. Once we were bald and a few dollars poorer, we left by a back door and stood in another gaggle until everyone was sheared. Standing there in fatigues and black boots with bald heads, everyone looked like everyone else. We had just given up our last shred of identity as a civilian.

I remember looking at the parking lot where the barbers apparently parked — the cars were all Cadillacs and Lincolns; not a Ford or Chevy in the lot. This group of barbers must cut a lot of hair. More feather merchants.

When everyone was done, the Drill Sergeants began to instruct us on how to form up into something like an organized group of soldiers. They showed us how to stand at attention, parade-rest, at-ease and salute. We practiced commands including Fall In, Attention, Parade-Rest, and At-Ease. We practiced a command called "Dress Right Dress" that aided us in lining up with the proper spacing.

The Drill Sergeants walked up and down the ranks checking our positions of attention, parade-rest and our hand salutes. This included more shouting and something new — pushups. When a soldier made a mistake, "Drop and give me 10" was the usual reply.

What I did not know was that many of the men in this group of new soldiers were from the Pittsburgh area. I had flown into and out of the Greater Pittsburgh International Airport, located in Moon Township on the outskirts of Pittsburgh, one time, but that was all I knew about Western Pennsylvania.

Two of the soldiers were whispering to each other and laughing as a Drill Sergeant passed behind overhearing them. He moved in front of one of these soldiers and asked in a wet, barking shout, just what was so funny that it had to be shared right then and there. The troop did not reply. He moved closer to the soldier, looked at his name tag, and showered his face with the question, "Private SomeName, where are you from?" The soldier replied, "Moon, Drill Sergeant." At that point the

Drill Sergeant literally blew up. "Listen college boy. I may not be a college graduate like you, but I know that there is no one living on the moon now or ever (Apollo 11 had not yet landed on the moon). Drop and give me 20!" The Drill Sergeant went on for a few more rants while this soldier was doing the pushups when the soldier who was being whispered to began to laugh. The Drill Sergeant noticed this and stepped in front of him asking in another verbal shower, "What is so funny, Private SomeOne?" The startled soldier did his best to answer but only a squeak came out. Then the Drill Sergeant asked, "Where do you come from, Private Someone?" The soldier squeezed out, "Mars, Drill Sergeant". (Mars is a small town north of Pittsburgh.) At this the Drill Sergeant went totally nuts, and we all found ourselves doing pushups while listening to an even louder lecture on respect for Drill Sergeants and the importance of answering questions truthfully. We continued to do pushups — a lot of pushups.

From there the rest of basic training was in many ways essentially all downhill.

Telephoning the Army's Surgeon General

Linda was starting her fourth year at the Woman's Medical College (WMC) in Philadelphia when I got orders for Vietnam. I was at Ft. Campbell, Kentucky in a basic combat training company as the executive officer (second in command) and training officer. My orders were to report to Ft. Bragg, North Carolina in September for three months at the Kennedy School for Special Warfare (Special Forces) for training to serve as a member of a MAT team. Following that, I would have thirty days of leave, beginning in late November, and then report to Ft. Bliss, Texas for three months of Vietnamese language training at the Defense Language Institute, Southwest. From there I would report to Vietnam. This was unusual in that most soldiers assigned to Vietnam had their leave just prior to departure instead of before an extended training sequence. But these were unusual times.

We decided to get married at the beginning of my thirty day leave and I would spend the first part of my leave time in Philadelphia with Linda, while she continued her studies. WMC (today it is the Drexel University College of Medicine) was established in 1850 to train women as physicians. By 1969 women doctors were still uncommon in the profession. As such, the women of her class were activists in many ways. Several were part of the occupation of the Registrar's office at Columbia University during a protest of the Vietnam war. Linda's decision to marry a soldier did not draw negative reactions from her classmates. In fact, they were supportive and the genesis of the events on which this story centers.

In 1970, the Army operated William Beaumont Army Hospital in El Paso, Texas as a stand-alone military installation. It was near Ft. Bliss but not a part of Ft. Bliss. It had its own commanding officer who was a physician. After my leave was up, I was going to Ft. Bliss for language training. One of Linda's classmates suggested that we call the Army and ask if she could accompany me and do some of her training at William Beaumont. The third and fourth year of medical school involves "rotations." A rotation is one or two months of working with physicians while treating actual patients in the hospital wards. Woman's Medical College allowed its students to do these rotations at other hospitals by mutual arrangements. Linda talked to the Dean, and she agreed to rotations at Beaumont if the Army was willing to work out the details and conditions. Now all we had to do was, "Call the Army."

In early December, 1970 Linda and I had been married only a few days. There was no internet, but there were listings of Federal telephone numbers in the front pages of the telephone book. Somehow, some way, we found the telephone number for the Surgeon General of the Army[58]. With nothing to lose — I was the lowest rank an officer could have and I was going to Vietnam — I dialed the number. A male voice answered with, "Surgeon General SomeName's office." I said who I was and asked

---

[58] This is not the same person as the Surgeon General of the United States. The Surgeon General of the Army is a doctor and an Army General.

if I could talk to the General. I receive the usual Army reply of, "Wait one" and was put on hold. A brief time later, a voice on the line said, "This is General SomeName, Lieutenant. What can I do for you?" After stammering through my first sentence, he asked to speak to Linda. I handed the phone to her and she calmly explained who she was and what was she was trying to do. They talked for a while, and she hung up. Linda said that he would have someone call me back in a day or two with the details, but it was going to happen. She would be accompanying me to El Paso for the three months prior to my departure for Vietnam. So, we waited.

I had to report to Ft. Bliss right after New Year's Day. We waited, but there was no return call about Linda's rotation.

Finally, as the days between Christmas and New Years started to wane, I called the Surgeon General a second time and, once again he got on the phone. I introduced myself and handed the phone to Linda. They had a very short conversation. The General thought this matter had been "handled," and he promised her that someone would get back to her very shortly.

Very shortly was only a few minutes, when the phone rang. The voice on the other end said that the rotations had been arranged with WMC and that William Beaumont was expecting her right after the New Year. She would do two months of surgery and one month of pediatrics. He gave her the name of the person to whom she should report. He went on to say that someone had failed to call her earlier with this information and then said, "Goodbye." Everything had been arranged with her medical school and William Beaumont as the General had promised.

This was an incredible Christmas present, and I still wonder how many Second Lieutenants have ever called the Surgeon General of the Army with a personal request like this.

William Beaumont was beginning a rotation program with a Texas medical school in the coming fall, so Linda would be a good test run for the program. The medical staff at Beaumont warmly welcomed Linda and treated her like a doctor. Their first problem was finding a white coat with the hospital logo that would fit her. (Make a note — order smaller sizes of white coats for the fall rotation class — the trial run with Linda was already paying benefits.) During the surgery rotation she performed surgical procedures. Treating wounded Vietnam veterans was also part of her surgery rotation giving her some firsthand knowledge of the hazards of combat in Vietnam. Linda earned an honors grade on her surgery exams when she returned to Woman's Medical College in April.

Acknowledgements

There are many people to thank for contributions and help with this book, and I hope that all are remembered here. My sincere apologies to any I have missed.

Jim Rice and Gary Weinreich, who served with me in Dong Xoai, contributed stories that are found in these pages. They read early drafts and dug deeply back into their memories to help me correct the errors and add depth to the stories. Jim Rice provided the photograph of his dog, Deros (Figure 26.3) and the District Team NCO (Figure AP2.9).

George Milman whose father piloted my father's B-17 in WW2 was on another MAT team while I was there. He contributed two stories, one of which a number of the readers of the early drafts found quite moving. He provided the photographs of Loi (Figure 21.3) and the kite gang (Figure 21.4).

Ralph Simpson graciously gave me permission to use his image of the Whiz Wheel (Figures 33.1 and AP1.17).

The remainder of the pictures were taken by Gary Weinreich and me. We shared all of our images over the past forty-nine years so I am no longer sure who the photographer is of each image.

The scans of documents and maps were made from the papers I brought back from Vietnam in 1971.

While I may not be a very good writer, apparently I am very talented in embedding deeply hidden errors within the text as I type. This talent presented a major challenge to the following people:

Brian Walrath was one year ahead of me in every phase: Basic Training, Infantry OCS, MAT Team member and MAT Team leader. He was on MAT Team 24, an element of Advisory Team 16 in Quang Nam Province in I Corps the year before I arrived at Dong Xoai. He found a video I had published on YouTube in 2018 about MAT teams and contacted me. He then offered to read the manuscript. He did much more than read it; he scrubbed it thoroughly, finding the errors which had escaped the following set of proofreaders. Being an Infantry veteran and former MAT team member, he found technical errors that others would not find and offered suggestions on parts that made the work a smoother read. He has written a book about being in the Army and a Lieutenant on a MAT team at that time for private reading that is quite fascinating, and I am encouraging him to publish it in the future.

The following did a detailed reading of what was supposed to be the penultimate draft: Terry Brink, Jacobo Carrasquel, Joyce Chilton, Gordon Lam, Richard McJunkin, Eric Minde. Like Brian, they scoured the draft finding many of my hidden mistakes. Their suggestions helped make some of the stories clearer.

Rick Duncan found numerous errors and offered detailed advice about the book's organization and structure as well as suggestions on some of the segments that were unclear.

Linda Roberts read an early draft and learned much about my tour of which she was unaware. Her questions on various stories helped me in rewriting them to make them clearer to non-veteran readers.

The following read various stories as they were being written and offered advice, corrections, and suggestions: Maria Emerson, John Haretos, Chris Kissell, Bev Randolph, and Kay Zoldos.

Penny Byrnside was a very early reader who endured reading all forty-four stories when they were in a very rough draft form providing strong encouragement and very helpful suggestions.

Appendix 1 - Vietnam 1971: Situation, Organization, Equipment, and Terminology

The Situation on the Ground:

In 1971 the Vietnam War was winding down due to Congressional mandates that led to a program called Vietnamization. After the Tet Offensive in 1968, US support started being withdrawn, and the total war effort was slowly shifted to the government of Vietnam and the ARVN (pronounced: r-vin) — the Army of the Republic of Vietnam.

As part of the winding down, the 12-man Green Beret (Special Forces) A teams and their supporting B and C teams were withdrawn. In many places they were replaced by 5-man Mobile Advisory Teams (MAT teams). The MAT teams were deployed to continue the work of training and advising the Regional Force (RF) companies in the districts and the Popular Force (PF) platoons in the villages. The A-Teams had recruited, equipped, trained, and led these forces until they were withdrawn.

Now there would be two very significant changes. Unlike the A-Teams who led these units, the MAT teams would have only an advisory role; the Vietnamese were in command. The other change was combat support. There were no B and C teams to provide such support. Tactical support included artillery support and helicopter support for resupply, air mobile assaults, medical evacuation, and gunship sweeps. Material support consisted of ammunition, weapons, jeeps, trucks — anything a unit needs to fight a war. MAT team material support was "supposed" to come through the ARVN supply lines.

An important part of the MAT teams' work with the RF and PF was that of liaison between these units and American units for any tactical help that could be acquired when it was available. This included helicopter and artillery support. The RF companies and PF platoons were at the far end of the ARVN supply lines, and material support could be scarce. MAT team Sergeants helped fill these gaps by making scrounging and trading runs to American units and, on rare occasion, committing theft. Viet Cong battle flags complete with bullet holes and blood (often made for MAT advisors by women in the villages, sprinkled with chicken blood, and shot at by local soldiers) and Montagnard cross bows were good trading stock. Vietnamese and Montagnard villagers were more than willing to make these items and sell them to us.

Figure AP1.1 An advisor who has just bought a cross bow from a Montagnard.

Vietnam was divided into 44 provinces (equivalent to states). The provinces were divided into districts (equivalent to counties). Population centers of the districts were the villages, which were collections of hamlets. Most hamlets were segregated by culture, race, religion, or ethnicity: Vietnamese, Cambodian, Montagnard, Hoa Hao, Cao Dai, Catholic, etc.

Governmental Organizations in Vietnam in 1971

Vietnam	Leader	United States Equivalent	Leader
Province	Province Chief appointed	State	Governor
District	District Chief appointed	County	County Executive
Hamlet	Hamlet Chief elected	Neighborhood	???

Militarily, the US divided the country into four Military Regions or Corps: I, II, III, IV. I Corps (pronounced "eye core") was north at the border between North Vietnam and South Vietnam. IV Corps (pronounced "4 core") was the southernmost area that included the Mekong delta.

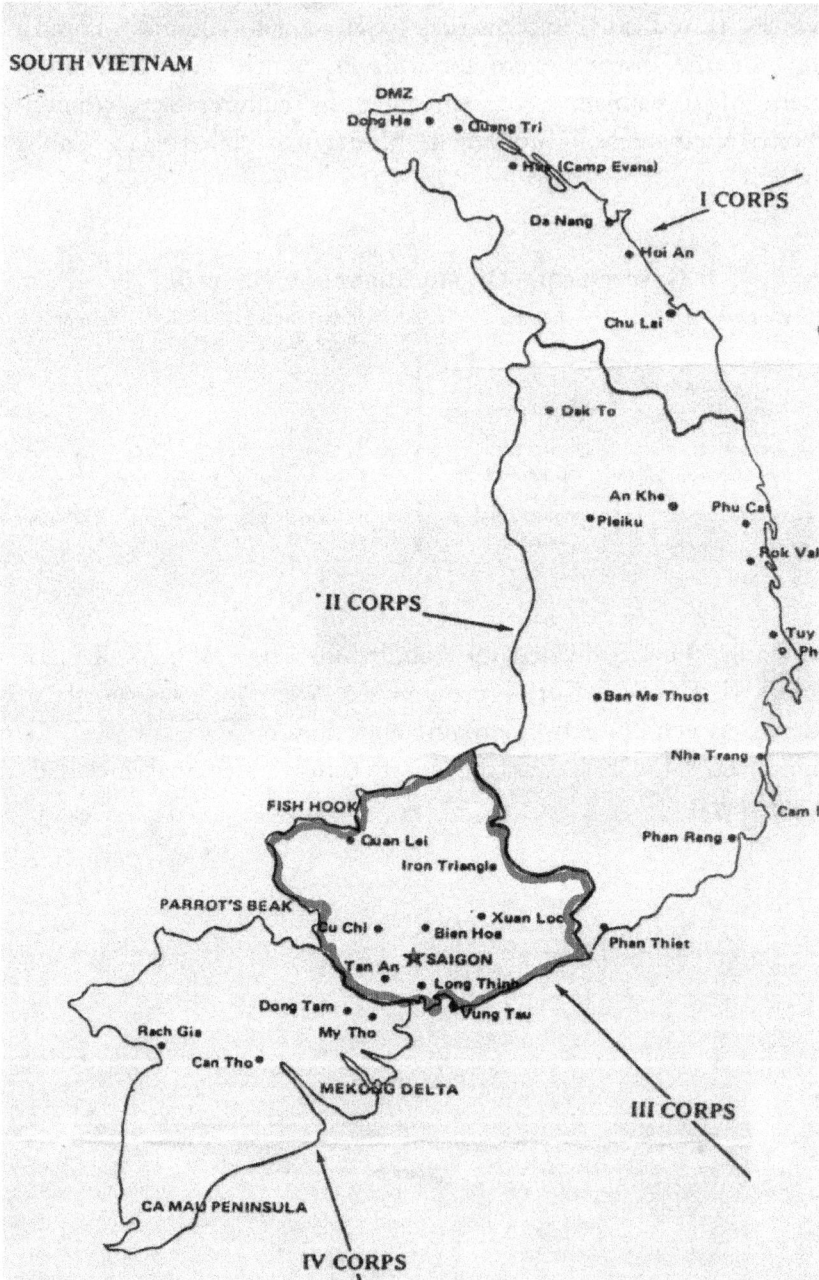

SOUTH VIETNAM

DMZ
Dong Ha • • Quang Tri

• Hue (Camp Evans)

Da Nang •   I CORPS

• Hoi An

Chu Lai

• Dak To

An Khe
• Pleiku   Phu Cat

Rok Val

'II CORPS

Tuy
• Ph

• Ban Me Thuot

Nha Trang •

FISH HOOK   Cam

• Quan Loi   Phan Rang •
Iron Triangle

PARROT'S BEAK   • Xuan Loc
Cu Chi •   • Bien Hoa   Phan Thiet
Tan An ☆ SAIGON
• Long Thinh
Dong Tam •   • Vung Tau
Rach Gia •   My Tho
• Can Tho •
MEKONG DELTA   III CORPS

CA MAU PENINSULA

IV CORPS

Figure AP1.2   US Military Region or Corps Map of Vietnam.

III Corps or MR3 included Saigon, Ben Hoa and my province, Phuoc Long. The province was in the northeastern corner of III Corps bordering II Corps on the East and Cambodia on the North.

Figure AP1.3   III Corps or Military Region 3.

Phuoc Long Province had four districts. I was in the southern district of Don Luan about 25 miles from the Cambodian border and about 40 miles north of Saigon. The province had no rural population to speak of; the French and American wars with the North had put an end to that. By 1971 most of the people in Phuoc Long lived in hamlets clustered close together in the main village of each district.

I was based in the village of Dong Xoai. The village had five hamlets: 2 Vietnamese, 2 Montagnard, and 1 Cambodian (refugees from that

297

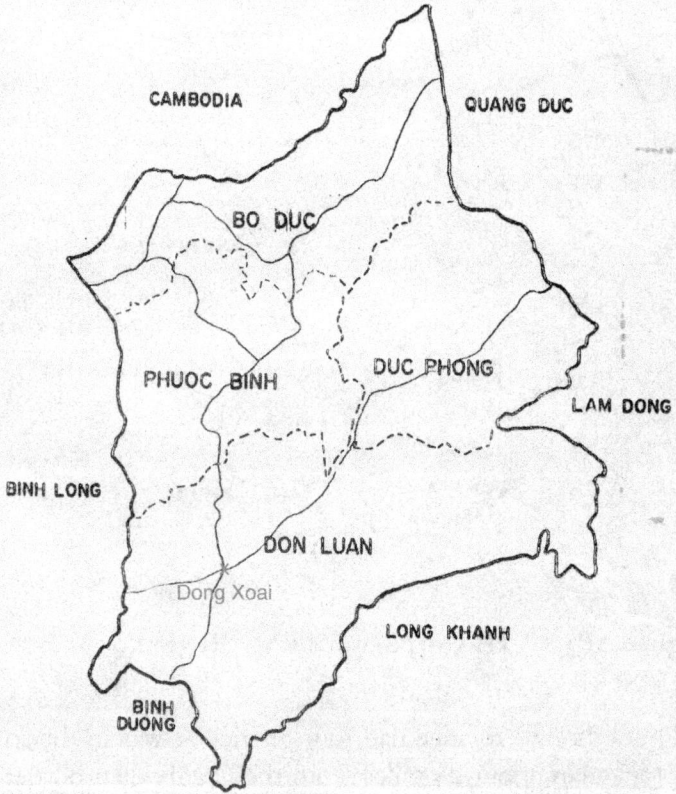

INFORMATION BRIEF
PHUOC LONG PROVINCE
VIET NAM

CAMBODIA

QUANG DUC

BO DUC

PHUOC BINH

DUC PHONG

LAM DONG

BINH LONG

DON LUAN

Dong Xoai

LONG KHANH

BINH DUONG

CORDS MR 3
JULY 1971

Figure AP1.4   Districts in Phuoc Long Province

country who were resettled there by the Vietnamese government). Farming was small and local to the villages. The village was at the intersection of two major roads, one extending from Ben Hoa to the Cambodian border. The big industries were lumber and rubber. The lumber operations were strictly local. However, rubber was another story. Michelin and other French corporations had numerous rubber plantations in Phuoc Long that at one time were self-contained communities, similar to the coal towns of the last part of the 19th and first part of the 20th century in West Virginia and Kentucky. Michelin was trying to restart operations at a few rubber plantations in the province while I was there. The rumor was that the company paid the Viet Cong protection money to be left alone, but we were never able to prove that. Before the French war started, the French maintained resorts in the province, where the wealthy could come and stay to hunt tigers and elephants.

The jungle in which we operated was either single canopy or double canopy. A canopy is a layer of vegetation. Movement in single canopy jungle was often very difficult due to the density of the growth. The term, "Wait-a-minute vine" was often used to describe the dense vegetation that made movement extremely difficult, however we did not cut our way with machetes. That would leave a trail of where we had walked and make it easier for "someone" to follow us. Double canopy jungle had a second layer of vegetation above the first blocking out much of the sunlight. This second layer played havoc with radio communications and helicopter support.

Personnel and Teams in Rank Order:

MACV — Military Assistance Command Vietnam — the overall command for the advising efforts in the War.

COMUSMACV — COMmander United States Military Assistance Command Vietnam; the General in charge of the war. William Westmoreland was probably the most notable general to serve in this position. Creighton Abrams was in charge in 1971 when I was there.

Army of the Republic of Vietnam — ARVN — The country's regular army. To my knowledge, the ARVN never operated in Phuoc Long while I was there.

Province Chief — Equivalent to the governor of an American State — appointed usually from the Vietnamese military.

Province Senior Advisor — PSA — An Army Colonel who worked directly with the Province Chief and was the Commanding Officer of the American advisors in the Province.

S-2 — Intelligence Officer — Typically an Army Major who worked for the PSA at Province. Working with his Vietnamese counterpart, his responsibility was to collect and interpret intelligence that was used to plan operations against the Viet Cong.

S-3 — Operations Officer — Typically an Army Major who also worked for the PSA at Province. Working with his Vietnamese counterpart, his responsibility was to plan operations against the Viet Cong based on the intelligence supplied by the S-2. These operations usually involved the MAT teams based in the districts.

S-4 — Supply — S-4 was responsible for supplying the District Teams, MAT Teams, and the Province Team with some of the materials needed to conduct their missions, which included mail and some of our food.

District Chief — Equivalent to the elected leader of an American County — appointed usually from the military.

District Senior Advisor — DSA — Usually an Army Major who worked directly with the District Chief and organizationally was the MAT team's immediate commanding officer.

District Team (at Dong Xoai) — Composed of four US soldiers: District Senior Advisor, District NCO, a Military Intelligence team of two men: a Captain and an NCO.

Intelligence Team — Part of the District Team — they worked with their Vietnamese counterparts to identify Viet Cong sympathizers and

VC agents in the village and hamlets. They also gathered information from Montagnards and our agents on Viet Cong movements and supply caches; information that was used to plan operations against the Viet Cong.

MAT Team — Mobile Advisory Team composed of five men: Team leader who was a Captain, Assistant Team Leader who was a Lieutenant, two NCOs, and one Medic. The team worked directly with the Regional Force (RF) companies, the Popular Force (PF) platoons and the Peoples Self Defense Force (PSDF) in the District.

Medic — An NCO with medical skills and training for the care of traumatic wounds received in combat.

Montagnard — The hill people of Vietnam. They were considered second class people by many Vietnamese. They hated the Viet Cong and were good allies of the Americans. The Montagnards in our area spoke the language of the Stieng tribe, not Vietnamese, that had no written language.

NCO — Non-Commissioned Officer — a Sergeant.

Popular Force — PF — PF soldiers were guaranteed that they would be based in and never operate outside their village area. They received less pay, training, and equipment than the RF troops. MAT 111 worked with the PF platoons.

Regional Force — RF — RF soldiers were guaranteed they would be based in and never operate outside their home district. For this condition of service, they received less pay, less training, and less equipment than the ARVN. They had no direct helicopter support and only limited artillery support. MAT 111 worked with the RF companies at Dong Xoai.

RTO — American **R**adio **T**elephone **O**perators are highly trained communication personnel. For the MAT team however, the RTO was the person who carried the radio — usually a Vietnamese soldier.

Ruff Puff — This vocalization of the letters RF-PF was one name used by some Americans to refer to the RF and PF soldiers — often considered derogatory.

Little People — The slang name used by some advisors when they talked about the Vietnamese. I found this term to be offensive. I cannot say how the Vietnamese felt.

Military Ranks:

A Colonel outranks a Lieutenant Colonel. Both are addressed as "Colonel".

A First Lieutenant outranks a Second Lieutenant. Both are addressed as "Lieutenant". In combat units, Lieutenants were often addressed as "L T." For some of us, it is/was a point of pride to be called, "L T."

In 1971 the Army had 9 enlisted ranks from E1 to E9. Each rank has a corresponding title or name. Soldiers with ranks E5 to E9 were considered Non-Commissioned Officers or NCOs. The word "Sergeant" is in the rank name within this group: Sergeant, Staff Sergeant, Sergeant First Class, Master Sergeant, Sergeant Major. Except for the Sergeant Major, they were addressed as Sergeant.

Weapons and Equipment:

Figure AP1.5   The AK-47 — The rifle used by the Viet Cong and is still used today in conflicts around the world.

Figure AP1.6   The M-16 rifle (left) and the M-60 machine gun.
Both weapons were used by the American forces.

**Figures AP1.7 and AP1.8
The 40 mm M-79
Grenade Launcher.**

The M-79 Grenade Launcher fired a variety of 40 mm rounds. The HE (High Explosive) shell was fired in a high arc allowing an infantry unit to put explosive fire down on an enemy position. The weapon had other types of shells available including the buckshot round and illumination round. The weapon loaded like a single barrel shotgun.

Jim Roberts

Figure AP1.9   The .50-Cal Machine Gun.

The .50-caliber machine gun that was used by Americans fires 400 rounds per minute. The .50 Cal had a range about 3000 meters. This model is identical to the .50 caliber machine gun used in World War 2 and Korea and is still used today.

Figure AP1.10   The 81 mm Mortar.

The 81 mm mortar was an infantry weapon that fired explosive shells in a high arc with a maximum range of about 3 KM. Unlike the howitzers (shown below), the shell fired from the mortar is placed in the top of the tube and allowed to slide down the tube striking a firing pin at the bottom, which fires an explosive charge that launches the shell. The shell being held is an illumination round that opens at the height of its arc and deploys a magnesium flare suspended by a parachute.

The location of the mortar is called the "mortar pit." The black ring on the walls of the pit with white vertical stripes is for aiming the mortar.

The baseplate of the mortar on which the bottom of the tube rests is not visible. It has been forced into the ground by previous firing of the mortar during Viet Cong attacks.

Figure AP1.11   The 105 mm Howitzer.

105 MM Howitzer is essentially a cannon that is loaded from the back. The barrel diameter in millimeters or inches was used to identify the type of Howitzer; The Regional Forces (RF) at Dong Xoai had two 105 mm Howitzers. It can fire a 33-pound shell about 11 kilometers or 6 miles. This howitzer was manufactured the year I was born.

Figure AP1.12   The 155 mm Howitzer.

155 MM Howitzer is a larger version of the 105 mm Howitzer. It can fire a 95-pound shell about 15 kilometers or a little more than 9 miles. A US battery of three guns was located at Dong Xoai for a few weeks. The unit was withdrawn as part of Vietnamization, and the guns were transferred to the ARVN.

C4 — A white clay-like explosive that came in rectangular bars measuring roughly 2"x2"x"12". Its intended use was for destroying bunkers, caches of weapons and ammunition. We used it for that and for heating C-Rations and canteen cups of water.

Pop Flares or Parachute Flares — A hand-held pyrotechnic similar to the star cluster that was used to illuminate a ground position. When fired, it opened at the top of its arc deploying a small parachute and igniting a magnesium flare that burned with an intense white light while it slowly descended. It provided light for about 20-30 seconds. Care had to be used deploying these. The soldier had to make sure there were no helicopters in the area because the light from one of these would destroy the night vision for the helicopter crew for 10 to 15 minutes.

Rocket Propelled Grenade — RPG — Viet Cong weapon; shoulder fired rocket with an explosive charge — very effective and still used today in conflicts around the world.

Figure AP1.13   The Smoke Grenade.

Smoke Grenade — A non-explosive grenade that produced smoke. Colored smoke grenades generated a specific-colored smoke for about 40 seconds. These were used to mark positions on the ground for helicopters when they were providing close tactical support firing their weapons near an American ground unit and to aid a helicopter pilot judge wind speed and direction when trying to land. When a smoke grenade was deployed, the soldier on the ground did not identify the color; the radio message was, "Smoke out, over." The pilot would reply,

"I identify red smoke, over." To which the soldier on the ground would reply, "Roger, out." The Viet Cong, using captured smoke grenades would also deploy smoke grenades to lure the helicopter into a trap. If the ground soldier identified the color when he threw the grenade, the Viet Cong could deploy the same color, so having the pilot identify the color reduced this chance. A white smoke grenade was also available. These produced a heavy dense white smoke for about 100 seconds and were used to cover movement. Both types burned very hot and could start grass fires during dry season.

Rucksack, ruck, pack — Back pack carried by soldiers; it had an aluminum frame with a three-compartment bag attached to it. The bag had reinforced points for attaching other equipment.

Star Clusters — A hand-held pyrotechnic similar to a pop flare that launched a fireworks type charge into the air that exploded into several brightly burning segments of the same color. Like smoke grenades, different color clusters were available. These were used to mark positions at night. Also like the colored smoke grenades, the pilot identified the color of the flare. Care in using them was essential. Helicopters operating at night in an area involved in enemy contact did not display running lights. The soldier on the ground had to be careful not to launch the flare in the direction of the helicopter. A closely exploding flare could reduce the helicopter crew's night vision.

Web Gear — A belt with places to attach equipment. It has a set of suspenders to transfer weight to the shoulders. On operations I attached two one-quart canteen carriers, two magazine pouches that had loops to carry two fragmentation grenades each, and a bayonet to the belt. The canteen carriers each had a plastic canteen for water, a metal cup with a folding handle for heating water. The suspenders had attachment points for other equipment such as a flashlight, smoke grenades, first aid pouch with a large field dressing or bandage to cover a large wound.

Communication:

Figure AP1.14   A Portable Field Radio.

PRC 25 — Portable field radio used by Americans; it had a glass tube.

PRC 77 — Newer version of PRC 25; it was solid state; no tubes.

Both radios — PRC stands for Portable Radio Communicator — pronounced, "Prick". It weighed 13 pounds plus a 3-pound battery that was good for 1 day of use. Transmission range with the 3-foot-long flexible antenna was about 11 km / about 6.2 miles.

Call Sign — Each person in a unit had a radio call sign which consisted of two random words, a number and a letter. The last month I was in country, Phuoc Long Province's call sign for all advisors was "Brief Alarm". Each unit in Phuoc Long had its own number. Dong Xoai's number was 65. The MAT team's number was 33. Each person in the unit had a letter of the alphabet. My letter was "Q" or "Quebec" which was pronounced "key BECK". The NCO that I always worked with in the field was "T" or Tango. My call sign was "Brief Alarm 33 Quebec". After answering the initial radio call, this was shortened to just "33 Quebec".

Commo — Radio or wire-based communications. Frequently used as the overall ability to communicate with another party, "Do we have commo with Province?"

Green Machine — The KY-38 Nestor was a radio transmission scrambler that prevented anyone listening to the call from eavesdropping unless they had the same device with the same settings. The settings were changed every night at midnight.

Figure AP1.15   Two TA-312 Land Line telephones and a PRC77 Handset.

Land Line — TA-312 Army telephones that worked on battery power. These two phones were connected by wire to the District Chief's headquarters and the Regional Force headquarters. The black handset is to a PRC-77 field radio.

Phonetic Alphabet — Specific words that stand for each letter of the alphabet. Every soldier memorized this list of words in Basic Training. These words are used in radio transmissions, so the letters can be understood. There can a great deal of noise during combat and a radio transmission can have static making letters, such as "A" and "K" or "B" and "D" difficult to differentiate. The replacement words "Alpha," "Kilo," and "Bravo," "Delta," are easier to discriminate. "Quebec," was the word for the letter "Q" and Tango was the word for "T."

Radio Terminology — Terms used for radio communication:
    OVER — On the radio, "I am finished for now; it is your turn."
    OUT — On the radio, "This is the end of the transmission."
    ROGER — On the radio, "I understand."
    WILCO — On the radio, "I will comply."

SOI — Signals Operating Instructions — a small paper booklet issued to each member of the team every month that had all of the call signs, radio frequencies for units operating in the province, and the whiz wheel sheets (1/day).

Land Navigation:

Encrypt — A method of substituting letters of the alphabet for your numerical grid location on a topo map or a radio frequency so a listening enemy would not know your position or the frequency.

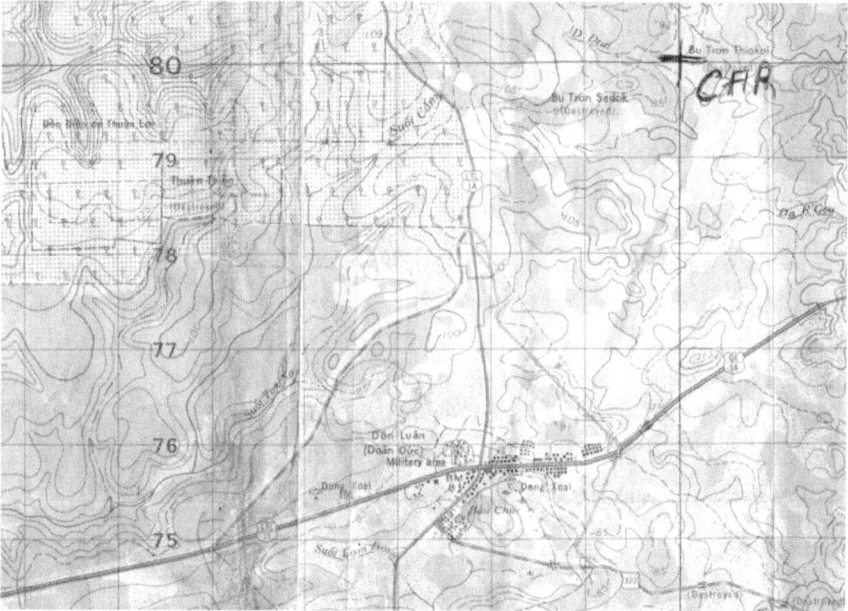

Figure AP1.16   The Topographic map of the village of Dong Xoai.

Topo — Topographic map of the area that showed the land forms: hills, depressions, valleys, ridges, saddles[59], the relative steepness of the land forms, water courses, vegetation covering, and a grid system to allow one unit to tell another unit (via radio) their location.

The point marked, "CAR" in Figure AP1.16 was one of several designated locations for positioning artillery and helicopter gunship fire and for rallying, if we had to escape and evade the camp during an attack.

---

[59] A land form that has two sides higher and two sides lower.

Whiz Wheel — The small plastic device used to encrypt map coordinates. In Figure AP1.17 all of the letters and numbers you see are on a removable piece of paper that slides into the clear plastic device. There is one piece of paper like this for each day of the month. The slightly darker circular disk that has the black ring rotates. On this disk are a thick black circle and a slightly larger thin circle with straight lines radiating from the circle. The inner ring of alphabet letters is the "Set Ring". You rotate the darker disk so the very small circle is over a letter of your choosing. In the image, the small circle is set over the letter, "A". With this setting each digit from 0 to 9 has a randomized set of letters. With this setting, the number 1 can be represented by the letters, "V," "K" or "B". This whiz wheel allowed us to quickly send a map location over the radio to another unit. Map coordinates were designated by six digits. The first three were the horizontal grid location and the second three were the vertical grid location. If I was at map coordinates 352 - 278, I could communicate the location on the with the following encryption: Echo, Tango, Charlie, Uniform, Oscar, Zulu. With the person on the other end of the transmission's wheel set letter A in the small circle, he could decrypt the coordinates.

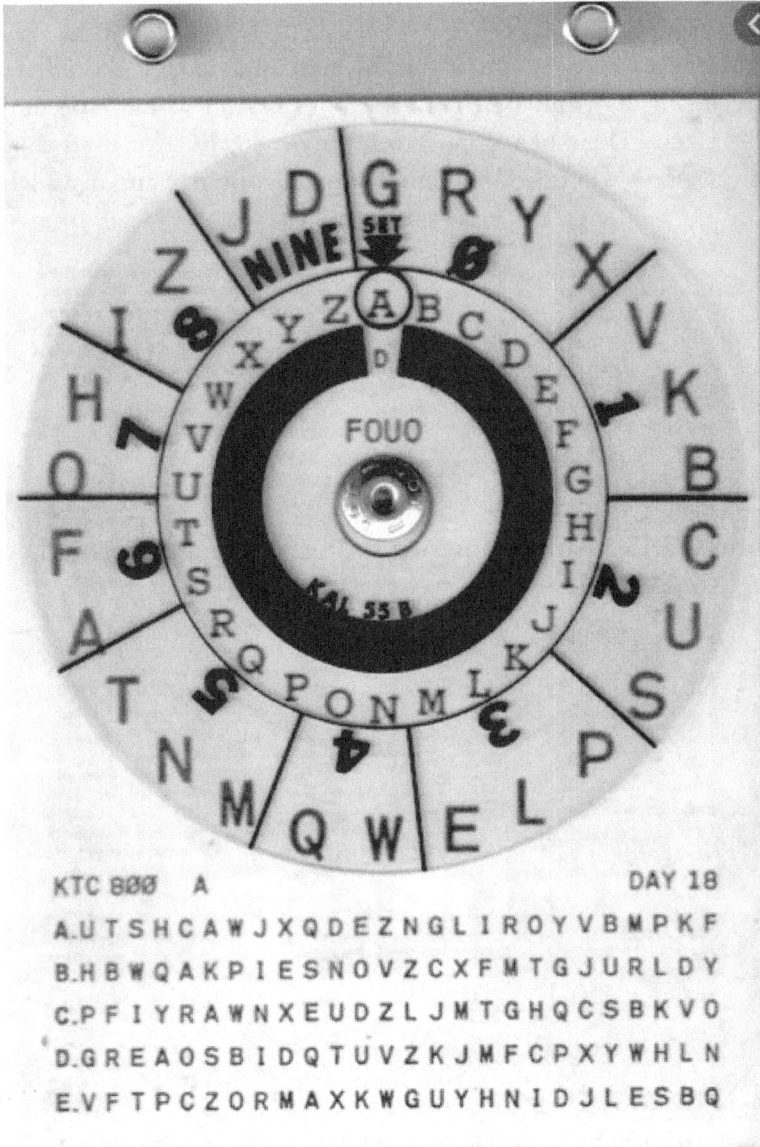

Figure AP1.17   The Whiz Wheel used to encrypt map
coordinates. Courtesy of Ralph Simpson.

Aircraft:

Air America — An airline owned and operated by the CIA. They made regular runs from Ben Hoa to Song Be and would stop at Dong Xoai, if asked. Their helicopters were unarmed, but we used them for resupply at times when US or Vietnamese helicopters were unavailable.

Figure AP1.18   An Air America Porter on the dirt airstrip at Dong Xoai.

Figure AP1.19   An Air America Huey on the landing pad at Dong Xoai.

O-1 Bird Dog — A light unarmed single engine airplane capable of carrying a pilot and an observer. The plane could land and take off from the dirt air strip at Dong Xoai. The high wing design and slow flight speed made it ideal for aerial reconnaissance. Look closely at smudge marked by the arrow on the front of the plane. It is a bright orange kangaroo silhouette put there by a passing Australian soldier. The Australians put them on everything when they visited an area. We found one under our jeep hood.

Figure AP1.20   An Army Bird Dog on the dirt air strip at Dong Xoai.

Cobra — An attack helicopter that is really a flying weapons platform with a 36-inch-wide fuselage. It was used for close ground support of the troops on the ground — close ground support means that in communication with someone on the ground (me), they could fire their weapons at targets **very** close to my position with "relative" safety.

Jim Roberts

Figure AP1.21   A Cobra taking off from the helipad at Dong Xoai.

Figure AP1.22   The pilot is checking out one of the weapons systems on the Cobra.

Huey — The helicopter that became the symbol of the war; typically used to move troops and supplies. Later in the war when I was there, some of the early models that had less power and could not carry many troops were converted to gun ships with mini-guns that could fire 2000 bullets a minute. It was also called a chopper, copter, bird, and slick.

Figure AP1.23   An Huey taking off from the helipad at Dong Xoai.

Lift — One round trip by a flight of helicopters to deliver or pick up troops on the ground.

LOH — A Light Observation Helicopter (called a "loach") that is very small and maneuverable but carries no armor. Its only weapon was a hand-held M-60 machine gun.

Figure AP1.24   A Loach on the helipad at Dong Xoai.

LZ — Landing Zone for helicopters for inserting and extracting soldiers.

Medivac — A Huey helicopter configured to carry wounded soldiers. One of the crew members was a medic.

Figure AP1.25   A Medivac landing at Dong Xoai.

PZ — Pick Up Zone - a term used for the extraction LZ.

Slick, Chopper, Bird —Slang names for a Huey.

Work Ship, Work Chopper — A Huey helicopter assigned to the province almost every day to provide support including noncombat movement of military and civilian personnel, delivering and picking up mail, transporting injured villagers and RF or PF troops, and resupply of units that had been in contact with the enemy. It was occasionally used for reconnaissance. The S-3 would use the work ship to fly out to contact a MAT Team on an operation when the MAT Team was out of radio range of District or Province.

Other Terms:

C-Rations or Cs — Food carried on missions. There were 12 different meals. In addition to olive green cans of food, each ration also included a spoon, a few matches, 3 sheets of toilet paper, and a large green wooden toothpick, called a "stimudent," for cleaning your teeth. Because we had no method of resupply on a 5 or 7 day operation, we had to carry all of the food we needed, but carrying 13 or 19 [60] complete rations would not fit into our packs and would be prohibitively heavy. Choosing what to take and packing it for an operation was a mental and a physical challenge. We were usually hungry when we were in the field.

DEROS — Date Eligible for Return from OverSeas — This was the end of your assignment or tour in Vietnam. Every American serving in Vietnam knew their DEROS. Most of us, if we still have a working memory, remember our DEROS. It is something that few veterans ever forget.

Many GIs maintained the count of "days and a wakeup" until their DEROS. The "wakeup" day was not counted because that was the day

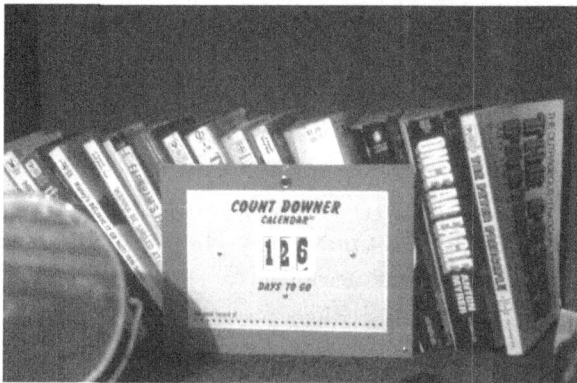

Figure AP1.26   A "commercial" DEROS calendar.

---

[60] Typically, you did not eat a breakfast ration on day 1 and a supper ration on the last day of the operation.

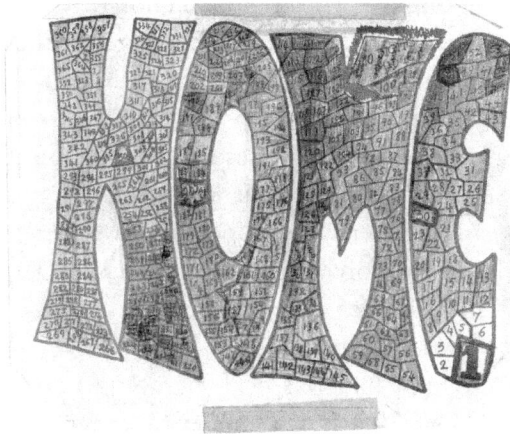

Figure AP1.27   A "home made" DEROS calendar provided by a Donut Dolly.

you left. Some soldiers used commercial devices to keep track of the count of days and others used simpler, handmade countdown sheets:

Deuce-and-a-Half — A two and one-half ton truck used to transport troops and supplies.

Flank Security — Moving in a single file column can be risky. Where possible, two soldiers would be positioned to either side (flank) of the moving column to look for traps and ambushes. Dense jungle vegetation and the terrain often prevented this.

MPC — Military Pay Certificates or Monopoly Money — colored currency bills used in place of actual US currency in an effort to thwart black market dealing by the US soldiers.

Night Defensive Position or Perimeter — **NDP** — A secluded and defendable position for spending the night; typically, a circular formation with the command elements in the center.

Point, Walking Point — The lead element of a column of moving soldiers was called the point. Soldiers who were in the point element were said to be, "Walking point." This was usually two very experienced men who could be trusted to find signs of enemy movement, potential ambush locations, and booby traps across the line of march. Walking point was dangerous because of the chance of triggering a booby trap or initiating an ambush. Different units operated in different ways but my counterpart, the Regional Force Captain with whom I operated in the field, was always #3 in the line of march. #4 was his radio operator and I was #5 followed by my interpreter

If you are wondering why I was near the point, Infantry officers lead from the front. "Follow Me" is the motto of the United States Army Infantry School and those two words were on the OCS patch I wore on my shoulder while I was in Officer Candidate School.

Figure AP1.28 The "Follow Me" patch worn by Officer Candidates in Infantry OCS. The "subdued" patch on the right is worn on fatigues.

Leading from the front is why Lieutenants have a high causality rate in combat. One in ever twenty names on the Walls of the Vietnam Memorial is that of a Lieutenant. Over 3,000 Lieutenants died in Vietnam.

Appendix 2 - The Soldiers and People of Dong Xoai and Phuoc Long

I am not using the names of most of the Advisors at Dong Xoai because I do not know if they would appreciate seeing their names in print. All but one of the names that are in this appendix are being used with their permission.

The Americans with whom I served at Dong Xoai were outstanding soldiers and I was very fortunate to be stationed there with them. The Officers in the Vietnamese Regional Force (RF) companies were also very good soldiers. They maintained the training of their troops and were well respected by these soldiers. There are stories of nepotism among the command ranks of some RF units in Vietnam but that was not evident in Don Luan District, the location of Dong Xoai — at least not to me.

Moving up to Province, I am not sure I can say the same thing with confidence. I worked for the Province Senior Advisor (PSA) who was a Colonel, his S-2 (Intelligence Major), and his S-3 (Operations Major). The three officers who were in those slots when I arrived were good officers. My interactions with them in preparation for operations were always positive. During my tour, these three DEROSed and were replaced by officers about whom I am not sure. The new S-2's intelligence briefings were vague and less helpful. The new S-3's operations seemed to have bothersome loose ends. It is uncomfortable to be inserted by helicopter for a mission knowing that the S-3 is, "working on finding a unit to extract you." To be fair, by the time these replacement officers arrived, Vietnamization was in full swing, and

Jim Roberts

American units were being pulled out at an increasing rate. It is possible that these two officers did the best they could in these circumstances. Maybe they deserve the benefit of the doubt.

My interactions with the new PSA usually centered on being chewed out. I do not know if I was a just bad officer or if he had little time for Lieutenants. In contrast, he did write a glowing letter of commendation for me when I left, and he forwarded the recommendation for my Bronze Star to III Corps HQ.

MAT 111 was based at the Regional Force (RF) camp in the village of Dong Xoai. We were there to continue the work begun by the Special Forces in 1965. We worked with the RF companies and the Popular Force (PF) platoons to help them maintain their skills and to accompany them on operations. We also coordinated advising efforts with Province based advisors in areas of economic development, public health, and other civic areas. One aspect of our mission was to "win the hearts and minds of the people in the village and hamlets." Part of this effort was the hiring of local Vietnamese to work for us. Mind you, we had to pay them out of our own pockets, but this employment was expected by the "higher ups." As part of this, we employed a cook and two house maids.

The cook's name was Tei Lai and she was a good cook, though everything she made was prepared as a Vietnamese meal — even a standard American dish like spaghetti. How she managed to do that remained a mystery but she did serve good food, and we were well fed. Rice was a part of every meal, even the spaghetti,

Figure AP2.1   Tei Lai, our cook and her son.

and she cooked far more than we could eat. The left-over rice went home to feed her family. I hope they had more than one meal a day. Tei Lai arrived early in the morning to begin breakfast. Memory is strange; I bought the food for the team but I do not remember what we ate for breakfast or lunch. The other members of the teams with whom I am in contact do not remember either.

We hired two house maids to clean our rooms and the common areas, wash our clothes, and polish our boots. They were supervised by our

Figure AP2.2   Tei Lai and the two maids.

cook. They did the job with exuberance; there is no other way to describe it. If I changed into my tennis shoes and shorts and went out to run after lunch, my boots would be polished and my fatigues washed and hanging on the barbed wire to dry when I returned. They washed our jungle fatigues with a scrub brush on a wash board to within an inch of their lives. They could not remove some of the stains but they did get the dust, dirt and the odor of sweat out.

I had very little personal interaction with the District and Village

Figure AP2.3   Barbed wire — our clothes line.

officials. That was taken care of by the District Senior Advisor and the MAT Team leader. My main interaction was with the Regional Force (RF) Captain with whom I worked on operations in the district. He is the soldier holding the papers in figure AP2.4. The soldier next to him is his executive officer (second in command). 33 Tango is on the left side and I am on the right. I referred to the Captain as Captain Ky in these stories but that was not his name. I have dug deeply into my memories but cannot find a name that fits. It is not there and that is truly sad. We had tea once or twice a week after lunch during my tour, and we helped each other with our language skills. His English was much better than my Vietnamese. His family fled the North when he was a small child and he had been fighting the war his entire adult life. He had been trained by the Green Berets and had passed his training on to his officers and NCOs. His troops were also well trained and respected his leadership. Captain Ky and his troops are one reason I can write these stories today.

Tactically, Captain Ky never really needed my advice. On operations whenever we took a break, he would always confer with 33 Tango and me about our location. We would compare our thoughts, and we were usually very close in our thinking. When we differed on our position and were within artillery range, he would call the Vietnamese artillery unit or,

Figure AP2.4   33 Tango, Captain Ky, his XO, 33 Quebec.

if one was available, I would call an American unit and have them fire a round to a specific coordinate on the map. We would request a white phosphorous round to explode in the air so we might possibly see it. The artillery unit would notify us when they fired and then call "splash" 2 seconds before the rounded exploded. Counting the seconds until we heard the explosion and pointing our compasses towards the white puff of the phosphorous or the sound of the explosion, we could confirm our location with reasonable accuracy. As far as who was right, it was probably 50/50 — at least that is how I remember it.

Captain Ky and I worked well together. 33 Tango worked well with his executive officer so, we made a good four-man team. I wish I could have taken his company with me on my operations in other districts as my tour wound down. He gave me a blue beret with a silver bar when I DEROSed — the unofficial ceremonial head gear for RF troops. It was unauthorized but I wore it anyway.

The MAT team had an interpreter provided by the RF company,

Sergeant Yung. He was a very good interpreter. He could read and write English, in addition to speaking English very clearly; something that is important during the cacophony of combat. Unlike some of my later interpreters, Sgt. Yung was not afraid to translate bad news or a disagreement between Captain Ky and me. He was also willing to share the risks. I walked near the point with Captain Ky and he was always right behind me. Sgt. Yung could not accompany me when I operated with units outside the district because as an RF soldier, he never worked outside the Don Luan district. The interpreters with whom I worked outside the district were inaccurate and never wanted to walk with me near the point because it was too dangerous.

Figure AP2.5 Sgt. Yung, the MAT team interpreter.

Our field radios had two frequency preset positions. Whenever I was talking with the S-3 (Operations) on the radio, Captain KY would switch his radio to our frequency and Sergeant Yung would translate for him. We would do the opposite when Captain Ky was talking to the Vietnamese S-3.

Our MAT Team had the honor of being invited to Sergeant Yung's wedding in the village. It was quite an elaborate affair in the middle of a war and the festivities continued for several days. It was the cultural highlight of my tour.

Figure AP2.6   Sgt. Yung's family getting ready for his wedding at the Advisors' team house.

Figure AP2.7   The Wedding Ceremony.

The overall American commander at Dong Xoai was the District Senior Advisor (DSA). He was a Major on his second tour in Vietnam. He had arrived before me in February, 1971, replacing a well-respected DSA. Under his watch, things seemed a bit "fuzzy." For example, when I arrived, one of the first questions I asked was, "Where is the escape route through the mine field and barbed wire, if we are being overrun?" His answer was, in essence, "Somewhere over there. It's marked with some cloth, I think."

Figure AP2.8   The DSA.

The District NCO, an E-7 Sergeant First Class was, on his third consecutive tour and was asking to be extended a fourth time. He was an outstanding "combat" soldier who knew that, as a soldier, he fared much better in a wartime environment. He was our main mechanic and he kept our generators and jeeps running. Due to his extended time in country, he "knew" where to get what we needed and "who" would trade for the things we could not get through the Vietnamese or US supply lines.

Figure AP2.9   The District Team NCO.

The District Team had within it a two-man Intelligence Team who worked with the Vietnamese Intelligence officers to gather information about the Viet Cong operating covertly in the village and the Viet Cong squads operating in the District. This team was led by a Military Intelligence Captain. I had only social contact with him at meals and in the evenings at the team house. The work he and the Intelligence NCO were doing was classified, on a need-to-know basis, so we rarely talked at length.

Figure AP2.10   The Intel Team captain.

The Intelligence NCO, Sergeant Gary Weinreich, known in these stories as "YB" was a kindred spirit. Like me, he took lots of pictures. We merged our image collections together years ago so I am not sure what pictures in this

Figure AP2.11   Gary Weinreich, the Intel Team NCO. We called him YB.

set of stories were taken by him or me unless they are of him or me — then the photographer is obvious. Gary and I have been in contact ever since I returned in December, 1971. I managed to smuggle out the tail fin section of the mortar round that hit his room wounding him. I mailed it to him in December, 1971 as a "Christmas Present," and he replied with a Christmas Card sent to, "L T's War Souvenirs". Correspondence from him always had this same address until we began to use e-mail. We visited the Vietnam Memorial in Washington, DC — The Wall — together in the spring after it was dedicated and have visited each other several times in the intervening 49 years. We are in frequent contact, and he has been reading the drafts of the stories, providing corrections and comments as they were being written. He lives in Arizona with his wife.

At the time of my arrival at Dong Xoai in May, 1971, the two MAT NCOs had been there almost 11 months. Both were on their second tours and DEROSed about a month after I arrived, so I never worked with them in the field. They were replaced by two NCOs from a deactivated MAT Team in another district in the province.

One of the "new" NCOs who arrived shortly after I did to replace the two NCOs who had DEROSED was E-7 Sergeant First Class Linsley Moore. He was on his second tour and had seen a great deal of action during his first tour. He operated with the MAT Team leader, so we never worked together in the field. We did talk during the evenings. He was a good soldier and stayed in the service for 30 years retiring as a Command Sergeant Major — the highest enlisted rank in the Army. He lives in Alabama today with his wife.

Figure AP2.12   SFC Linsley Moore

Figure AP2.13   33 Tango

The other NCO, 33 Tango, who arrived with SFC Moore was L J Turner. His first name was 'L' and his middle name was 'J.' He was the NCO with whom I worked on operations and was also an E-7 Sergeant First Class. He gave me his address and phone number when he DEROSed. I called the number when I returned to the states, and the nice lady who answered the phone replied that she, "Had never heard of him." Letters to the address he gave me went unanswered.

He had joined the Army right out of high school in 1951, but did not make it to Korea; not having completed his training before that war ended. He was in his 20th year and would retire when he DEROSed. He was on his third tour of Vietnam and was really not supposed to be here. Apparently, he managed to anger someone in personnel and that person's revenge was his posting to Vietnam — on a MAT Team. As you will or have read, he was a good NCO for me, a green Lieutenant in a combat zone. When we realized that we were going to be working together, we had a long talk in which he explained how he got here and the reason for his attitude. Right then and there we made a deal; he would try to keep me from making dumb Lieutenant mistakes, and I would do my best to get him to his DEROS. What he taught me became vital to my survival on the missions I drew after he left. He is the one reason I usually avoided the common Lieutenant error of speaking out of turn. Whenever we were in a discussion about a mission with the DSA or the S-3, I would look at him before I spoke and he would usually shake his head, "NO." On one mission we were about to initiate contact. I was kneeling down near Captain Ky when I found myself being pushed from behind down to a position that was flat on the ground. Angrily, I glared back and there was 33 Tango with his hand on my rucksack, "What the hell are you are doing?" I whispered angrily He replied, "Get down all the way? If you get hit, I have to come forward to take care of you! You promised that you would get me on my DEROS bird, so get down, stay down, and keep your promise!" With that he turned and moved back to his position. Lesson learned!

Figure AP2.14 The Team Medic. We called him "Bac Si."

Our medic, or "Bac Si" as we called him (Vietnamese for "doctor") was an E-6 Staff

Sergeant on his second tour. SOP for MAT Teams was that the medic did not go to the field. He did MedCaps (Medical Civic Action Patrols) in the village hamlets. He was always accompanied by another team member and our interpreter. Occasionally, a visiting civilian doctor would join him on the MedCap.

He took care of YB when he was wounded and looked after our daily health concerns. One thing we really hated was his Monday dispensing of our Malaria prophylaxis. Another thing we hated was his periodic injections of Gamma Globulin (GG) to thwart Hepatitis and other diseases. The dosing was 1 CC of a thick liquid for every 10 pounds of body weight. For someone weighing 200 pounds, that was 20 CCs (about 4 teaspoons), which was BIG volume — administered half in each buttock. Of course, he had to endure the same injections. The thick GG serum did not disperse quickly so each injection took some time, and sitting was very painful for several days. Jeep rides were not a favorite activity on the days following the shots.

The medical bunker was built and stocked for Green Beret medics, who had very advanced medical training including surgery to stop severe bleeding in wounded soldiers. He used those supplies to good advantage on several occasions.

Bac Si also did the village food shopping with our cook, which was the major source of the fresh food we had to eat. He was pulled back to Province after our two NCOs DEROSed, leaving only the Team Captain and me on MAT 111.

The MAT Team leader, Captain Jim Rice had arrived in Vietnam in early November, 1970. He

Figure AP2.15   Captain Jim Rice, the MAT Team leader.

volunteered for a MAT assignment to help further his career plans — leadership of a combat unit was a plus in your military record when being considered for promotion. He was an Air Defense Artillery officer and the Viet Cong had no air forces in the war. The North Vietnamese Air Force did not fly over South Vietnam. Rather than take a staff job, he opted for command of a MAT unit and attended the 2-week MAT school at Di An when he arrived. His decision to volunteer was a good one for him, me, and the team.

The word "rice" translates to "gao" (pronounced "gow") in Vietnamese. The rank of Captain in Vietnamese is "Dai Uy" (pronounced "Die" "Wee"), so we commonly called him, Dai Uy Gao. We never worked together in the field; he operated with SFC Moore and I operated with SFC Turner. Typically, Captain Rice dealt with the District and Village officials and took the larger size operations mounted by the Regional Force (RF) companies. I took care of the internal matters of the MAT Team, training of the RF and PF (Popular Force) soldiers, worked with the Peoples Self Defense Force (PSDF), and worked on the smaller RF operations. Captain Rice would remain in the Army for 26 years, retiring as a Full Colonel.

There are two other interesting (to me, at least) parts of our stories. One is a set of coincidences:

Our first names are "Jim".

We both got married on our way to Vietnam.

We both got married in November, 1970.

Both of our wives are named, "Linda".

The second interesting part was finding Dai Uy Gao 46 years after I left Dong Xoai. As the internet became a mature reality and the web browsers developed some decent search engines, I would sit down at my computer several times a year and run searches on "MAT Teams," "Dong Xoai," and the names of the advisors on the team. Over time as more data was put on the web and the search programs improved, I found clues and hints of information about advising and MAT Teams. One day I found the DSA's name on the list of the Army Command and General Staff College students for 1972. Eventually I found a newspaper article about a life time service award for an activity being given to a Jim

Rice. A memory returned that he had talked about this activity during his tour so I dug deeper and found an address. Digging still deeper, I found a phone number and called it. A voice answered and I asked if he knew Jim Rice and if that Jim Rice was ever in the army. The voice said, "Yes" to both questions. I explained who I was and asked if he could put me in contact. Surprisingly, he did; he gave a total stranger a private phone number that he thought belonged to his boss. I called that number. After several rings, a voice from my distant past said, "Hello." I replied, "Dai Uy Gao?" After a pause, the voice said, "L T?" But it was not his phone that he answered. The phone number was his daughter's. He just happened to be visiting her that day and was sitting on the patio with her phone on the table beside him. Instead of letting it transfer to voice mail when it rang, he decided to answer it.

A last note on Dai Uy Gao. We exchanged email addresses and in my first mail, I started it out addressing him as Jim. And that did not work. I still address him as "Dai Uy Gao" and he calls me "L T". It is the same for Garry Weinreich; we begin our emails, "Y B" and "L T." Some things are apparently never lost.

Figure AP2.16   Jim Roberts a/k/a 33 Quebec.

The last person in this overview is me. These are real stories about actual events from my tour, written as I remember them though some of the details are fuzzy, if not completely gone. I tried to fill in the blanks with narrative that is accurate for the time and situation in a way that tries to give you a sense of the emotions and concerns during my tour in Vietnam. I hope this has been successful.

As you read these stories, you may have noticed discrepancies and disagreements in the facts from story to story. This is how memories work. Dai Uy Gao, YB, and I developed a time line of events and the coming and going of individuals, but we did not agree on everything. Some of those areas of disagreement can be found in the stories.

If you want to know a bit more about the development and deployment of MAT Teams in Vietnam and me, there is a YouTube video you can watch. I wrote and produced it in 2018. It is about 30 minutes long and has pictures and movie scenes taken by YB and me during our tours of duty. You can go to YouTube.com and search for Brief Alarm. You should see the image in Figure AP2.17 somewhere in the search results. Clicking this link will take you to my YouTube channel.

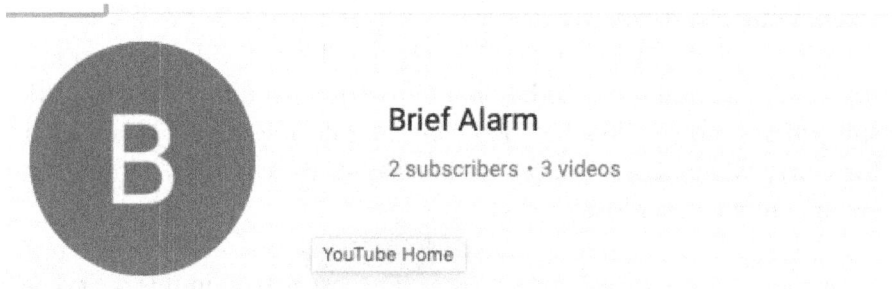

Figure AP2.17   The Brief Alarm YouTube channel.

Three videos related to Vietnam are there. The video, "Vietnam - For MAT teams It Was A Very Lonely War" with the image of a Huey tells the background story of MAT Teams and of my tour.

You can also enter this link in a web browser:
https://www.youtube.com/watch?v=NWVLwlxMO90

Or you can search the YouTube site using the string:
Vietnam - For MAT teams It Was A Very Lonely War
to find the video. The word, "Very" is important — there are lot of "Lonely War" videos.

I hope you found reading these stories a worthwhile use of your time, and that you have some appreciation of the diverse missions the veterans of wars past and present have been given in their service to the country.

33 Quebec, out.

Abbreviations

ADA	Air Defense Artillery
AIT	Advanced Individual Training
AO	Area of Operations
ARVN	Army of the Republic of Vietnam
C4	Composition #4 (an explosive)
CIB	Combat Infantry Badge
DEROS	Date Eligible for Return from OverSeas
DSA	District Senior Advisor
DX	Dong Xoai
E&E	Escape and Evasion
IG	Inspector General
KM	Kilometer
LRRP	Long Range Reconnaissance Patrol
LZ	Landing Zone
MACV	Military Assistance Command Vietnam
MAT	Mobile Advisory Team
MM	Millimeter
NCO	Non-Commissioned Officer (a Sergeant)
NVA	North Vietnamese Army
OCS	Officer Candidate School
Op Con	Operational Control
Op Order	Operations Order
PF	Popular Force
PSA	Province Senior Advisor
PSDF	Peoples Self Defense Force
PZ	Pickup Zone
RF	Regional Force
R&R	Rest and Recuperation or Rest and Relaxation
RTO	Radio Telephone Operator
S-1	Adjutant or Personnel Officer
S-2	Intelligence Officer
S-3	Operations Officer

S-4	Supply Officer
SFC	Sergeant First Class (E7)
SOI	Signals Operating Instructions
SOP	Standard Operating Procedure
SSG	Staff Sergeant (E6)
VC	Viet Cong
XO	Executive Officer (second in command)
YB	Young Buck (short for Young Buck Sergeant Gary Weinreich)

About the Author

Jim Roberts was born at Wright Patterson Air Force Base near Dayton, Ohio. As an Air Force Sergeant's son, he attended public schools in West Virginia, Panama, Nebraska, and Mississippi. He was a classroom teacher for 45 years teaching science to grades 7 through 12 for 15 years and computer programming to college students for 30 years.

Photo by Michael Sahaida

He was retired as a Teaching Professor in the School of Computer Science at Carnegie Mellon University (the School's choice; not his) in June, 2011 and returned that fall to teach at CMU's College of Fine Arts for three more years. He also taught for three semesters at the

University of Pittsburgh. His name appears as a coauthor on three printed textbooks that have sold over 50,000 copies.

Jim was an avid backpacker and white water paddler. He taught outdoor skills and topo map reading in the outing program of the Pittsburgh Council of the American Youth Hostels. He and his wife, Linda taught white water canoeing for the council.

Over the years Linda and Jim have enjoyed hiking, cycling, canoeing and camping, sea kayaking, cross country skiing, and diving; pursuing these activities throughout the United States and places such as Belize, Puerto Rico, St. John, Alaska, Canada, Belize. and Mexico.

Today, they both continue to enjoy the outdoors with hiking, cycling, canoeing, and sea kayaking.

Charlie Cong's a fighting man.
Lives and fights in Vietnam.

Hey people, don't you know?
I don't really wanna' go.

But people, can't you see?
I'm doin' this for you and me.

Charlie Cong's a fighting man.
Fights and dies in Vietnam.

Made in the USA
Middletown, DE
14 December 2021